Fear of a
Hip-Hop Planet

Fear of a Hip-Hop Planet

AMERICA'S NEW DILEMMA

D. Marvin Jones

PRAEGER

AN IMPRINT OF ABC-CLIO, LLC
Santa Barbara, California • Denver, Colorado • Oxford, England

Library of Congress Cataloging-in-Publication Data

Jones, D. Marvin.
    Fear of a hip-hop planet : America's new dilemma / D. Marvin Jones.
        p. cm.
    Includes index.
    ISBN 978-0-313-39577-2 (hardcopy : alk. paper) —
ISBN 978-0-313-39578-9 (ebook)   1. Hip-hop—United States—Public opinion.   2. African Americans—Social life and customs.   3. Public opinion—United States.   4. United States—Social life and customs.   I. Title.
    E185.86.J647   2013
    973.932—dc23   2012037962

ISBN: 978-0-313-39577-2
EISBN: 978-0-313-39578-9

17 16 15 14 13   1 2 3 4 5

This book is also available on the World Wide Web as an eBook.
Visit www.abc-clio.com for details.

Praeger
An Imprint of ABC-CLIO, LLC

ABC-CLIO, LLC
130 Cremona Drive, P.O. Box 1911
Santa Barbara, California 93116-1911

This book is printed on acid-free paper (∞)

Manufactured in the United States of America

Contents

CHAPTER 8
"We are Oscar Grant!," 245

CHAPTER 9
Race and Reconciliation, 251

EPILOGUE
The Last Word, 259

Preface

Hip-hop was investigated and found to be the root of all evil in America. Kool-Aid was the antidote. All the media marketed it, especially Fox News. White women with blue hair gave it to their kids.

The Kool-Aid was not laced with poison, there was no alcohol mixed in. But it acted like a drug.

The police drank it first. Once they drank it they stopped arresting people who actually had committed a crime. It was all about the profile. They arrested kids wearing dropped pants or hoodies and sporting gold teeth.

Black leaders stood in line to get theirs. One sip and their fists unclenched. They would go to bed with fire in their eyes singing "Fight the power, Fight the power." They woke up as Republicans. Reverend Al Sharpton called off rallies in support of Trayvon Martin to make time for TV appearances denouncing Snoop Dogg and Nelly.

The Kool-Aid was passed around at cocktail parties. Bill Cosby was hired to be its pitchman. He gave it out in gift bags whenever he made his speeches. Some say Clarence Thomas invented the Kool-Aid.

Introduction

It is 1967. Newark is burning in gritty black and white. America watched in shock as "Negroes" smashed windows, battled police, and carried away everything from groceries to dining room sets. Twenty-six people died.[1] More than 1,100 were injured.[2] Three days later Detroit exploded. As if someone had lit a fuse the conflagration spread to 75 other U.S. cities.

Convinced this was the work of communists, President Lyndon Baines Johnson appointed the governor of Illinois to lead a fact-finding team.[3] Governor Otto Kerner famously reported, "Our nation is moving toward two societies: one black, one white, separate, and unequal."[4] The prophecy has come to pass. We are two societies. But the color line has been replaced with the line between the suburbs and the inner city.[5]

This line separates not white and black but two continents. These two places are as different from each other as Europe was different from its colonies. In suburban America there are rolling lawns, places to work, decent schools, safety, and late-model cars. In the past this was home to Ward and Beaver Cleaver, now it is home to the Huxtables as well. But on the urban continent houses with plywood sheets for eyes stare blankly across a moonscape of social decay. As William Julius Wilson noted, "work has disappeared."[6]

Looking at Drake and Clayton's Bronzeville I can illustrate the magnitude of the changes that have occurred in many inner city ghetto neighborhoods. A majority of adults held jobs in 1950 . . . by 1990 only 37 percent of all males 16 and over held a job . . . today the nonworking poor predominate in the highly segregated and impoverished neighborhoods. The rise of the new poverty represents a move

Riot damage in D.C. (Library of Congress)

away from an institutional ghetto toward a jobless ghetto, which features a severe lack of opportunities and resources.[7]

This "jobless ghetto" is relatively new. It is an urban desert that has emerged over the past 40 years. As Houston Baker notes,

Disaster struck more than four decades ago in the form of an American polity's decision to go global, restructuring the nature of work inside the country's traditional borders and outsourcing millions of American jobs abroad. . . . Work has disappeared and with its disappearance, hope became a lottery ticket.[8]

In this postindustrial dystopia, schools have become disaster factories. There are classrooms packed with students but there are no materials.

The science labs at East St. Louis High are 30 to 50 years outdated. . . . The six lab stations in the room have empty holes where pipes were once attached. . . . I don't even know where to begin. I have no materials with the exception of a single textbook given to each child.[9]

At these schools failure has been normalized, and violence at the school is routine. "A staggering 50% of all minority kids who enter the 9th grade do not graduate."[10] In the film *Hard Times at Douglass High*,[11] a moving scene featured the head of the English Department at a Baltimore inner city school. He stated that when a reading test was given to 300 or 400 ninth-grade students, only 3 or 4 passed at grade level, the vast majority were at least three grade levels behind.[12]

Here, in the inner city, helicopters circle constantly overhead. In some cities blue lights blink at you from each lamppost, silent monitors to pinpoint gunfire. I grew up here, in Baltimore, in the seventeen hundred block of Lafayette Avenue. My block was a stone's throw away from where many of the drug sales depicted in *The Wire* were shot. Recently, I visited my old neighborhood. I saw those blue lights blinking at me. I had a Twilight Zone moment. I checked the signpost up ahead to see if this was the street where I grew up. The signpost was right. But this was clearly not the same place. This was some place foreign, futuristic, and strange. Whatever name we give to this other country that the inner city has become it is now the most militarized place on earth. But for all the helicopters and surveillance, automatic rifle fire can often be heard punctuating the silence on any given night. Violent crime is so omnipresent that Lil Wayne calls the inner city a "city of death."[13] "I'm from the city of death, nigga!" says Lil Wayne. "We kill niggas for nothing."[14]

Sometimes it is gun battles between rival drug crews; sometimes it is the violence of local gangs[15] competing for turf, sometimes it is the petty violence of young black men killed over an insult, a girl, or a gold chain. But grim statistics anchor the description of Lil Wayne. Since the 1990s homicide has been the leading cause of death among young black men between the ages of 15 and 24.[16] It's gotten worse: from 2002 to 2007, the murder rate among young black males increased 30 percent, while it dropped among every other segment of the population.[17]

The conventional wisdom seems to be that ghetto culture is criminogenic:[18] The aberrant and pathological values of the ghetto breed[19] violence and crime. Thus, the patterns of violence that occur in the ghetto are "contagious."[20] Taken literally, it is as if young black men—"The 'Boyz in the Hood"—are infected with a virus as a result of living in the ghetto environment. In a real sense this is true. But what they are infected by are conditions of joblessness and poverty. These conditions in turn trace back to deindustrialization, the suburbanization of investment, the resegregation of schools, and the intensifying abandonment of these areas by both the larger society and a black middle class that has moved away.

Marooned in these postindustrial colonies, the youth have issued their own declaration of independence from the mother country. These 21st-century Thomas Jeffersons do not wear horsehair wigs or write about "we the people." Their declaration of independence, their constitution, and their revolution is their culture.

Still sweltering under the *very same* conditions, which led to the urban rebellions of the 1960s, they have attempted to again set fire to America's urban areas. But they have picked up the mike instead of the Molotov cocktail. If their chapter in history had a title it would not be the era of black power, it would be the era of black noise.[21] They challenge not political order but cultural order, through forms of dress, music, and language, which flies in the face of mainstream values and the values of middle blacks as well. Through this rebellion of music, dance, and dress they seek to emancipate themselves—or at least create a sense of independence and freedom. Identity in the past was associated with national categories of race. Identity has become local, defined less by race than by whether or not you are from the hood. The hood has become the capital of both a new American art form and a new social identity all under the banner of the hip-hop nation.

Vulgar to some, lyrical to others this brash new urban culture is the social equivalent for the hip-hop generation of what the civil rights movement was to an earlier generation of middle-class blacks. The saggy pants they wear (an outgrowth of prison culture in which belts are not allowed), the gold teeth that Bill Cosby laughs at, even the N word by which they call themselves are emblems of solidarity and belonging. These ghetto motifs are as defining to the millennial underclass as the Afro was to their counterparts back in the day.

In the 1960s one of the heroes of my generation was Malcolm X. Malcolm was associated with a forgotten era of ferment and possibility I would call the black power era.

The civil rights narrative has replaced the narrative of black power. Malcolm's story may be lost to the mainstream in this generation, but for the 1960s he captured the zeitgeist of black thought. Spike Lee, through Denzel, tried to capture that revolutionary spirit on film.[22] He might as well have tried to capture lightning in a bottle.

Although whites at the time were not interested in Malcolm's message, they wanted to understand the source of his power. Thus, a television interviewer asked James Baldwin how Malcolm X had achieved such prominence with the masses of blacks. Baldwin replied, "He corroborates their reality."[23]

Hip-hop has captured the lightning. The Gangstas are the heirs of Malcolm. They corroborate the reality of the urban underclass. By his very name hip-hop's Nigga signifies his rejection of the official story of progress or inclusion. *Nigga* is not just another word for black. "Products of the post-industrial ghetto, the characters of Gangsta rap constantly remind listeners that they are still second-class citizens—Niggas—that nothing has changed for them."[24] To be a Nigga is to say to the world "Assimilation is a false notion of freedom."[25]

In the film *Guess Who's Coming to Dinner*,[26] Sidney Poitier arrives at the mansion owned by Spencer Tracy to date his daughter. The black middle-class dream is to be Sidney: to arrive.

The masses of black people do not aspire to be Sidney Poitier, or to arrive for dinner at the big house on the hill. Like Nino Brown taking over "The Carter"[27] they want to take over the house—the house of popular culture—to be the new cultural address everyone wants to come to.

Across the border, in the suburbs, the dominant society has responded to this aggressive form of hip-hop with widespread moral panic. Tipper Gore famously linked rap music to rape.[28] A women's college protested against Nelly as if he were David Duke with gold teeth.[29]

Rappers are attacked for their music as if it were something toxic, or addictive. Perhaps it is. They are attacked for their dress as if saggy pants were a crime.[30] They are attacked for their language as if the N word they use so frequently was some kind of assault. Of course it is. The violence of strong lyrics is creative. It is not intended to maim or kill; rather their riot of words, attitude, and dress is a new America trying to be born. Perhaps historians will say it was hip-hop that gave birth to the 21st century.

This war against Gangsta rap is waged from as a kind of pincer movement, by the dominant society on one side and by the burgeoning black middle class on the other.

For the dominant society the raison d'être of the conflict is the fear of cultural penetration. In the 1960s whites feared integration—blacks crossing over into the suburbs from the inner city to live next to them. Now the dominant society fears the crossover of urban culture into middle-class suburban households. In the era of integration, great white fear was that blacks, urban primitives, would be a source of violent crime. Interestingly, the mainstream portrayal of Gangsta rap is that it "glorifies, encourages, and 'causes' crime."[31] Bill O'Reilly compared the menace of one Gangsta rapper to that of Cambodia's murderous Pol Pot,

O'Reilly:	You can't draw a line in the sand . . .
Bain:	. . . (Unintelligible. . .
O'Reilly:	. . . and say, Ludacris, because he's a subversive guy, that, number one, advocates violence, number two, narcotics selling and all the other thing . . .
Bain:	But Bill, if you look at the research . . .
O'Reilly:	. . . but he's not as bad as Pol Pot, so we'll put a Pepsi can in his hand.[32]

In tandem with this portrayal linking, Gangsta rap to crime is the notion that Gangsta rap leads to moral decay. Reverend Calvin Butts said famously, "unless we speak against this [rap music] it will creep continually into our society and destroy the morals of our children."[33] Said William Bennett, "I think that nothing less is at stake than the preservation of civilization. This stuff by itself won't bring down civilization, but it doesn't help."[34]

This sociopathic image of Gangsta rap is, in a superficial way, anchored in the lyrics. Since the days of Ice Cube's "Fuck the Police," Gangstas routinely perpetrate criminal acts within the story lines of their songs. Carjacking, armed robbery, beat downs of their rivals, freewheeling drug use abound as rappers appear on stage like so many "Wilding Willie Hortons."[35] Ludacris croons: "I caught him with a blow to the chest. My hollow put a hole in his vest. I'm 'bout to send two to his dome. Cry babies go home!"[36] 50 Cent rhymes, "Run up on a nigga, pop one on the floor, Tell em' come up off that shit fore' we start poppin' some more."[37]

The missing context here is that rap involves metaphorical battle between masters of ceremonies, (MCs), who deploy the mike "as a Tec-9, or AK-47." "Flowing lyrics become hollow point shells." Part of this misreading comes from the fact that because Gangstas are seen as criminals their lyrics become "autobiography."[38] This thug image is cultivated by the rappers themselves, who typically perform under fictitious names, often of famous Gangsters. Rick Ross takes his name from a legendary local drug lord. Biggie Smalls was a gangster in the Bill Cosby film *Let's Do It*

Again. The original 50 Cent was "a Brooklyn stick-up kid infamous for his 'I don't give a fuck fearlessness.'"[39]

But the most scandalous charge leveled against hip-hop is its portrayal of women. With its explicit lyrics, and army of scantily clad women, hip-hop has become the poster child for concerns about the exploitation of black females. There is no doubt that the characters in hip-hop portray an ethos of pimps up and hos down. Women are variously money hungry jezebels—recall Kanye's "I ain't saying she's a gold digger"; or sexually manipulative "bitches"—recall Bell Biv Devoe's "never trust a big butt and a smile"; or simply "pussy to be bought,"[40] as Nelly's video suggests, with a credit card or cash.

Because of images like these, conservatives like C. Delores Tucker have indicted hip-hop as a subversive influence that "coerces . . . motivates, and encourages black youth to . . . abuse women." A few years ago, Calvin Butts entered his verdict on the charge, famously bulldozing a mountain of Gangsta CDs.

Ironically, it is a predominantly suburban-white-audience that buys most of the CDs.[41] What they want, like tourists on safari, is a trip to the ghetto in images and lyrics. Without the violent lyrics and portrayal of criminal lifestyles, Gangsta rap would not sell. Thus Craig Watkins argues, "In exchange for global celebrity, pop prestige and cultural influence hip-hop's top performers had to immerse themselves into a world of urban villainy."[42]

Analysis like this caricatures hip-hop as hate: it is reduced to nothing more than the exploitation of stereotypes for fun and profit. It is just a hot mess of ghetto culture.

Of course it is true that Gangsta rap is densely popu typical images. But the attack on hip-hop is not rooted i lyrics. It is rooted entirely in the narrative of black devia

To white dominated mass media, the controversy over Gangsta rap makes great spectacle. Besides the exploitation of these issues to attract audiences, a central motivation for highlighting Gangsta rap continues to be the sensationalist drama of demonizing black youth culture in general and the contributions of young black men in particular. It is a contemporary remake of "Birth of a Nation." only this time we are encouraged to believe it is not just vulnerable white womanhood that risks destruction by [the Gangstas] but everyone . . .[43]

It is Ellison who says "change the joke, slip the yoke."[44] By embracing the stereotype of black men as thugs and gangsters, for example, rappers seek to invert the hierarchy implicit in the degrading labels of thug and gangster. Racism, today, relies on spatial metaphors. It is sometimes expressed in the top-bottom notion implicit in white superiority/black inferiority.

Black people already experience degradation. Real black men are degraded by poor educational opportunities and by being forced to choose between menial jobs and selling drugs. Products of the same failing schools, black women are often forced to choose between the same menial jobs and working on the stripper pole. What emerges from these wretched choices is that the game—from gangs, to hustling, to selling drugs—has become a defining aspect of ghetto life. It is something blacks are born into which few escape from. Hip-hop in its realism opens a window on this drama and invites the listeners to experience—to participate—in the game vicariously. As the line between those in the game, the players (objects) and the spectators (subjects) begins to blur so does the top-bottom hierarchy on which race depends.

> The "top" attempts to reject and eliminate the "bottom" for reasons of prestige and status, only to discover, not only that it is in some way dependent on the . . . other . . . a psychological dependence upon precisely those others which are being rigorously opposed and excluded at a social level . . . but also that the top also includes the low.[45]

Hip-hop is not a source of degradation so much as it is a response to it.

Race also operates on an inside/outside metaphor. Blacks were kept out of white schools and white suburbs because they would contaminate white society with their criminality, their low sexual mores, and the like. Butts and Tucker track this metaphor by portraying hip-hop as something through which toxic images from the ghetto will *come in* to corrode decency. Hip-hop implicitly challenges this inside/outside dichotomy. Stripper clubs are becoming mainstream. Popular culture and the "porno sphere" are increasingly blurred[46] as the Internet has expanded, amplifying the exploitation of women. Hip-hop is not creating social reality; it is its reflection. It is not bringing in violence or abusive attitudes toward women; it is exposing what is already inside.

You are the key to my locker room. And while it is true that your music holds some of fifteen-thirty year old black men's uglier thoughts about me; it is the only place where I can challenge them. You are also the mirror in which we can see ourselves and there's nothing like spending time in the locker-room to bring sistas face to face with ways we straight up play ourselves. Those are flesh and blood women who put their titties on the glass. Real life women who make their living by waiting back stage and putting price tags on the punnanny. . . . As for the abuse the process is painful but wars are not won by those afraid to go to the battleground. . . . Hip-hop and my feminism are not at war . . . but my community is. And you are critical to our survival.[47]

Hip-hop is not driven by villainy or hate. The true issue with hip-hop is that it embraces a set of values diametrically at odds with those of the dominant society and middle-class blacks as well.

Rappers exchange hard-edged street toughness for middle-class respectability, educational achievement for knowledge of the game, and they exchange in their lyrics the rules of moral behavior for a sense of defiance and being bad. The iconography of hip-hop expresses this defiance by portraying pimps, and hustlers and thugs as representatives of the black experience, and puts their worldview out there without apology much like a cinema verité set to rhyme.

Appreciating the new black aesthetic and the new politics of identity hip-hop symbology represents requires a radical shift in perspective. It cannot be understood from a vantage point outside the culture that produced it. It can be understood only from the standpoint of hip-hop itself. In this the current debate reprises the debate around the black arts movement, which is the precursor to Gangsta rap.

In the aftermath of the assassination of Malcolm X, as the fuse of race relations slowly burned toward an explosive fervor. Playwrights like Baraka, Shange, and Hansberry attempted to use "art" as a "political weapon."[48] Alain Locke had exhorted black artists to break with all "established dramatic conventions"[49] and "develop" their own "idiom."[50] Replete with profanity, populated with winos, prostitutes, con men, and revolutionaries these works did just that. The stage became a site of protest. Baraka, the father of black arts, said his theater was "a weapon to help in the slaughter of these dimwitted fat-bellied white guys who somehow believe that the rest of the world is here for them to slobber on. . . . White men will cower before this theatre because it hates them."[51]

In *The Dutchman,* for example, Baraka presents America as a kind of racial hell in which a white woman can stab a black man to death in the middle of the day with no consequences. "Once dead the rest of the subway's passengers dispose of the body by dragging it out of the car."[52]

Larry Neal in his manifesto about this new movement openly embraced a militant black separatism,

> As such it envisions an art that speaks directly to the needs and aspirations of Black America. In order to perform this task, the Black Arts Movement proposes a radical reordering of western cultural aesthetic. It proposes a separate symbolism, mythology, critique, and iconology. The Black Arts and the Black Power concept both relate broadly to the Afro-American desire for self-determination and nationhood.[53]

Many whites were deeply offended. "Written over 35 years ago . . . many viewers are still offended by the play."[54] Incensed, the mainstream attacked this with both feet. This was "black racism!," cried many critics.[55] Louis Gates exposed this furor as so much cultural relativity. He argued that black art could be understood only on its own terms.[56] In essence Gates exposed the fact that whites had adopted a God's eye view and that this false claim of objectivity prevented them from appreciating the black experience.

It is this same "objectivism" that lurks within the critique of hip-hop. It is a true fact that these artists use words like "bitches" and "hos." I do not defend this. But it is not a question of defense, but rather of perspective.

My point about Gangsta rap is precisely the same as that made by Henry Louis Gates about the black arts movement: Gangsta rap can only be understood on its own terms, from inside the culture that produced it.

> [T]he black aesthetic should repudiate the received terms of academic, or white literary critical methods and theories . . . [a] corollary is that the experience represented by an author in a text is so unique in Western culture that only black critics are able to make normative judgments because only they can guage how "true" or "real to our lives" any particular text might be.[57]

Labels like "pathological" and "violent" are as culturally contingent here as they were in the earlier era of black arts movement—which was the precursor to Gangsta rap.[58] On its own terms Gangsta rap is clearly a response to life and conditions in the ghetto. As such, a "distinction can be drawn between the pathological social conditions in which black urban poor live and the culture they have created to deal with those conditions."[59] In context the new urban culture is a part of the cure, not part of the disease.

The urban griots tell stories that describe, explain, and interpret the lived experience of the ghetto. Through a richly symbolic order they disseminate the shared ideology of a marginalized group. No one—including black middle-class academics who grew up in the wood rather than the hood—is likely to understand the stories. The telling of these stories is church for them, it is their political movement, it is the father they did not have. And despite the masculinist character of the genre one black woman who grew up within the crucible of urban culture embraces it as a place of honesty and freedom:

> We're all winners when a space exists for brothers to honestly state and explore the roots of their pain and subsequently their misogyny. . . . It is criminal that the only space our society provided for the late Tupac Shakur to examine the pain, confusion, drug addiction, fear that led to his arrest and his assassination was a prison cell.[60]

It functions not merely as the mirror of the ghetto, it is its voice. In reading Robinson Crusoe, Toni Morrison reflects on the fact that Man Friday—who really has no name—does not achieve personhood because he cannot speak.[61] The urban underclass is like Man Friday. Many, from middle-class politicians to black academics promoting their books on Nightline, claim to speak for them. But rarely do they speak for themselves. Gangsta rap gives them a way to speak.

What they speak is a testimony. Light passing through water is distorted. Urban cultural production is similarly distorted by the medium of a mainstream culture, which captures, commercializes the content, and distributes it to a mostly suburban audience. But this stream of expression remains our only means of accessing the urban black experience, the only means by which those within it can be heard.

In criminal court the witness to a crime may be someone with a criminal background himself. To investigate the crime you must still listen to the witness and suspend judgment to understand the story.

The major crime in our society, the American dilemma of the 21st century is not Gangsta rap. It is the gulf between the suburbs and the inner city. What was racism has realigned itself along the fault line that divides urban and suburban space both as geographical and cultural space. In the past you were a beast if you were a black man, now the beasts are the ones wearing the saggy pants, in twisty braids, found on street corners in the wrong zip code. The new racism is entangled with a moral panic, which blurs the urban masses and urban culture and demonizes both.

For the larger society the debate about Gangsta rap works to simply silence the witness. It does not illuminate; it obscures.

Structure and Organization

The threshold question is: What is hip-hop? Hip-hop is many things.

> Hip-hop is the plunder from down under, mackin' all others for pleasure. Hip-hop is the Black aesthetic by-product of the American dream machine, our culture of consumption, and subliminal seduction. . . . There is no such thing as good hip-hop, or bad hip-hop, progressive hip-hop, or reactionary hip-hop, politically incorrect hip-hop or hip-hop with a message. It's either hip-hop or it ain't.[62]

For the urban youth who produce it, for the predominantly white audience that listens to it, it is music before it is anything else. But for our purposes it represents a quiet riot set to rhyme. It is a continuation of the politics that began in the streets of Newark by cultural means. To understand the politics that hip-hop represents—a politics of race, space, gender, and class—we must put it in historical and social context.

Part I: Racing Culture/Erasing Race

> America is a fatal division of being, a war of impulses. America knows that split is in her and that that split might cause death; but she is powerless to pull the dangling ends together. An uneasiness

haunts her conscience, taints her moral preachments, lending an air of unreality to her actions, and rendering ineffectual the good deeds she feels compelled to do in the world. America is a nation of riven consciousness but from where did the split, the division come?[63]

In part I, "Racing Culture/Erasing Race," we explain in detail the political context of hip-hop. We will explore what the debate about hip-hop as art has obfuscated: The scapegoating of hip-hop is part of the machinery of denial and evasion concerning how the race is implicated in the ghetto. As we blame the lyrics of Gangsta rap for violence, teenage pregnancy, and the like, race is "invisibilized"[64] as a source of the problem.

The starting point in understanding this process of denial is to understand how our vocabulary has changed in the post–civil rights era. The framing has changed to accommodate the post–civil rights vision of racial transcendence, while the underlying apartheid has remained the same.

Black and white no longer describe the problem. The color line has become more porous: The fragmentation of the black community into an urban underclass and a middle class that has "made it" into the suburbs (the Huxtables); the ascendancy of a black man to the presidency; and the increased visibility of blacks in roles as celebrities, sports figures illustrate just how porous the once impenetrable color line has become.

Because of our success in civil rights, new walls have come up. This dividedness has simply shifted from physical separation of the era of Jim Crow to a cultural schism. I still remember driving through Detroit. I have a friend who works at the law school at the University of Detroit. To drive to his house from the law school one must drive through the black ghetto. The dividing line between the Detroit ghetto and the affluent predominantly white suburb was dramatic, stunningly clear. We went from archetypical urban blight to rolling lawns in the twinkling of an eye. But the objective differences between the two spaces have been conflated with differences between people. Spatial metaphors like inner city and underclass replace the color scheme of the past. Race has been spatialized.

There is also a shift from biological hierarchy—inferior/superior—to one of cultural difference: us versus them. "Us" represents mainstream middle-class culture and values. "Them" represents the ways of life of the urban underclass, a muttering scowling mass criminogenic, dangerous, and lurking in the shadows. It is no longer a problem of color—blacks are on both sides of the divide—but of menace by a criminogenic urban underclass. Cultural alterity has replaced race: it is the new race.

The cultural schism that race has morphed into has in turn been spatialized.

This framework in which race is hidden within spatial metaphors and a narrative of urban cultural menace is illustrated powerfully in the war on drugs. The massive incarceration of black men is widely attributed, in the mainstream, not to race, directly, but to the disparate impact of the war on drugs. It just so happened that Reagan and his predecessors chose to wage the war on drugs in low-income communities. But why were low-income communities targeted? I argue it is because the same moral panic, once associated with "biological inferiority," is now focused on concern that the inner city is a place of urban primitives who must be targeted and controlled. Cultural menace, twisty braids, dropped pants, and gold teeth serve the same function today as biological menace in the "bad old days of segregation."

Chapter 1: From Plantation to the Hood: A Play in Three Acts

I explain this shift in chapter 1, "From Plantation to the Hood: A Play in Three Acts."

"Act One: The Dickensian Aspect" takes us from the Great Migration to the ghetto of today. The history of the urban ghetto chronicles the successive rise of two black metropolises in the same inner city space. Both cities have "a Dickensian aspect" in their abject squalor. The first city, or black ghetto, comes about over a period of about 70 years. This is the ghetto of Kenneth Clark, the ghetto I grew up in which sociologists call, the institutional ghetto. The second city is relatively new; it is the ghetto built on the wreckage of the old. This is the jobless ghetto produced by a convergence of globalism, the suburbanization of investment, technological change, urban renewal, and other transformations. The result is that the 21st century ghetto is a postindustrial wasteland.

In "Act Two: Another Country" I chronicle how Hollywood constructed a fictional ghetto. In this stereotypical ghetto the urban underclass are portrayed much like the rapacious "negroes" who populated the film *Birth of a Nation*.[65] Perhaps we are having a *Birth of a Nation* moment. The real ghetto arises as a result of migration, economic, and global forces that concentrated poor blacks in urban enclaves. The Hollywood ghetto

Dr. Kenneth Clark. (Chicago Urban League records, CULR_04_ 0220_2469_003, University of Illinois at Chicago Library, Special Collections)

arises out of decades of horror films, decades of biased news reporting, and an underlying narrative that says that the ghetto is criminogenic, a place of homicide, rape, robbery, and menace.

Race as a universal has been decommissioned as the basis on which people are targeted for official abuse. What replaces it is more complex—a combination of race, culture, and zip code. The linchpin of this transformation is the war on drugs. In "Act Three: The War on Black Men," I show how the war on drugs relies on the images and constructs—mirroring those created by Hollywood—to result first in massive incarceration and second the transformation of the ghetto into the most militarized community on earth. It is of course not merely the ghetto that is transformed. I argue that we are witnessing the erasure of race and the racing of urban space. (Urban space and urban culture are signifiers of each other here.)

In 1982, Ronald Reagan declared war on drugs.[66] Shortly thereafter Reagan and later Clinton pursued a policy of targeting low-level drug dealers in urban areas.[67] With these marching orders, the black community disproportionately became the target. In 1980, 143,000[68] black men languished in American prisons and jails. Today there are 846,000.[69] "On any given day one out of three black males is in prison, on probation, or parole."[70] The average prisoner is black or Hispanic.[71] The ghetto is more and more like a prison and "the prison more like a ghetto."[72] Dubber calls this a "police regime."[73] More accurately one law professor calls it "petit apartheid."[74]

How is this justified? The police regime that has grown up in the midst of democracy in the inner city is not freestanding. The astonishing numbers of black men handcuffed, locked down, and thrown away have been understood as a problem of institutional racism. It is a problem understood as arising in the decision-making sphere. I am arguing the problem arises in the meaning-making sphere. The stereotypical images, the way the ghetto has been constructed in film, are critical to the projects of the drug war and massive incarceration. The social imaginary and the social real are intimately intertwined.

Chapter 2: Thinking with the Nigga

This political context is essential to understanding the debate about hip-hop music. Nelson George, a brilliant critic of hip-hop as music, says that the main fact that has to be understood about rap music is the context of the epidemic of crack cocaine. I disagree. I think the main fact that explains hip-hop is that the ghetto has become a kind of prison—as a result of structural conditions. The goal of the hip-hop artist is to get out. Gangsta rap has been called nihilistic because it glamorizes criminal lifestyles. The notion is that this is just black noise, that Gangsta rap is to music what senseless violence is to social life. In contrast to these claims I try to show that far from being merely noise there is a powerful outsider narrative in play. In chapter 2, "Thinking with the Nigga," I identify the ideological themes in this outsider narrative that define the community, the hood, and operate as strategies for survival and escape.

The central figure in Gangsta narratives is the Nigga. For the critics of Gangsta rap the Nigga personifies thuggishnes and self-hate. I want to claim the Nigga. For all his vices he has artistic use:

Yet despite its vices and vulgarizations, its sex informalities, its morally anarchic spirit, [it] has a popular mission to perform. Joy after all has a physical basis . . . [It's] spirit, being primitive, demands more

frankness and sincerity . . . and so this new spirit of joy and spontaneity may itself play the role of reformer.[75]

The civil rights narrative is a narrative of citizenship and belonging. It
is African American. To understand the Nigga and the radical honesty he
presents, it is necessary to look at things from a different point of view:
to make a paradigm shift, if you will. The shift is from a linkage with
America to a linkage with the ghetto. In effect one needs the perspective
of ghetto-centrism. (Or really, if I can say it as I feel it—Nigga-centrism.)
    In recovering Gangsta rap as a political narrative—as a counterstory
to those who seem to say we have transcended race—it does not matter
for my purposes whether it functions as art. What does matter is that it
provides a kind of reporting on lived experience of the urban youth in the
inner city that is available nowhere else. But it is only available if we make
the shift to ghettocentrism.

Chapter 3: The Beauty Shop

The characters of Gangsta rap are always getting out of limousines, dressed
in furs, or lounging by the pool, and surrounded by gorgeous, scantily clad
women in bathing suits. While Terrence Howard humanized the pimp in
Hustle and Flow, Gangster rap presents him unapologetically using abus-
ing black women who are constantly referred to as bitches and hos. The
height of this outrage for many was when Nelly slides a credit card down
the crack of a woman's behind—suggesting black women were sex available for anyone with the cash. For many this makes hip-hop a force of evil,
for others at least a source of stereotypes and degradation.
    In chapter 3 I show how the interpretation of hip-hop's images of
women is a matter of perspective; as beauty or ugliness is in the eye
of the beholder, so is hip-hop's ugliness or beauty.[76] We start with the
perspective that seems to be the consensus of both the dominant society and the black middle class. This is the notion that hip-hop is hateful toward women, was built on the exploitation of black women, and
should be held in contempt. The essence of this view is that hip-hop
artist wield cultural power and the pimp/player/ho imagery reinforces
stereotypes.

I contrast this perspective with the bell hooks view that hip-hop merely reflects, rather than creates, the problem of white male patriarchy. I give bell hooks's perspective a local reading: I trace these patriarchal notions to the gangster image propagated by James Cagney and others. The pimp and the gangster are two sides of one coin. bell hooks's view assumes that the pimp is normative: that he represents an actual embrace of street values, and demeaning images.

A contrasting perspective but parallel to that of bell hooks is the notion that the pimp figure is a metaphor or figure in hip-hop, as the bad nigger was in the toasts of folklore. In this perspective the pimp is symbolic, not real, essentially an expression of yearning of black men for recognition.

The final perspective I present is that of hip-hop's badwomen. These sexy MCs wear the term bitch proudly, and brag about using their sexuality making money off powerful men.

All of the perspectives represent competing interpretations about the relationship between the production of stereotypes in music and the perpetuation of stereotypes in the society. All of the perspectives represent a degree of truth. Do we avoid these stereotypes, or do we act them out? Even become them? Hip-hop errs in the direction of bringing wreck. While there are many contradictions here, the bottom line is this: hip-hop's B-Boys and Sexy MC's may trope on stereotypes but they did not create them. The stereotypes create in a pimp/ho/player nexus that exists in the social real, a nexus fused within the crucible of oppression that the ghetto represents.

Part II: Family Affairs

This is a dispute within the family: It is conflict of mothers and daughters, and fathers and sons as much as it is a conflict of class.

The civil rights generation became today's black middle class. This is a middle class produced by affirmative action programs of the 1970s. As they moved up vertically they moved spatially, geographically, as well. In 30 years, 7 million blacks have made it out of the ghetto into the suburbs.[77] Greater America—but at a price. The price of being middle class, as we develop further below, is conversion to the good life. This conversion entails acceptance of basic neoconservative values around family, the work ethic, law and order, and middle-class sexual mores. But that is not all.

To fully assimilate they must reject any association with their uncouth, uneducated ghetto counterparts: The black middle class defines itself by contrast to and disassociation from the black majority in the ghetto. It is this rejection of their ghetto counterparts that the middle class said Amen to when they thunderously applauded Bill Cosby.

> Ladies and gentlemen, the lower economic and lower middle economic people are [not] holding their end in this deal. . . . (Clapping) I'm talking about these people who cry when their son is standing there in an orange suit. Where were you when he was two? (Clapping) Where were you when he was twelve? (Clapping) Where were you when he was eighteen, and how come you don't know he had a pistol? (Clapping) And where is his father, and why don't you know where he is? . . .
>
> 50 percent dropout rate, I'm telling you, and people in jail, and women having children by five, six different men. Under what excuse . . .
>
> Looking at the incarcerated, these are not political criminals. These are people going around stealing Coca Cola. People getting shot in the back of the head over a piece of pound cake! Then we all run out and are outraged, "The cops shouldn't have shot him." What the hell was he doing with the pound cake in his hand? (Laughter and clapping) . . .
>
> Are you not paying attention, people with their hat on backwards, pants down around the crack. Isn't that a sign of something, or are you waiting for Jesus to pull his pants up (laughter and clapping) . . .
>
> We are not Africans. Those people are not Africans; they don't know a damned thing about Africa. With names like Shaniqua, Shaligua, Mohammed, and all that crap and all of them are in jail.[78]

It is as if we have all been cast in *Medea's Family Reunion* where the high society, well-to-do blacks do not get along with their cousins from the hood.

But the conflict goes deeper. The black middle class is divided in itself over who it is. In a real sense in seeking to re8ress the urban primitives they repress a part of themselves.

True reunion, true integration of the black self requires a tricky psychotherapy. The psychological therapist summons repressed memories. The social therapist must summon collective memory.

Chapter 4: Souls on Ice

In chapter 4, "Souls on Ice," I mix autobiography with history. I take the black middle class back to its own beginnings and highlight the moral choices they made—we made—that have precipitated this conflict between classes. I discuss how the streams of suburbanization, the failure of the civil rights movement, and an internal dividedness led them to become what Houston Baker calls "the assimilados."[79]

Chapter 5: Black Skin, New Masks: Hip-Hop and the New Politics of Blackness

At the same time as this is a dispute between different classes and generations, it is also a reflection of an internal division within the black self. Armed with this historical background in chapter 5, "Black Skin, New Masks: Hip-Hop and the New Politics of Blackness," I try to show how the debate about what hip-hop is reflects a conflict over the meaning of blackness.

The black middle-class indictment against hip-hop is that the Gangsta's parading across the stage, as well as the brothers in the hood parading in saggy pants are a minstrel show. They are walking stereotypes costumed for commercial effect at the expense of black people. In the words of Chris Rock they are "fake niggas": as false as the "negroes" of the 19th century who paraded in blackface. In this chapter I turn the tables and look at the ways in which we, the black middle class, are vulnerable to the charge of being fake.

The problem is the bargain. The black middle class can achieve the highest levels of economic and political success, but there is a catch. They either cannot see racism or they must, in our supposedly postracial society, function as if it no longer defines them. In a Fanonian sense they must wear a mask.

We contrast this with the cultural stylings of the urban underclass and discuss how the saggy pants, car culture, and music simply make explicit the very racial contradictions to which the black middle class is blind. In essence, each generation of blacks must choose between the black skin and white mask as versions of identity. I try to show that the Gangsta's embrace of stereotypes is in a sense an embrace of the black skin.

Part III: Solutions

A state of emergency exists in the inner cities of this country. It is a crisis that involves inner city schools that have long been warehouses for urban black youth, it involves the collapse of the economic infrastructure of the inner city, it involves massive incarceration and race-targeted violence by the police. The discourse about the intersection of race and culture has focused on N word, on whether the images produced by urban poets promote violence. This abstract discussion ignores the emergency. The purpose of this book is to flip the script, to shift the discussion back to issues of real black men, real black women, and systemic injustice.

The emergence of Gangsta rap reflects the pervasive and systemic social isolation of the urban underclass. The music is emblematic of the rift between two Americas. The rift is geographic, socioeconomic, and cultural. *The issue is, how do we enfranchise and integrate the urban underclass into the larger society?* More specific to the art form: how do we channel the rage, the alienation, and the yearning the political discourse hip-hop represents into something good?

In part III I identify concrete strategies for how we fix the schools, how we take back hip-hop from the corporations that have appropriated it and distorted its content and shape. Of course I have no magic wand. But I think it is Obama who suggests that the way change begins is by "changing the conversation."

The first step in changing the conversation is to contemporize our notion of the source of change in society. I adopt what I call a post–civil rights stance, synonymous with the stance of hip-hop itself. The stance of civil rights was the stance of governmentality. What I mean by governmentality is that the government, particularly the federal government, is the source of all power and agency. We reject that. Here we adopt a bottom-up concept of change, as opposed to top-down. Traditionally, local knowledge and local control were used against blacks during the school desegregation battles in schools. This same local knowledge/local control can become the pillar of a new strategy of empowerment.

Chapter 6: Lessons from the Second Civil War

In chapter 6, "Lessons from the Second Civil War," I recover the story of a 1960s experiment. I show how local urban communities can take control of their schools.

In Ocean Hill–Brownsville the local Board incorporated African dance and culture into the curriculum.[80] I argue that taking democratic participation seriously requires incorporation of urban cultural production in the curricula of public schools. The two things—local control and the integration of urban culture into public education—areintertwined. The traditional objection to local control has been that the urban underclass lacks the skills to participate at a high level in management. We discuss ways in which lawyers and academics can support this movement for empowerment.

Chapter 7: The Trial of Howard Colvin

The television series *The Wire* tells a story about Bunny Colvin, the fictional Commander of the Western District of the Baltimore City Police Department. Bunny is shown attending a meeting in which Commanders are evaluated on their "arrest statistics." The police department has become like a corporation, where they focus on a bottom line—read the number of arrests—to the exclusion of all else. This is what the drug war has come to. There is no consideration of the fact that after 30 years they are not winning the war, and to the contrary, the use of resources to fight this war is preventing Bunny and others from fighting violent crime. Bunny Colvin leaves the meeting, goes to the bathroom, and throws up. Recovering himself he takes the elevator back to his office. Stanislaus Valcheck, Southeastern District commander, enters the elevator and asks Bunny Colvin how he is going to find a way to reduce crime in the Western District, while at the same time making his share of drug arrests. In the elevator Bunny gets an epiphany, "I might legalize drugs!" This epiphany gave birth to a social experiment in which he creates a safe zone, an area of abandoned houses where drug dealers can sell their drugs without fear of arrest. The area is called Hamsterdam, a combination of a notion that the Baltimore drug dealers are guinea pigs and an analogy to Amsterdam in Holland where drugs have been decriminalized.

Colvin's experiment lasts only until it is discovered by his superiors. In a single morning the Baltimore Police Department mounts a military style raid on the open air drug market brazenly sanctioned by Bunny Colvin. They arrest scores of drug dealers and drug addicts, all to "The Ride of the Valkyries"[81]—a timeless classical score by Wagner, but known to popular culture as the music from the film *Apocalypse*

Now[82] (which depicts the U.S. war against the Viet Cong). Thus, in *The Wire* series, in essence the illicit truce declared by Colvin was over and the war against drugs resumed. Colvin was one of the casualties of this resumption of the war. He is forced to resign and in effect apologize for dereliction of duty.

In chapter 7 we re-present the ideas of Captain Colvin. I present a fictional speech—that Captain Colvin never gave (but should have), which summarizes why the war on drugs failed. It also says why Captain Colvin's brilliant experiment was not only right but should be explored by social scientists, urban mayors, and legal scholars. Following this chapter I present a short epilogue on how a "New Hamsterdam" might work.

Chapter 9: Race and Reconciliation

It has much to do with the rhetoric of war. Wars, as Kenneth Nunn has noted, are fought against groups, not inanimate objects like drugs.[83]

The rhetoric of war mapped easily onto existing stereotypes of blacks and other urban minorities as the source of crime. What emerges is an us-versus-them mentality. It is this us-versus-them mentality that is in play not only in terms of massive incarceration but when black men are profiled, or—like Sean Bell—shot by police. The social practices—our *petit* apartheid—and the us-versus-them mentality are two strands of a single knot of oppression.

To untangle the knot we have to change the culture of "us and them."

Apartheid in America, de jure segregation, ended when the evening news exposed its human consequences: the brutality of blacks being water-hosed, bitten by police dogs, attacked as they marched in places like Selma and Montgomery. Exposing this humanized blacks and broke down the us-versus-them barrier necessary for segregation to exist. The systemic injustice in the inner city persists in part because its human consequences have not been exposed. There is a conspiracy of silence that surrounds police shootings and police brutality.[84]

I propose the same kind of amnesty hearings in inner cities, as were held under Mandela in South Africa. Police must be given amnesty to share their fears and confess to instances of wrongdoing, particularly in cases of police shootings of unarmed black men. This will change the culture. We explore the potential of this effort at reconciliation and the extent to which Gangsta rap can help to drive the discussion of these issues.

Chapter by chapter I show in concrete specificity how local knowledge and urban cultural productions can be a catalyst to empower urban minorities: to transform schools, communities, and ultimately the vibrant art form of hip-hop itself.

Notes

1. Paul Finkelman and Peter Wellenstein, *The Encyclopedia of American Political History* (Washington, DC: Congressional Quarterly Press, 2001), 74.
2. Finkelman and Wellenstein, *The Encyclopedia of American Political History.*
3. Nicolas Lehman, *The Promised Land: The Great Black Migration and How It Changed America* (New York: Alfred A. Knopf, 1991), 190.
4. Otto Kerner, U.S. Riot Commission, *Report of the Nat'l Advisory Comm'n on Civil Disorders* (Washington, DC: National Advisory Commission on Civil Disorders, 1968), 1.
5. One of the effects of deindustrialization is that the office building has replaced the factory in urban areas. Along with that a predominantly white professional class has moved into close proximity to the postindustrial ghetto. See John Mollenkamp, *The Contested City* (Princeton, NJ: Princeton University Press, 1983). Thus, urban/suburban is more of dividing line between different socioeconomic spaces—still heavily linked to race—than a dividing line of geographical space.
6. William J. Wilson, *When Work Disappears: The World of the New Urban Poor* (New York: Alfred A. Knopf, 1996). See also Fred R. Harris and Lynn Curtis, *Locked in the Poor House: Cities, Race and Poverty in the United States* (Boston: Rowman and Littlefied, 2000); Julius Wilson has demonstrated how work has disappeared in the inner city.
7. Wilson, *When Work Disappears*, 19–23.
8. Houston A. Baker, *Betrayal: How Black Intellectuals Have Abandoned the Ideals of the Civil Rights Movement* (New York: Columbia University Press, 2008), 102.

9. Jonathan Kozol, *Savage Inequalities* (New York: Harper Collins, 1992), 29.

10. Robert Holland and Dan Soifer, "How School Choice Benefits the Urban Poor," *Howard Law Journal* 45 (2002): 337.

11. *Hard Times at Douglass High: A No Child Left Behind Report Card*, DVD, directed by Alan Raymond (New York: HBO films 2008).

12. D. Marvin Jones, "The Original Meaning of Brown: Seattle, Segregation and the Rewriting of History: For Michael Lee and Dukwon," *University of Miami Law Review* 63 (2009): 629.

13. "These niggas know where I'm from. I'm from the city of death, nigga. We kill niggas for nothing." Lil Wayne in interview, *DJ Absolute Show*, December 2006, quoted at http://hollyhoodbuzz.blogspot.com/2006_ 12_01_archive.html.

14. Lil Wayne interview, *DJ Absolute Show.*

15. This violence ripples out to claim the lives of black children who refuse conscription into the gang. See "Teen's Beating May Be Gang Related," United Press International, September 25, 2009. http:// www.upi.com/Top_News/2009/09/25. Discussing the case of Derrion Albert, a Chicago teen who was "beat[en] to death" because, in the words of his pastor, "he refused to join a gang."

16. Jewell T. Gibbs, *Young, Black and Male in America: An Endangered Species* (Dover: Auburn House Publishing, 1988), 261.

17. Jennifer Ludden, "Bucking Trend, Homicides among Black Youths Rise," NPR, December 29, 2008, http://www.npr.org/templates/story/ story.php?storyId=98794212.

18. Black-on-black violence as a construct represents the convergence of several competing narratives. Thomas Sowell, for example, features the black family as the source through which negative values and behaviors are transmitted. Underclass families are marked by, "emptiness, agonies, violence and moral squalor." Thomas Sowell, "Tools for Rising Above Are Withheld Today," *Sun Sentinel* (Ft. Lauderdale), November 6, 2001. This story has a "principal villain": the black male child. See David Wilson, *Inventing Black-on-Black Violence: Discourse, Space, and Representation* (Syracuse: Syracuse University Press 2005), 59. With "brutish bodies and brutish minds they are predisposed to being violent." Wilson, *Inventing Black-on-Black Violence*. These strands merge together in a "culture of poverty"

thesis "according to which the black urban poor are conceived of as an isolated group of individuals whose behavior is aberrant and dominated by pathological cultural values." Tommy Lee Lott, *The Invention of Race and the Politics of Representation* (Maiden, MA: Blackwell, 1999), 111.

19. Ironically, it was Kenneth Clark who popularized the notion of the ghetto as a place of pathology. See Kenneth Bancroft Clark, *Dark Ghetto: Dilemmas of Social Power* (Middletown, CT: Wesleyan University Press, 1965), 81. "The dark ghetto is institutionalized pathology; it is chronic self-perpetuating pathology." But Clark uses the term in the context of a macro-structural analysis of the problems of "the ghetto."

> The publication of the Dark Ghetto in 1965 marked the beginning of a series of thoughtful studies of life in impoverished inner-city neighbor-hoods . . . These studies were distinctive in their focus on the macro-structural constraints that have compelled many ghetto residents to act in ways that do not conform to mainstream social norms and expectations. (ix)

20. Clark extended the disease metaphor—that is, ghetto culture is "pathological"—to the notion that it is also "contagious."

> Neither instability, nor crime can be controlled by police vigilance or by reliance on the alleged deterrent forces of legal punishment, for the individual crimes are to be understood more as a result of the *contagious sickness* of the community itself than as the result of the inherent criminal or deliberate viciousness. (*Dark Ghetto*, 81)

Clark was talking about the effects of institutionalized racism. Clark's "contagion thesis" has largely been appropriated by neoconservatives. In fact the Broken Windows theory created by conservative New York mayor Rudy Giuliani was predicated on this notion of urban disorder as infectious. See Ronald Bailey, "Is Crime Contagious: Experiments Vindicate the Broken Windows Theory," *Reason Magazine*, November 25, 2008.

21. See Tricia Rose, *Black Noise*: *Rap Music in Contemproary America* (Middletown, CT: Wesleyan University Press, 1994).

22. Spike Lee and Arnold Perl, *Malcolm X*, directed by Spike Lee (Burbank, CA: Warner Bros., 1992).

23. James Baldwin, Fred L. Stanley, and Louis H. Pratt, *Conversations with James Baldwin* (Jackson, MS: University Press of Mississippi,

1989), 43. "That's Malcolm's great power over his audiences. He corroborates their reality, he tells them they really exist."

24. Robin D.G. Kelly, "Kickin Reality, Kickin Ballistics: Gangsta Rap and Post-Industrial Los Angeles," in *Droppin Science: Critical Essays on Rap Music and Hip-Hop Culture*, ed. William Eric Perkins (Philadelphia, PA: Temple University Press, 1996), 137.

25. Christa D. Acampora, *Unmaking Race, and Remaking Soul: Transformative Aesthetics and the Practice of Freedom* (New York: State University of New York Press, 2007).

26. *Guess Who's Coming to Dinner*, directed by Stanley Kramer (1967; Culver City, CA: Columbia Pictures, 2004, DVD).

27. Thomas L. Wright and Barry M. Cooper, *New Jack City*, directed by Mario Van Peebles (Burbank: Warner Brothers, 1991).

28. Tipper Gore, "Hate, Rape and Rap," in *Rap and Hip Hop: Examining Pop Culture*, ed. Jared Green (Farmington Hills, MI: Greenhaven Press, 2003), 110–13.

29. Kathy Willens, "Black College Women Take Aim at Rappers," *USA Today*, April 23, 2004. Rapper Nelly discovered his sister had bone marrow cancer. Nelly started a foundation and persuaded Spellman College to co-sponsor an event to increase awareness concerning the disease. But Nelly had produced a video, "Tip Drill," airing on BET's after hours uncut video show. The misogynistic lyrics and images had inflamed many members of Spellman's historically all-female student body. Student protests forced Nelly to cancel the event. My sense is that the images in this video did have a clearly sexist dimension—a credit card slides down the crease of a woman's backside. However, there is another side to this debate. Is Nelly glorifying stripping, the selling of black women's bodies? Or is he holding up a mirror? See discussion in Willens.

30. One of the themes I am developing here is the remaking or recoding of race as culture. Moral panic is conserved: it shifts from color to an intersection of color and cultural alterity. My earlier work was a brooding meditation on this recoding. See D. Marvin Jones, *Race, Sex, and Suspicion: The Myth of the Black Male* (Westport, CT: Greenwood, 2005).

31. Dan Frosch, "Colorado Police Link Rise in Violence to Music," *New York Times*, September 3, 2007.

Frosch reports:

> [T]he police here are saying Gangsta rap is contributing to the violence, luring gang members and criminal activity to nightclubs. The police publicly condemned the music in a news release after a killing in July and are warning nightclub owners that their places might not be safe if they play Gangsta rap.

32. Bill O' Reilly, "Factor Follow-Up Interview with Jackson Bain," *The O'Reilly Factor*, August 28, 2002.

33. Tricia Rose, *Hip-Hop Wars: What We Talk about When We Talk about Hip-Hop—and Why It Matters* (New York: Basic Books, 2008), 95.

34. Rose, *Hip-Hop Wars*.

35. Murray Forman and Mark Anthony Neal, *That's the Joint!: The Hip-Hop Studies Reader* (London: Routledge, 2004), 335.

36. "Cry Babies (Oh No)," on an album called *Word of Mouf*, performed by Ludacris, (New York City: Def Jam South, 2001).

37. Ron Browz, "I'll Whip Yo Head Boy," on album called *Get Rich or Die Tryin'*, performed by 50 Cent (Santa Monica: G-Unit/Interscope Records, 2003).

38. Rose, *Hip-Hop Wars*.

39. Derrick Parker and Matt Diehl, *Notorious C.O.P.: The Inside Story of the Tupac, Biggie, and Jam Master Jay* (San Clemente: Tantor Media, 2007).

40. T. Denean Sharpley-Whiting, *Pimp's-Up, Ho's Down: Hip-Hop's Hold on Young Black Women* (New York: New York University Press, 2007), 4.

41. Richard W. Oliver, *Hip-Hop Inc: Success Strategies of the Rap Moguls* (New York: Thunder's Mouth Press, 2006), 172.

42. Samuel C. Watkins, *Hip-Hop Matters, Politics, Pop Culture, and the Struggle for the Soul of a Movement* (Boston, MA: Beacon Press, 2005), 45.

43. Marjorie Ford and Jon Ford, *Mass Culture and the Electronic Media* (Boston, MA: Houghton Miflin, 1999), 63.

44. Ralph Ellison, *Shadow and Act* (New York: Random House, 1995).

45. Brian McNair, *Strip-Tease Culture: Sex, Media and the Democratization of Desire* (New York: Routledge, 2006), 87.

46. McNair, *Strip-Tease Culture*.

47. Joan Morgan, *When Chicken-Heads Come Home to Roost: A Hip-Hop Feminist Breaks It Down* (New York: Simon and Schuster, 1999), 70.

48. Philip U. Effiong, *In Search of a Model for African-American Drama: A Study of Selected Plays* (Lanham, MD: University Press of America, 2000), 32.

49. Paul Carter and Gus Edwards, *Black Theatre, Ritual Performance in African Diaspora* (Philadelphia, PA: Temple University Press, 2002), 4. "Negro art . . . must more and more have the courage to be original, to develop . . . its own idiom, to pour itself into new molds."

50. LeRoi Jones, *The Revolutionary Theatre*, quoted in Carter and Edwards, *Black Theatre*, 239.

51. Sharon Monteith, *American Culture in the 1960's* (Edinburgh: Edinburgh University Press, 2008), 55.

52. Effiong, *In Search of a Model for African-American Drama*, 22.

53. Emmanuel S. Nelson, *African-American Dramatists: An A–Z Guide* (Westport, CT: Greenwood Press, 2004), 28.

54. Karen L. Rood, *American Culture After WWII* (Farmington Hills, MI: Gale Research, 1993), 29.

55. James Edward Smethurst, *The Black Arts Movement: Literary Nationalism in the 1960's and 1970's* (Chapel Hill: The University of North Carolina, 2005), 391; Imamu Amiri Baraka and William J. Harris, *The Leroi Jones/Amir Baraka Reader* (New York: Thunder Mouth Press, 2000), 382, see also Henry L. Gates, *Figures in Black: Words, Signs and the Racial Self* (New York: Oxford University Press, 1989), xxvii.

56. Gates, *Figures in Black*, 31.

57. Fahamisha P. Brown, *Performing the Word: African-American Poetry as Vernacular Culture* (Rutgers, NY: Rutgers University Press, 1999), 91.

58. Brown, *Performing the Word*.

59. Tommy L. Lott, *The Invention of Race: Black Culture and the Politics of Representation* (Malden, MA: Blackwell Publishers, 1999), 112.

60. Morgan, *When Chicken-heads Come Home to Roost*, 80.

61. The concept of voice is as important here as it is in the study of black drama or literature. It is again Henry Louis Gates who says that

> [T]he concept of voice (finding the authority to speak)—who speaks, to whom, or what—signifies the difference between the Anglo and African American traditions. . . . For African-American poets the empowering response is from the people: call and response . . . the African-American

poet seeks the authority to speak by trying to recover an un-exiled continuity between speaker and listener.

Barbara Bowen, "Untroubled Voice: Call and Response in Cane," *in Black Literature and Black Literary Theory*, in Henry Louis Gates, 31.

62. Yvonne Bynoe, Stand and Deliver: Political Activism, Leadership and Hip-Hop Culture, (Berkeley: Soft Skull Press, 1992), 147.

63. St. Clair Drake and Horace R. Cayton, *Black Metropolis: A Study of Negro Life in a Northern City* (Chicago: Chicago University Press, 1993), xxi.

64. Loic Wacquant, *Deadly Symbiosis: When Ghetto and Prison Meet and Mesh* (Cambridge, MA: Cambridge University Press, 2010), 98.

65. *Birth of a Nation*, directed by D. W. Griffith (originally released 1915, Epoch Film Company).

66. "Reagan in Radio Talk, Vows Drive against Drugs," *New York Times*, October 3, 1982, 1:38.

67. Michael Tonry, *Malign Neglect: Race, Crime and Punishment in America* (New York: Oxford University Press, 1996), vii.

68. Demico Boothe, *Why Are So Many Black Men in Prison?* (Baltimore, MD: Full Surface Publishing, 2007), 86.

69. Boothe, *Why Are So Many Black Men in Prison.*

70. Wacquant, *Deadly Symbiosis*, 96.

71. Wacquant, *Deadly Symbiosis*, 97.

72. Wacquant, *Deadly Symbiosis*, 97.

73. Markus Dubber, *Victims in the War on Crime: the Use and Abuse of Victim's Rights*, New York: NYU Press, (2006), 15.

74. Dragan Milovanovic and Katheryn K. Russell, *Petit Apartheid in the U.S. Criminal Justice System* (Durham, NC: Carolina Academic Press, 2001).

75. Alain Locke, *Harlem, Mecca of the New Negro* (1925), quoted in Lewis Porter, *Jazz, A Century of Change* (CT: Schirimer Books, 1997), 126.

76. In critical theory we call this the problem of "incommensurability." All truth is paradigm dependant. Each community of interpretation operates from a different model in terms of how it defines, race, respectability, gender, and so on. There is no neutral place to stand between these competing worldviews.

77. Sheryll Cashin, *The Failures of Integration: How Race and Class Are Undermining the American Dream* (Jackson, TN: Public Affairs Books, 2005), 134.

78. Bill Cosby, "Speech at NAACP Gala Celebration of the Brown Decision," Constitution Hall, Washington, DC, May 17, 2004, quoted in Juan Williams, *Enough: The Phony Leaders, Dead-end Movements, and Culture of Failure That are Undermining Black America—And What We Can Do About It* (New York: Crown Publishing, 2006), 9.

79. Baker, *Betrayal*, 91.

80. Generally, Jerald E. Podair, *The Strike That Changed New York: Blacks, Whites and the Ocean—Hill Brownsville Crisis* (New Haven, CT: Yale University Press, 2004).

81. Richard Wagner, "The Ride of the Valkyries," from *Die Valkyrie*, performed by the Vienna Philharmonic Orchestra in Francis Ford Copola, *Apocalypse Now* (San Francisco: California Zoetrope Studios, 1979).

82. See Copola, *Apocalypse Now.*

83. Kenneth Nunn, "Race, Crime and the Pool of Surplus Criminality: Or Why "War on Drugs" Was a "War on Blacks," *Journal of Gender, Race, & Justice* 6 (2002): 381, 389.

84. Transparency and Conspiracy: Ethnographies of Suspicion in the New World Order, edited by Harry G. West , Todd Saunders, (Chapel Hill: Duke University Press 2003); see Mary F. Berry, *Police Practices and Civil Rights in New York City* (Washington, DC: The U.S. Civil Rights Commission, 2000), 38. As the Dorner case suggests, this conspiracy of silence is policed against other policemen who try to blow the whistle. Serpico style Dorner tried to blow the whistle on practices of the Los Angeles Police Department and ended up being terminated unjustly. Tragically this led, according to police, a rampage in which Dorner murdered innocent people. Dorner is not a hero. Unlike Django, Dorner killed innocent people not slave owners and overseers. There is no justification for killing innocent people. Like King we must categorically reject the temptation of violence as a means to political ends. Otherwise we trade places with those who oppress. But the point here is that is a conspiracy of silence among police departments, which urgently needs to be addressed.

Part I

Racing Culture/Erasing Race

Racist representation of African American youth in the mainstream media has shifted. Where in the past it was typically signified through stereotypical caricatures, today it is also signified through the use of racially coded spaces, like the post-industrial city. In the midst of various political, cultural and socioeconomic factors the inner city, and people that inhabited it, became Hollywood's new symbol for vulgarity, inhumanity, and intellectual inferiority. Instead of depicting all Blacks as threatening, ruthless, or academically inept, inhabitants of the ghetto, who were believed to live a certain type of lifestyle, became the media's new "other."[1]

Introduction

The act of writing requires "a constant plunging back into the shadows of the past."[2] What is true for writing in general is true for film, especially when one tries to capture the black experience. The artist here must plunge into our racial past to help us to remember the choices and steps, which brought us to this place. In the film *Precious,* Tyler Perry takes us back to the past—to Harlem of 20 years ago—to tell a story about a talented, star-crossed teenage girl named Precious. But what Perry produces is a parade of contemporary stereotypes, not a recollection of Harlem as it was.

To stereotype black people is the moral equivalent of an act of violence against them. It is representational violence. Violence, of course, can be justified—if it serves the purposes of social realism. Since John Singleton's *Boyz in the Hood* and *Menace to Society,* a generation of Hood films have mobilized violent images. But the Hood films were expressions of a ghettocentric imagination. Like hip-hop music, these films do the job of a ghetto-based CNN: they vividly documented the raw conditions of ghetto life.

Precious though was not John Singleton style ghettocentrism, it was Eurocentrism. This was not realism but caricature—no single black family could have captured all of the pathology, the cooning of the people portrayed.

Set in Harlem in the late 1980s, the movie focuses on Clariece Jones, a teenager known as Precious, who is sexually and emotionally abused by her enraged, foul-mouthed mother, Mary (played by the actor and comedian Mo'Nique). They rely on welfare; Precious

35

is H.I.V.-positive; and the first of her two children (both by her father) has Down's syndrome. Precious fantasizes about having a light-skinned boyfriend and about herself as a thin, white girl.[3]

Every negative cliché about ghetto blacks was on display—from a collard greens and pig feet eating family, to an illiterate welfare queen (the mother), to a violent abusive father, to the black family that can't speak English, to the "I hate I'm black I wish I was white" syndrome portrayed by Precious. It is not merely that the black family has such problems as ignorance, self-hatred, and child abuse but they personify these problems. As Courtland Malloy wrote, "Maybe there is something to the notion that when human pathology is given a black face, white people don't have to feel so bad about their own. At least somebody's happy."[4]

The degradation of the black underclass was so explicit it prompted one reviewer to exclaim, "Not since *The Birth of a Nation* has a mainstream movie demeaned the idea of black American life as much as 'Precious'."[5] But criticism by a few progressive black journalists was marginalized as a kind of minority report.

Precious, a clichéd portrayal of the ghetto, was nonetheless greeted with mainstream critical acclaim.

At the 25th Independent Spirit Awards, *Precious* took top prize for best feature. Mo'Nique—you go girl—won an award for Best Supporting Actress in her role as the abusive mother. Geoffrey Fletcher won an academy award for his adaptation of the novel *Push.*

In context this was a celebration of minstrelsy. Of course, *Precious*'s defenders described the film as inspirational, as a statement of hope. But as Aisha Harris writes, "the glimmer of hope is hard to see when the movie concludes with Precious living in a halfway house and infected with HIV from her father who raped her and left her with two children."[6]

Race Porn

The dominant society has an illicit appetite for portraits of blacks in the ghetto as an unreachable, unredeemable underclass.

Tyler Perry did not create a scenario of hope, rather he pandered to and commodified this story of nihilism and hopelessness. The picture seems to say, "The stereotypes are true."[7] It is in this vein that Courtland Malloy

wrote, "In 'Precious' Oprah and Perry have helped serve up a film of pruri-
ent interest that has about as much redeeming social value as a porn flick."[8]

Farah Jasmin Griffin notes there are three safe places in the black community: the mother, the family, and the church.[9] But here in the context of
the claustrophobic and incestuous violence on display, the mother and the
family—of Harlem, East Baltimore, and South Bronx—are the source of
the violence. The church in the Harlem of *Precious* is inexplicably non-
existent. The only hope for Precious is messianic members of the black
middle class.

Precious's teacher Rain and her lesbian lover who take her in personify hope. The middle class blacks are role models. The black middle class
is also judge and jury. Mariah Carey, the dowdy social worker who interro-
gates Mo'Nique and exposes her complicity in her daughter's abuse, personifies this function. From behind her social worker's desk, Carey passes
judgment not only on Mo'Nique but on the black family of the ghetto. The
film seems to say that a black family is the source of its own sociopathol-
ogy. And it says it in a booming authoritarian voice.

In many ways, the author of this story is not Geoffrey Fletcher but
Daniel Patrick Moynihan. His 1967 report, The "Negro Family: The Case
for Action,"[10] is the source of the narrative that *Precious* retells. Moynihan
largely attributed the social disparities of the ghetto to the collapse of the
nuclear family. "At the heart of the deterioration of the fabric of Negro
society is the deterioration of the Negro family."[11] More specifically he
tied ghetto poverty to the pattern of single parent households headed by
women. "Black family structures are seen as deviant because they challenge patriarchal assumptions . . . "[12]

What is stereotyped in *Precious* is not merely the black family, or the
black single mother, but the ghetto itself.

The ghetto is a jungle where mothers abandon their young, where fathers rape their daughters, and there is no God.

This captures a critical change in the way race is performed on our
screens. As one writer puts it, "race becomes space." As Murray Forman
writes, "new signifiers of blackness are also closely aligned with the vital-
ized significance of place, for they are often though by no means always
grafted onto one another."[13]

Historically, we thought of space as transparent, apolitical, and innocent. But space as Murray Forman tells us serves as a tool of thought

and action.[14] Race, space, and class have historically been systematically ordered in the collective consciousness, especially among white middle class[15] Said another way,

> Racist representation of African American youth in the mainstream media has shifted. Where in the past it was typically signified through stereotypical caricatures, [t]oday it is also signified through the use of racially coded spaces, like the post-industrial city. In the midst of various political, cultural and socioeconomic factors the inner city, and people that inhabited it, became Hollywood's new symbol for vulgarity, inhumanity, and intellectual inferiority. Instead of depicting all Blacks as threatening, ruthless, or academically inept, inhabitants of the ghetto which were believed to live a certain type of lifestyle, became the media's new "other."[16]

Precious lives in a world within a world. There is an invisible line that separates the world—the space—Precious lives in and the world—the space—of Blue Rain. This is symbolic of the invisible but unmistakable line that separates the ghetto from the world the middle class moves in and has its lattes. One space is safe, the other deadly. One space is inhabited by normal people and the other by violent, abusive sociopaths.

The notion is that once you cross the line, that is, once you leave the suburbs and enter the inner city, you have entered into an urban nightmare. This nightmare space is coded as black. That is ghetto space—ghetto conditions—and its people are conflated. This conflation enables verbal shorthand:

> [M]ost people know in advance that Harlem and the Bronx are predominantly inhabited by blacks, Latinos, or immigrants, distinguishing it from Manhattan and other boroughs. This assumed knowledge makes it easier to graft onto these places further images (as well as stereotypes) pertaining to the cultures that cohere there.[17]

As race becomes space, the stigma always associated with race defines the sense of place, "No one could agree on exactly where the South Bronx is but they all said that wherever it is it has a bad reputation."[18]

If race and space have become two sides of one coin, race and criminality have as well. In an earlier conversation—in my book *Race, Sex, and Suspicion: The Myth of the Black Male*—I noted how in the past the subordination of blacks rested on a notion of biological inferiority, but that increasingly, this story of biological inferiority is being replaced with a notion of criminality or disease.[19] We are portrayed as criminals, thugs, and abusers. Black women have HIV. Black men will jack your car or steal your purse.

This conflation of blackness and criminality is referred to as the narrative of black deviance. But it is no longer blackness as a universal which drives the narrative; it is a more local version of blackness. For example, in my tailored suit and tie, brightly polished shoes, and sophisticated bearing, I am welcomed into art galleries, law firms, and into elite spaces. Whites may sit next to me on the train. I am not threatening. The men scowling in twisty braids and baggy pants—and to a lesser extent women in Harlem gaming the welfare system—are threatening, and they are key figures in the story. This narrative of black deviance today has black men and as we see in *Precious,* black families from the ghetto in mind. The anchoring notion is that the ghetto is an alien place. In *Blues People,* Imamu Baraka makes a point that what made blacks different was not merely that they were a different color but that they were foreign.

> When black people got to this country, they were Africans, a foreign people. Their customs attitudes, desires were shaped in a different place, a radically different life . . . an African who was enslaved by Africans can still function as a kind of human being. . . . However the African who was unfortunate enough to find himself on a fast clipper ship to the new world was not even accorded membership in the human race.[20]

Otherness as foreignness becomes key to the narrative. The spatial isolation of the ghetto enables this sense of foreignness. Foreignness is the root of the notion of black deviance. Thus in *Do the Right Thing,* the action revolves around a pizzeria, owned by Sal, located smack-dab in the Brooklyn Ghetto. Sal personifies generations of white businessmen who profit from businesses of the ghetto but who buy a notion of the black poor around them as culturally alien. Pino, Sal's son, captures this when he says, "Everyday I come to work, it's like 'Planet of the Apes'."

Cinematic productions like *Precious* reinscribe this signifying chain of race, space, and alien culture: bad families, bad fathers, bad mothers, and bad behavior are identified with those people who live in certain zip codes. You know the ones with the twisty braids, gold teeth.

Film as Legitimation

Tyler Perry's movie was acclaimed because it was perceived as authentic. "The perception of naturalness makes stock characters particularly revealing of cultural assumptions . . . stock figures are part of the cultural coin of the moment; their use is remarkable only when they are supplanted by newer, more contemporary currency."[21]

What is the source of this claim of authenticity? It is authenticity validated by common sense. Of course as Waheema Lubiano has written, "whenever one can say something is common sense we are describing ideology."[22]

The picture of the ghetto as a place of pathology and dysfunction embodies the common sense of the black middle class about why the ghetto is in the condition that it is.

In this common-sense view, the ghetto is an already read text. It is a set of preexisting images. In this preconceived image of the ghetto, the ghetto appears both dangerous and alien. The hard working people who live in the inner city disappear. All we see on our screens is a netherworld of dysfunctional families, bad actors, graffiti-covered walls, and dead end streets.

This preconceived image erases both the story of how the ghetto came to be, and the structural racism that continues to exist.

As David Leonard writes,

These films don't merely reinscribe dominant stereotypes that play to uncertainties and fears that naturalize social decay in the name of increased state intervention within communities of color. They also offer narratives that successfully deny racism and [p]rovide legitimacy to claims of colorblind America, all the while justifying a coercive and violent state presence within American ghettos needed to protect and contain those whose poor choices make them a threat to Americans.[23]

Such legitimation films as *Precious* are part of the reason why the ghetto persists:

Like the moralistic interpretation of ghetto poverty offered by . . .
William Bennett or the coverage of the "Crack epidemic" on network
news shows, they mystified the source and nature of the real social
and economic problems faced by our major cities. So much so that it
serves to perpetuate the conditions even as they selectively exaggerated their severity.[24]

Of course violence within and between black family members is em-
barrassingly evident from the evening news. Tony Morrison explores this
often-incestuous violence in her novels.

The traumatic, unspeakable secrets around which each novel is struc-
tured are acts of familial, black-on-black violence. I am thinking of
Cholly's rape of his own daughter in The BLUEST EYE; of Eva's cre-
mation of her still living son and the National Suicide Day proces-
sion that ends up burying itself alive in SULA; of the life insurance
salesman's suicide flight and Milkman's leap into the killing arms of
his brother in Song of Solomon, of Sethe's infanticide in BELOVED;
of Joe's murder of his lover and his wife's knifing of her corpse in
Jazz.[25]

But Morrison, while painting her social realist image of the black family, is careful first to show that the wound to the black family in the present is the result of an original wound perpetrated by the dominant white
society.

While each novel performs an important work of cultural memory by
narrativizing a specific era of African-American history, each novel
also refers back to an "original" violation. . . . In *Song of Solomon*
the characters' actions can be traced back to the lynching of the first
Macon Dead; in *Tar Baby* to the slave economy upon which Valar-
ian's candy empire is built; in beloved the middle passage . . . in *Jazz*
to the history of lynchings and miscegenation that Joe and Violet attempt to escape by moving North.[26]

So what is missing and what makes *Precious* false is the absence of any
reference to the historical and structural dimensions of ghetto conditions.

As such, Tyler Perry's movie is the perfect metaphor for the dehistoricized way the ghetto is almost always portrayed in popular culture.

In this dehistoricized worldview, the mainstream seems to posit the conditions of the ghetto as just there, as something natural, a fact of life. This is reminiscent of the way Africa was dehistoricized and dehumanized during the colonial era: "[T]he European eye reduced the black man to merely part of nature, a thing outside of history or civilization, he became a 'fact of life before which those who have fashioned the colonial world become spectators in a mystery not of their own making'."[27]

Like Africa the ghetto has a history. This history was summed up in the Kerner Commission report in 1968. "What white Americans have never fully understood but what the Negro can never forget—is that white society is deeply implicated in the ghetto. White institutions created it, white institutions maintain it, and white society condones it."[28]

The double significance of these stereotypes is not only that black people are homogenized but also the role of white racism in the conditions is invisible. In the case of Precious, it is clear that she is failing in school, but there is no context provided of the extent to which inner city schools— underfunded and resegregated—are failing the students: To what extent has failure become a self-fulfilling prophecy at many of these schools?

Precious is not put in context. Worse, Precious, her mother, and her family's lifestyle are made to appear as somehow typical.

The people in the ghetto become a monolith. In the show *The Wire,* one of the most defining moments was when Kima Greggs sits in the window, holding a small child. As police sirens wail in the background, she sits looking out over the urban tableau. She looks out framed by the window of the row house and the expansive red brick walls so characteristic of Baltimore's inner city homes. She says good night to the ghetto: "Good night fiends/Good night hoppers/Good night hustlers/Good night scammers. Good night to everybody."[29]

Kima Greggs clearly has the idea that the ghetto is a place of rampant pathology and dysfunction. This image is a mixture of fact and fiction. For example, most people do not realize that, at least in Maryland—which is where the show *The Wire* is based—blacks' use of cocaine is statistically identical to the use of cocaine by whites.

Nonetheless, while blacks make up little more than a quarter of Maryland's population (28%), blacks comprise 68 percent of those arrested.

Equally important is the fact that it is only a minority of blacks who use drugs like cocaine. The majority of blacks in the inner city are law abiding.

But the perspective of Kima Greggs is typical of popular culture. Popular culture reduces the black community to its lowest common denominator. This reductive story is a kind of metonymy.[30] The part stands for the whole. This lumping is what happens in films like *Precious* and television series like *The Wire*. This prompted Elijah Anderson to say,

> I get frustrated watching it because it gives such a powerful appearance of reality, but it always seems to leave something important out. What they have left out are the decent people. Even in the worst drug-infested projects, there are many, many God-fearing, churchgoing, brave people who set themselves against the gangs and the addicts, often with remarkable heroism.[31]

In the next three chapters, we want to begin by providing the missing pieces. We want to explain how the ghetto was constructed as it is. This process has two parts: One part of the process has to do with the decision-making sphere. In this sphere, blacks made decisions to leave the South, whites in the North made decisions to segregate them. This process of migration of Southern blacks to Northern cities and the ghettoization that followed took place over a hundred years from 1870 to 1970. This produced the ghetto of *Precious,* of *Superfly,* and the ghetto of *Starsky and Hutch*. But the ghetto of today is relatively recent; it is the result of changes that took place over the last 30–40 years. This is a process of structural change. The ghetto of today is the ghetto produced by the forces of globalism, and by yet another migration, this time the migration of the black middle class, business, and investment to the suburbs. This is the ghetto where work has disappeared—the ghetto of crack epidemics, the ghetto of dislocation, the war on drugs, burnt-out houses, and of massive incarceration. It is the ghetto of Lil Wayne, Nas, T-Pain, Trina, and 50 Cent.

In this complex story of migration, ghettoization is the first act in the social construction of the ghetto. I title it "The Dickensian Aspect."

The second act has to do with the meaning-making sphere. In *Precious,* we talked about the disconnect between the problems of the ghetto as a function of structural conditions and the perception of the ghetto as a result of cumulative bad choices. What happened to account for this disconnect between the ghetto of the cultural imaginary—a place of black people behaving badly—and the ghetto in the social real as a product of history?

What happened was Hollywood. I title this second act "Another Country: The Nightmare on Our Screens."

The third act is the drug war. It functions first in the realm of structural conditions: It is responsible for most of the massive incarceration that is taking place. It only exacerbates the problem of violence and social disorganization. It also functions in the meaning-making sphere. It has in a sense changed the meaning of race. It contributes more than anything else to equating being in the ghetto and being in prison. Urban blacks internalize the oppressiveness associated with the place they are forced to live as the meaning of being black.

But I am ahead of my story. Let us begin with history.

Notes

1. Lamar C. Johnson, "Through Viewers' Eyes: Watching Race, Space, Place and the Hood Motif in Urban High School Genre Film," 2, http://juyc.info/pdf/Lamar_Johnson.pdf.

2. Ralph Ellison, *Shadow and Act* (New York: Random House, 1995), xix.

3. Sasha Stone, "The State of Race: It's the Movies," *Awards Daily* (Valley Village, CA), August 30, 2009.

4. Courtland Malloy, *Precious: A Film as Lost as the Girl It Glorifies* (Washington, DC: Washington Post), November 18, 2009.

5. Quoting Armand White, *Pride and Precious* (New York: New York Press), November 4, 2009, http://www.nypress.com/article-20554-pride-precious.html.

6. Aisha N. Harris, *Limited Black Film Genre Fosters Stereotypes* (Hartford, CT: Hartford Courant), A13, February 17, 2010.

7. See D. Marvin Jones, *Race, Sex, and Suspicion: The Myth of the Black Male* (Westport, CT: Greenwood, 2005). Increasingly one of the most fashionable forms of racism is this idea of "reasonable racism." This was a major theme of the *Race, Sex, and Suspicion*. The idea seems to be that yes we are stereotyping but this is "reasonable" because the stereotype is generally true. This cartoonish notion—"The stereotypes

are true!"—is at the core of racial profiling, particularly with respect to Mexican immigrants in the current Arizona immigration controversy and with respect to the Muslim mosque where Muslims want to build a place of worship near the world trade center. This same idea seems to drive the over-the-top use of ghetto stereotypes in *Precious*.

8. Malloy, *Precious.*

9. Farah Jasmin Griffin, *Who Set You Flowin: The African Migration Narrative* (New York: Oxford University Press, 1995), 113.

10. John Bracey, August Meir, and Elliot M. Rudwick, *Black Matriarchy: Myth or Reality?* (Belmont, CA: Wadsworth Publishing Company, 1971), 126.

11. Bracey et al., *Black Matriarchy*, 126.

12. Nelson M. Rodriguez and Leitlla A. Villa Verde, *Dismantling White Privilege: Pedagogy, Politics, and Whiteness* (Switzerland: Peter Lang Publisher, 2000), 12.

13. Murray Forman, *The Hood Comes First: Race, Space and Place in Rap and Hip-Hop* (Middletown, CT: Wesleyan Press, 2002), 28. Murray Forman, *The Hood Comes First*, 28.

14. Forman, *The Hood Comes First*, 4.

15. Forman, *The Hood Comes First.*

16. Johnson, "Through Viewers' Eyes".

17. Forman, *The Hood Comes First*, 28.

18. Forman, *The Hood Comes First*, 38.

19. Jones, *Race, Sex, and Suspicion.*

20. Imamu Amiri Baraka, *Blues People: Negro Music in White America* (New York: William Morrow and Company, 1980), 2.

21. Paul Loukides and Linda K. Fuller, *Beyond the Stars: Stock Characters in American Popular Film* (Madison: University of Wisconsin Press, 1993), p. 4.

22. Waheema Lubiano, *The House That Race Built: Black Americans, U.S. Terrain* (New York: Pantheon Books, 1988).

23. David J. Leonard, *Screens Fade to Black: Contemporary African American Cinema* (Westport, CT: Praeger, 2006), 25.

24. Steve Macek, *Urban Nightmares: The Media, the Right, and the Moral Panic Over the City* (Minneapolis: University of Minnesota Press, 2006), 203.

25. Sam Durrant, *Post-Colonial Narrative and the Work of Mourning: J.M. Coetzee. William Harris, and Toni Morrisson* (New York: State University of New York Press, 2004), 82.

26. Durrant, *Post-Colonial Narrative and the Work of Mourning.*

27. Jones, *Race, Sex, and Suspicion*, 88.

28. Philip J. Meranto, *Kerner Commission Report: Final Report and Background Papers* (Urbana: University of Institute of Government Affairs, University of Illinois, 1970), p. 11.

29. Sonja Sohn (playing detective Kima Griggs), *The Wire*, "Took," HBO Films, Episode 7, Directed by Dominic West, aired February 17, 2008. The scene was written by Richard Price, author of *Clockers* and is an adaptation of a scene from his book.

30. See Jones, *Race, Sex, and Suspicion.*

31. Brian Cook, "Joys of the Wire," *In These Times* (Chicago, IL), February 22, 2008 quoting Yale sociologist Elijah Anderson.

1

From Plantation to the Hood: A Play in Three Acts

Act One: The Dickensian Aspect

> From the deep and near south the sons and daughters of newly freed
> slaves wander into the city. Isolated, cut off from memory, having
> forgotten the names of the Gods and only guessing at their faces,
> they arrive dazed and stunned, their hearts kicking in their chest with
> a song worth singing . . . marked men and women seeking . . . a new
> identity as free men of definite and sincere worth . . . [T]hey carry
> as part and parcel of their baggage a long line of separation and dis-
> persement which informs their sensibilities. Foreigners in a strange
> land, they attempt to reconnect, reassemble themselves as free citi-
> zens . . . they search for ways . . . to give clear and luminous meaning
> to [a] song which is both a wail and a whelp of joy.[1]

One hundred years ago the American South was the home of 90 percent
of blacks bound to the land as sharecroppers.[2] They lived under conditions
of de facto slavery. As W.E.B. Du Bois wrote, "what rent do you pay
here? All we make, answered Sam."[3] From 1910 to 1930 more than
1.5 million blacks moved to the industrial centers of the North.[4] Some
historians attribute the shift from rural to urban to the fact that during World
War II the flow of immigrants into the United States was halted and many
Northern employers welcomed Southern blacks as fresh source of labor.
Others cite the boll weevil, which devastated the cotton crop and caused a
depressed agricultural market. But clearly a major factor was the desire to

47

escape the semiserfdom of Southern life. This racial caste system included the frequent spectacle of black bodies swinging from Southern trees. As Jacob Lawrence famously said of black migration, "another cause was lynching."[5] As historian Robert Norrell wrote, "Whites have allowed blacks to be lynched five at a time on nothing stronger than suspicion and to be whitecapped and their homes burned, with only the weakest and spasmodic effort to apprehend or punish the guilty."[6]

The caption to the picture read: "Where there had been a lynching the people who were reluctant to leave at first left immediately after this."[7]

Between 1882 and 1927 there were 4,951 lynchings in the United States.[8] Of those 3,513 were black.[9] Eighty-five percent of those occurred in the South.[10] Tolnay and Beck link the prevalence of lynching in the early decades of the 20th century to intensified competition over agricultural jobs.[11] "Called whitecapping for the style of headwear the white farmers donned, this violence was meant to enable whites to monopolize the diminished opportunities in southern agriculture. The price of cotton declined continuously over the last quarter of the 19th century while the southern population was growing rapidly."[12]

As Richard Wright wrote, "Water flows because of gravity, people flow because of hope."[13] The South was not Egypt. For black semifeudal serfs, however, the North appeared as a promised land.[14]" [B]lack migrants became a river across the land because their slave forebears had dreamed that the North Star pointed the way to a mythic "Freedom land" where blacks were free and unpersecuted."[15]

Black newspapers in the north cultivated this image linking the north with freedom. The Chicago Defender chronicled each lynching which occurred in the south while it "painted a glowing picture of northern cities."[16]

The First Ghetto

Between 1910 and 1920 New York experienced an 88 percent increase in its black population, Chicago a 148 percent increase, and Philadelphia a 500 percent increase. As this river of black aspiration and people flowed north they discovered that Northern racism was every bit as virulent as the Southern strain. The shock of blacks massively moving into northern urban centers sparked primitive violence reminiscent of the Southern Jim Crow regime. "In city after northern city a series of communal riots broke out between 1900 and 1920 in the wake of massive black migration."[17] "Race riots struck East St. Louis in 1917, Chicago in 1919. It is not possible to give accurately the number of the dead. At least thirty-nine Negroes and 8 white people were killed outright and hundreds of Negroes were wounded and maimed. The bodies of dead Negroes, testified one witness, were thrown into the morgue like so many hogs."[18]

This violence marked the beginning of the ghetto as blacks boiled out of white neighborhoods where they were extremely vulnerable. "Blacks who survived these 'white riots' were loath to return to their former dwellings where they feared (correctly) they would be subject to further violence. Following the riots there was an outflow of blacks from outlying neighborhoods to the emerging ghetto."[19]

Where communal violence failed, targeted violence was often used.

In Chicago fifty-eight black homes were bombed between 1917 and 1921, one every twenty days. . . . In Cleveland, a wealthy black doctor who constructed a new home in an exclusive white suburb had his house surrounded by a violent mob and when the attack failed the house was dynamited twice.[20]

One of the most famous incidents involved Dr. Ossian Sweet, a black man who purchased a house in a white neighborhood in Detroit.

Detroit–Ossian Sweet bought a house on an all white street, though other blacks lived only one street over. On the second day in the house, a mob of two thousand whites surrounded the home, pelted it with rocks . . . the house was later destroyed by arsonists.[21]

Although the wave of violence would subside in the 1920s, the hostility did not. It crystallized in a virtual wall of institutionalized segregation.

"Blacks were increasingly divided from whites by a hardening color line in employment, education, and especially housing."[22]

In Lorraine Hansberry's *Raisin in the Sun,*[23] Mr. Karl Lindner from the Clyburne Park Improvement Association offers Walter a tidy sum to buy back a house they can no longer afford. Lindner's soliloquy illustrated vividly how many Northern whites rationalized segregation, as something natural or inevitable.

[O]ur people out there feel that people get along better, take more of a common interest in the community when they share a common background. . . . I want you to believe me when I tell you race prejudice simply doesn't enter into it. It is a matter of the people in Clyburne Park believing rightly or wrongly, as I say, that for the happiness of all concerned Negro families are happier when they live in their own communities.[24]

Although fictitious, Lindner and the community association he represents are symbolic of the neighborhood-level efforts to maintain the color line.

In fact Lorraine Hansberry's play is a literary treatment of a controversy in which the Progressive Development Corporation "planned to sell ten to twelve new homes to blacks" outside of Chicago.[25] These neighborhood associations had a variety of means at their disposal.

They threatened boycotts of real estate agents who sold homes to blacks; they withdrew their patronage to businesses that catered to black clients; they collected money to pay black renters to leave the neighborhood and, most importantly they implemented "restrictive covenants" which were entirely legal until 1952. The restrictive covenant approach was widespread and included open federal government support.[26]

There was a thin line between private and public efforts to maintain discrimination. In 1927, the Chicago Real Estate Board organized a drive encouraging owners in the "better" city neighborhoods to adopt a model covenant.[27] The Federal Housing Administration also recommended restrictive covenants until 1950, two years after the U.S. Supreme Court found them unconstitutional.[28]

The collision between the intensity of black migration and a rigid color line set the stage for the rapid expansion of the ghetto.

Rapid black migration into a confined residential area created an intense demand for housing within the ghetto, which led to a marked inflation of rents and home prices. The racially segmented market generated real estate values in black areas that far exceeded anything in the white neighborhoods, and this simple economic fact created a great potential for profits along the color line, guaranteeing that some real estate agent would specialize in opening up new areas to black settlement.[29]

Like someone yelling "Fire" in a crowded theater, real estate agents pried open neighborhoods for black settlement by creating a panic leading to en masse white flight. "Real estate agents unscrupulously manipulated white fears to exacerbate the pattern of ghetto expansion and white retreat. This was done through the process of blockbusting."[30]

White homeowners would be told that blacks or other minorities are about to enter the neighborhood, and they would be offered a low price for their homes—often with a warning that the home would be worth less [once blacks moved in]. After whites sold at a low price, the house would then be sold to minority purchasers at a higher price. . . . The practice of blockbusting perpetuated segregation . . . and enhanced racial fears and prejudices.[31]

Natural boundaries interacted with this process of containment and retreat. "The expansion of the ghetto generally followed the path of least resistance, slowing or stopping at natural boundaries such as rivers and railroad tracks, or major thoroughfares and moving toward lower status rather than high status areas."[32] In many cities, like Miami, blacks tend to live on the "wrong side of the tracks." In Miami blacks traditionally lived on the west side of US 1 which is inland, while whites lived on the east side of the highway near the water. This exemplifies the characteristic pattern.

The new immigrants usually settle in pretty well defined localities in or near the slums, and thus get the worst possible introduction to city life. . . . Today they are found partly in slums and partly in those small streets with old houses, where there is a dangerous intermingling of good and bad elements fatal to growing children and unwholesome for adults. Such streets may be found in the seventh ward, between Tenth and Juniper streets in parts of the third and fourth wards. . . .[33]

Although its path was shaped and controlled by the pattern of white flight, the intensity of black migration could not be stopped.

Like a river depositing silt until it becomes a delta, the river of black migration gave rise to Boston's Roxbury, Chicago's South Side, Cleveland's Hough District, and Harlem in New York.

I struggle to imagine how cruel the conditions were for those early black immigrants to the North. Reminiscent of Middle Passage the new migrants had little personal space to live in. In Chicago's ghetto, 90000 people lived in one square mile, whereas the contiguous white areas contained only 20000."[34]

Detroit was as bad or worse.

There are practically no vacant houses in the Ghetto: three or four families to an apartment was the rule rather than the exception and Washington reported that 75% of negro homes have so many lodgers that they are really hotels. Stables, garages, and cellars have been converted into homes for Negroes. The poolrooms and gambling houses are beginning to charge *for the privilege of sleeping on poolroom tables over night.* (italics added)[35]

The lack of space was compounded by the conditions of the new dwellings themselves.

[G]enerally the houses were in a state of appalling disrepair. . . . Sanitary conditions were often disgusting . . . many of the homes had toilets located without partition either in a bedroom or in the kitchen. Washington reported . . . a shack of four rooms on Napoleon Street for which the widow pays 30$ per month in which the investigator on a stormy day saw the rain, literally, pour through the ceiling to the floor . . . There was no heat in the house because the pipe had burst and the landlord despite receiving 65$ a month refused to make repairs.[36]

James De Jongh writes that despite "a youthful population, the death rate [in Harlem] was 42% higher for Harlemites than the rest of the city."[37]

Like the slave ship the ghetto brought blacks together from both different regions and different social strata onto the same anvil of oppression.

Blacks were not only shaped on this anvil, they began culturally to do shaping of their own.

Black immigrants could not define the boundaries of the ghetto but they could pour their identity into it. The creation of jazz, the Harlem Renaissance, and the flourishing art in these communities were part of this outpouring. "So what began in terms of segregation becomes more and more, as elements mix and re-act, the laboratory of a great race welding."[38]

The hammer blows of segregation hardened a sense of a common identity: As boundaries hardened, so did race pride. Black institutions flourished.

Blacks increasingly patronized their own stores, churches, and places of amusement. A black-owned printing industry arose as black publications multiplied. The speech of a Chicago minister at the time captures the sense of common identity that was taking shape:

> Tomorrow I want all of you people to go to these stores. Have your shoes repaired at a Negro shop, buy your groceries from a Negro grocer . . . and for God's sake, buy your meats from a Negro Butcher. On behalf of the Negro Businessmen of Chicago I commend those Negro businessmen for promoting such an affair and again urge you to patronize your own.[39]

The second wave of black migration began in about 1940. Five million blacks moved from the South to the North and West between 1941 and the late 1970s. (About 1.5 million each decade from 1940 and 1970.)[40] In 1940, 49 percent of blacks lived in cities. By 1970, 81 percent were urban dwellers. Almost overnight in Los Angeles and the San Francisco bay area blacks created major populations. The path of migration went northwest as well as North. While it was a broad path it concentrated on a few major cities. This concentration of black immigration created the dense black demographics of urban centers in New York, Chicago, Detroit, Philadelphia, and St. Louis.

This last wave of inflows created the dark ghetto that was the focus of books like those of Richard Wright and James Baldwin in fiction and Gunnar Myrdal and Kenneth Clark in sociology. This became the iconic ghetto portrayed in blaxploitation films like *Shaft,*[41] *Superfly,*[42] *Foxy Brown,*[43] and *Across 110th Street.*[44] This ghetto was the one I grew up in. For all its problems it was a place of churches, black businesses, and where most people were working.

Even before the second wave of migration had ended, however, a third transformation began. A series of events took place that brought the ghetto into its present form.

As blacks became urbanized, they became proletarianized. The trigger for much of this movement was the need for workers in defense industries during World War II. Census tract data shows that as late as the 1970s blacks were largely a community of blue-collar workers. My father worked at Bethlehem Steel. The incredible upward social and economic trajectory of this migration was essentially the source of momentum for the civil rights movement.[45]

The explosive mixture of blacks concentrated in urban areas and a dramatic new militancy ignited white flight.

In the postwar era the mostly white upper middle class largely abandoned the central cities for the suburban fringe. With them went many of the businesses that once were the foundation of vibrant downtown economies. At the same time the nation's poor became concentrated in deteriorating inner city neighborhoods. According to Ronald Formisiano,

> White flight . . . [was] the greatest exodus in American history. It drained the white population out of the city limits and engorged the near and far suburbs . . . the suburbs were almost entirely white, while blacks, Hispanics and later Asians were ringed into the suburban noose.[46]

As Murray Forman puts it, "rather than repair the damage to our cities it seemed simpler, and less dangerous to rebuild the American City somewhere else."[47]

During the 1950s alone the white population of New York City declined by 7 percent. Chicago's white population declined by 13 percent and Philadelphia's by 13 percent.

The Second Ghetto

The civil rights era was constituted by the alliance of blacks, Jews, and Northern labor. That coalition broke up around 1968 as blacks shifted from civil rights to economic rights. As that coalition shattered, America began a hard turn to the right—the hard right. The Great Society programs gave way to a neoconservative vision that dominated government policy under President Ronald Wilson Reagan. With almost religious zeal Reagan's neoconservatives waged a war against social welfare programs. Armed with stories of welfare queens, famously Reagan talked about the woman in Chicago who received welfare under 127 different names and another in Pasadena charged with collecting $300,000 in a welfare scheme.[48] Reagan wove a narrative of the undeserving poor. Their campaign was highly successful.

During the Reagan and Bush eras alone federal aid to local governments was slashed 60 percent.[49] Federal spending on public housing dropped from $28 billion in 1977 to just $7 billion 11 years later.[50] Between 1975 and 1996 the inflation-adjusted value of the welfare benefit for a family of three with no other income fell 40 percent, and this was before the massive cuts implemented by welfare reform.[51] Payments to the urban poor rapidly declined while federal programs which benefited the middle class in the suburbs expanded. In the 1960s and 1970s the argument was that government should not gild the ghetto or subsidize slum areas.[52] Instead the ghetto should be dispersed. It was a catch-22: white resistance would not allow the ghetto to be dispersed and the federal government would no longer invest in the urban slums it had done much to create. In the Reagan era the issue of investment in inner cities was reframed through a narrative of imposition: urban blacks were demonized as welfare queens exploiting the system at the expense of whites.

The flight of federal support for the inner city was mirrored by that of private industry. Investment and jobs fled also. "The growing suburbanization of jobs, both in manufacturing and services, has isolated inner-city minorities from many work opportunities."[53]

> But inner city workers face an additional problem: the growing suburbanization of jobs. Most ghetto residents cannot afford an automobile and therefore have to rely on public transportation systems . . . recent research . . . strongly shows that the decentralization of employment is continuing and that employment in manufacturing . . . has decreased in central cities.[54]

As the social safety net unraveled, jobs began to disappear. Between 1965 and 1990 Black family income fell by 50 percent and black youth unemployment quadrupled.[55] The share of low-income households increased by one-third.[56]

In the 1980s America lost 1.2 million manufacturing jobs while adding 19 million jobs in the service sector—the vast majority of these jobs were clustered in the low-wage retail and personnel services sector.

Fifty percent of black males employed in durable goods manufacturing in five Great Lakes states lost their jobs as a result of computer-based automation or capital flight from 1979 to 1984.[57]

The share of the U.S. central city workforce employed in manufacturing declined from 24 percent in 1950 to 15 percent in 1990.[58]

From 1967 to 1987 Philadelphia lost 64 percent of its manufacturing jobs, Chicago 60 percent, New York 58 percent, and Detroit 51 percent.

As the industrial sector withered in many cities, the financial, technological, and professional sectors grew. At least by the late 1980s—and the early 1990s—affluent white professionals began to move back into the inner city.

A strong economy and the rise of an electronic information sector began to reverse the trend, stimulating urban real estate markets. Thousands of young single professionals have been lured back into the inner city by new opportunities . . . such trends have redefined the inner city as the new frontier in American capitalist conquest.[59]

This led to a polarized workforce especially in New York.

New York became sharply divided between an affluent, technocratic, professional white collar group managing the financial and commercial life of an international city and an unemployed and underemployed service sector which is substantially black and Hispanic. . . . [T]he growing predominance of white collar work on the one hand and wordlessness on the other have made New York's labor market resemble that of a Third World City.[60]

The urban scene was characterized by a paradox: there was close physical proximity but a vast economic gulf between whites and blacks. As the forces of deindustrialization and technological change closed the doors of upward mobility, low-paying jobs proliferated. "In the void left by manufacturing decline, and the removal of blue collar jobs overseas, came a profusion of low-skill service sector jobs, an abundance of jobs with few if any benefits: data processors, cleaners and janitors, retail clerks, catering staff, security guards, and street vendors."[61]

What emerges from this convergence of globalism, technological change, and demographic shifts is a community without an economic infrastructure. In the jobless ghetto of New York City, one in four black men between the ages of 16 and 24 has a job.[62] The jobless rate for black men in the city of Buffalo is 50 percent.[63] In Milwaukee, 53 percent of black men are unemployed or not even in the labor force.[64] "This compares to almost 85 percent [participation rate] forty years ago."[65] In Detroit 54 percent of black men are unemployed.

> Faced with a chronic shortage of jobs in the declining local labor market the percentage of Milwaukee's working age black males has declined from 73.7 percent in 1979 to a new low of 46.7 percent in 2009 (compared to 77.7 percent for whites).[66]

Other metropolitan cities at incomprehensible jobless levels include Cleveland, 52.3 percent; Chicago, 50.3 percent; and Pittsburgh, 50.3 percent.[67]

Overwhelmingly the media, academia, and popular culture assumes that the black men who are idle and unemployed standing on street corners, sitting on inner city steps, languishing on the edges of the 21st century are there because of their own bad choices.

This is a racial framing of a structural problem. Globalism and technological change have shifted the demand for unskilled labor. To blame the victims for tectonic shifts in the urban economic landscape is like blaming earthquake victims for homelessness.

The inner city in the 1980s was the site of twin, almost simultaneous disasters. The death of work in the inner city takes place in tandem with the death of educational opportunity in the inner city.

Desegregation began with the landmark Supreme Court case *Brown v. The Board of Education*.[68] The great case of the 20th century *Brown,* formally, overturned *Plessy v. Ferguson* and inaugurated the second reconstruction.

Plessy[69] had held infamously that segregating blacks on railroad cars was perfectly constitutional. The case put the imprimatur of the U.S. Supreme Court on the inherently contradictory concept of "separate but equal."

Legally, it constitutionalized—legitimized—what became a system of homegrown American apartheid. *Brown* represented the official rejection of this noxious doctrine. Of course the court did so strategically. In the 1950s, the United States was engaged in a struggle with the Soviet Union for the uncommitted nations. Desegregation was an imperative of the geopolitics of the Cold War.[70] America has always been schizophrenic on race. Jefferson who wrote the Declaration of Independence—"all men are created equal"—also owned slaves. *Brown* reflected this ambivalence. In *Brown I,* the court resounding denounced desegregation. The *Brown* Court said,

> To separate [children] from others of similar age and qualifications solely because of their race generates a feeling of inferiority as to their status in the community that may affect their hearts and minds in a way unlikely ever to be undone. . . . We conclude that in the field

The great Thurgood Marshall (center) celebrating victory with James M. Nabrit (right) and George C. Hayes (left). (Library of Congress)

of public education the doctrine of "separate but equal" has no place. Separate educational facilities are inherently unequal. Therefore, we hold that the plaintiffs and others similarly situated for whom the actions have been brought are . . . deprived of the equal protection of the laws guaranteed by the Fourteenth Amendment.[71]

But in *Brown II,* when required to propose a timetable for desegregation the Court specified that the standard would be "with all deliberate speed."[72] Officially, *Plessy* was dead. But the spirit of *Plessy* lived on in the dividedness of the Court's approach to what to do about it.

In 1988, that spirit crystallized in a series of decisions that quietly reversed the holding of *Brown.*[73]

The problem was the intersection of law and private choices. Efforts at integration resulted in white flight and residential segregation. All that was necessary for resegregation to take place was to insulate this process of resegregation from change. In a series of decisions, the decisions by the court ingeniously paved the way for resegregation. In part it was by emphasizing local control over federal power; in part it was by saying to federal courts that if whites moved into the suburbs they could not be pushed back into the inner city; and in part it was the doctrine of color blindness itself saying that school systems engaged in fateful discrimination when they tried to create a racial balance by considering race in selecting students for magnet schools. Between this color-blind approach, local control, and jurisdictional limitations on schools, *Brown* was, as a practical matter, reversed. Americans' ambivalence on race crystallized in the resegregation of inner city schools by 2000. As of 2002, almost 2.4 million students, or over 5 percent of all public school enrollment, attended schools with a white population of less than 1 percent. Of these, 2.3 million were black and Latino students. Demographically, these resegregated schools look no different from those in the 1950s.

In *The Wire,* David Simon portrays several children trying to survive in the mean streets of East Baltimore where I grew up. I was moved by their innocence, their intelligence, and their love of life. The series dramatized how these children went to schools in which failure had been normalized. A similar treatment takes place in *Hard Times at Douglass High,* the head of the English Department stated that when a reading test was given to 300 or 400 ninth-grade students only three or four passed at grade level, the vast majority were at least three grade levels behind.[74] Nationally, less than 50 percent of black males graduate from high school.[75]

The essence of segregated schools was not merely that blacks were separated from whites; it was that they got an inferior education. That is what is taking place at resegregated inner city schools under the guise of equal educational opportunity.

Both the media and public policy treat the problem of inner city schools as one in which black people have a virus that makes them unteachable. That virus is the pathology of ghetto culture. Ghetto culture bears the same stigma of inferiority as blacks' skin bore in the recent past. While it is tempting to individualize the problem, to look at trees, it is better to look at the entire landscape of unequal opportunity. The inner city is a desert where work has disappeared and schools have become warehouses. It is not the lyrics that are the starting point for understanding Gangsta rap; the historical and social context is the starting point.

Undereducated and barely literate, they have to choose largely between working for McDonald's and selling drugs on a corner. What Gangsta rap seems to say is "fuck flippin burgers." My answer is, "I feel you."

Act Two: Another Country: The Nightmare on Our Screens

> When you walk with Jesus, he's gonna save your soul/you gotta keep the devil way down in the hole.[76]
>
> —"Way Down in the Hole," introduction to *The Wire*

As the song plays—sung by the Blind Boys of Alabama—video of life in the Baltimore ghetto rolls on the screen. *The Wire* series is famously about the drug war in the ghetto. The song sets the mood for the HBO series. Against this background, the song knots together three things: sin, drugs, and *the ghetto*.

Race, of course, is no longer a question of color but a question of zip code: as we cross over from affluent areas to the ghetto, we shift from the realm of citizens to that of criminals. The boundary line between these two places is the new color line.

Another Country: The Nightmare on Our Screens

The meshing of race, space, and crime involves a relabeling of traditional categories. What emerges from this is a new vocabulary in which race is recoded as a set of spatial metaphors.

> In the aftermath of the civil rights movement of the sixties and sev-
> enties American culture has discovered that racial effects are more
> efficiently achieved in a language cleansed of overt racial reference.
> Although conceptual precision in discussion about American social
> life demands that racial discourse employ racial categories, such cat-
> egories may or may not make the explicit reference to perceivable
> and acknowledgeable racial characteristics such as skin color.[77]

Inner city or inner city youth or ghetto or ghetto culture is freighted with a set of assumptions and images.

The symbolic meaning of these spatial references to race is anchored in part by 40 years of books, beginning with Kenneth Clark's *Dark Ghetto* and continuing with a cottage industry of books by contemporary black conservatives, like Thomas Sowell, Shelby Steele, and John H. Mc-Whorter. The image of the ghetto is of an irredeemable space created out of the cultural pathology of the people who live there.

But more importantly, the symbolic meaning of ghetto space was created on our screens.

Dirk De Meyer, an urban historian, argues it began with the news in the 1980s—with "visualization" of "the black urban underclass."

> By the late 1980s images of unmarried ghetto mothers, crack
> users . . . were common on American television . . . these forms of
> programming encoded black urban poverty as distinctively separate
> from the worlds of the viewing audience. These images were not only
> "common," they were repeated daily in a ritual of racial caricature.[78]

Similarly, listen to Professor Herman Gray: "On the evening news net-work newscast there might be a black male correspondent covering the ar-rest of a black drug dealer, a black victim of a gang style killing, a teenage welfare mother . . . or [a depiction of] deteriorating inner cities."[79]

In 1990, Robert Entman did a famous study that quantified statistically the way blacks in the ghetto were caricatured. He looked at three 10-day periods covered by ABC, CBS, and NBC news.

1. About 77% of the stories, in which blacks were accused, concerned a violent or a drug crime. . . . In other words the overwhelming majority of black crime stories concerned violence or drugs."[80]

2. Blacks were twice as likely as whites to be shown in the grasp of a police officer.

3. The image of police breaking into a house was shown seven times during the period. In six of the cases, the occupants were black.

4. Ten stories during the period focused on people selling drugs. In six of those cases, such images were of blacks.[81]

Stereotypes found in news are harder to resist because the news is real. While the images are entirely stereotypical, they are presented as neutral. Entman notes that "the benign guise" of these stereotypical images encourages the racial coding of criminal behavior.[82]

The same racial coding of violence takes place on the silver screen. As Steve Marcel has noted, the horror film serves as a powerful vehicle in constructing this narrative of the ghetto as a world of sociopaths, both deadly and different from the world of mainstream whites.

According to film theorists, the horror film "addresses the anxieties of an affluent culture in an era of prolonged recession."[83]

The horror film works by thrusting its characters in a monstrous situation or terrible place. In the *Hood* horror film, monsters are replaced with Uzi wielding black teenagers and Transylvania with an impoverished slum or ghetto.

Judgment Night[84] is typical of the genre.

Premised on a crudely drawn binary opposition between the comforts of suburbia and the mortal dangers of the inner city it tells the story of a group of suburban men driving to a boxing match who take a wrong turn into a bad neighborhood on Chicago's South Side, witness a murder and spend the rest of the night running from the drug dealers who are responsible for the killing.[85]

In *Trespass*,[86] white middle class main characters are trapped in an abandoned East St. Louis factory where they are forced to fight for the lives against an Uzi wielding black gang.[87] These scenes of crossing over into the netherworld of urban decay "exude the Manichean, middle class paranoia that once you leave the bourgeois life you are immediately prey to crime, madness, squalor and poverty."[88]

Of course, the classic is *Bonfire of the Vanities*.[89] Sherman McCoy makes a wrong turn on the freeway and ends up in a war zone. Sherman McCoy is depicted as master of the universe. His world is destroyed when he and his girlfriend confront blacks walking toward him. She runs them over but McCoy is forced to take the rap. The film is bound up with a sense of both white guilt and the persecution of white males. But what comes through is the dividing line between safe and deadly spaces. The ghetto is an alien territory; a third world within our world in which sociopathic violence is the norm. It is a breeding ground for a pathological form of masculinity.

The horror story genre is only the most obvious mainstream effort to exploit the stereotypes whites have about the ghetto. There is a whole genre of films that while not explicitly focusing on race, use the ghetto as a backdrop and have major black characters. Whenever Hollywood situates itself in the ghetto, the film is populated with demeaning images.

In *Training Day*,[90] Denzel stars in a police drama which explores the question of police corruption. The film clearly individualizes the problem as a function of character rather than something rooted in the system itself. Alonzo Harris, senior narcotics detective, played by Denzel Washington, is a criminal with a badge. Jake Hoyt, the ramrod straight rookie, is the good cop. Jake is white. Alonzo is black.

When we meet Jake, he is with his wife and family. It is a place of warmth and of dreams. He speaks of the house he wants to buy, and his goals for his career. Jake moves up from patrolman to work with Alonzo as trainee detective in the drug war. The war is being fought in the Los Angeles ghetto. The ghetto in the film is called "The Jungle." It is so dangerous that Alonzo will not let Jake, a policeman, go there by himself. We meet crews, posses, crack addicts, and thugs, but no decent families.

This ghetto is portrayed as a criminalized culture, which Alonzo exemplifies. "The supposed scandal of a rogue cop is [contaminated] by an extant culture of criminalization that takes blackness as its master sign."[91]

In this jungle, the image of the black criminal and the animal are knotted together. Listen to an exchange between Alonzo and Hoyt. Alonzo, corrupting the law, has just released two would-be rapists.

Harris: You know they would have killed you without hesitating.
  Hoyt: That's why they belong in prison.
Harris: For what they did they got beat down. They lost their rock; they lost their money. Those eses from the Eastside are probably gonna smoke 'em. What else do you want?
  Hoyt: I want justice.
Harris: Is that not justice?
  Hoyt: That's street justice. Oh, just let the animals wipe themselves out.
Harris: God willing. Fuck 'em and everybody who looks likes them. . . . To protect the sheep you gotta catch the wolf. It takes a wolf to catch a wolf.

The line between corruption and decency is, at bottom, the line between law and anarchy. In turn, this is the line between civilization and the jungle—read the ghetto. In attempting to rule this jungle, Alonzo becomes an animal. Alonzo is the wolf, a renegade cop who preys on the other predators in this jungle. He is also in the imagery of the film compared to a gorilla. He intimidates the local thugs with threats of arrest: "I'm putting cases on all you bitches. You think you can do this to me. . . . You motherfuckers will be playing basketball in Pelican Bay [a notorious prison]. . . . Who the fuck you think you fucking with . . . I'm the police. I run shit here. . . . King Kong ain't got nothin' on me."

The film creates a signifying chain, linking together the images of criminal-animal-ghetto.

Jake redeems the police department: by choosing to respect the rights of others and rejecting Alonzo's corruption. Alonzo, toward the end of the film, is machine-gunned in a hit by the Russian mob. Alonzo is condemned by his poor choices; Jake is saved by his.

David J. Leonard notes how the racial narrative draws on the fact that Alonzo's ghetto is one "where blacks are in power." [92] This references the larger society where at the time Condoleezza Rice, Colin Powell, and a legion of black politicians represent the post-civil rights condition. If the ghetto does not progress, blacks have their own leaders to blame. God knows that many of our leaders have failed us, but in a real sense blacks are not in power. The power relationships between blacks and whites have not changed in the last 50 years. Somewhere between the post–civil rights narrative and the narrative of black deviance that links black men, wolves, and the ghetto, the film erases institutional racism.

The film *Crash*[93] is another example of this genre. There is an unforgettable scene when black thugs menace an innocent white family whose BMW has broken down. The human response is to assist the motorist. The response of the thugs was to jack his car.

The innocent white family is rescued by Danny Glover who confronts the thugs with a tire iron. He challenges their hostility as a kind of nihilism; he says, "Everything is exactly the opposite of what it is supposed to be."

Many will argue that ghetto life is nihilistic. But as Cornel West has written, "nihilism is to be understood here not as a philosophic doctrine that there are no rational grounds for legitimate standards of authority; it is far more the lived experience of coping with a life of horrifying meaning-lessness, hopelessness, and more importantly lawlessness."

The focus of these films is not the lived experience of blacks—their experience of oppression; it is the fears and anxieties of whites. In these films, none of the blacks we meet have any individuality. They are all faceless constructs. They exist to personify the criminogenic nature of the ghetto. Thus, it is the whole community that is demonized. As Henry Giroux writes,

> In the racially coded representations of violence in black films, vio-lence does not register as the result of individual pathology. Here the violence of representation serves to indict blacks as an entire racial group while legitimating the popular stereotype that their communi-ties are the central sites of crime, lawlessness and immorality.[94]

Conclusion

In the era of segregation we marked bathrooms, water fountains, schools—one for blacks one for whites. Now we mark territory or space. Race and space form an intersection in the urban ghetto, which is marked as the focal point of moral panic. The media has in effect placed a signpost in front of the urban ghetto, marked with a skull and crossbones, the sign reads, "Run for your life."

Moral Panic Requires a Vocabulary

In the past that vocabulary explicitly focused on race, the focus was blacks who were lazy, or dumb, or dangerous. This traces back to the stereotypes of Nat and Sambo. In the post–civil rights narrative, the central trope is the ghetto itself. The definitive quality of the tropological ghetto is that it is both a deadly and a different world. As Pino states, "Every day I come to work; it's like planet of the apes."[95]

It is this notion of the ghetto as both exotic and lethal environment, both a war zone—as Sherman McCoy might put it—and a foreign, alien place that is constructed for us by popular culture, especially in film.

This postracial narrative does not mention race but black urban poor become the scapegoats. This stereotyping and scapegoating narrative populates our screens in television and film. It is here that the cultural imaginary and real structural racism meet and reinforce each other.

The problem of the 20th century was the problem of the color line. The problem of the 21st century is the problem of the postindustrial ghetto. This postindustrial ghetto is the culmination of a racial project, which begins with slavery and ends up with massive incarceration. The prison and the ghetto are no longer distinct but increasingly resemble two elements of a single racial regime.

This existence of this racial regime in the midst of formal equality is made possible by the stereotypical images we have been talking about. As a black, Dr. Phil might say these demeaning images enable benign neglect.

Thus Robert Entman wrote, "These images matter because they are a central component of a circular process by which racial and ethnic misunderstanding is reproduced and thus become predictable influences in the criminal justice process."[96]

We struggle to understand why, if blacks and whites abuse drugs at statistically identical rates, blacks are incarcerated in such astounding disproportions. Why is the penalty for crack cocaine 100 times greater than that for powdered cocaine? Why do we accept without blinking attrition rates for black kids of 50 percent or more as normal? Why do we throw up our hands and give up on the ghetto? It is because through film and television we have succeeded in scapegoating ghetto culture.

The reality is that the conditions of the urban ghetto are a product both of structural racism and poor choices of the ghetto inhabitants themselves. But in the narrative, the problem of violence and crime simply *go with the territory,* while structural racism entirely disappears.

When we watch the horror film, the Hollywood Hood movie, *The Wire,* or the evening news, we don't see loving families, hard working people, the cherubic cheeks of innocent children; we don't see scholars, artists, or individuals at all. What we see is a landscape of violence, decay, hopelessness, and death. We see a place—a planet—different from our own. We see often across our screens pictures of starving children in distant lands, in Guatemala, Peru, or Haiti. The faces of the children, like Michael Lee and Dukwon, are as distant from us as the faces of the children in Guatemala or Peru. This is true because we do not see the ghetto as part of the same America in which we live. It is exotic, foreign, culturally a million miles removed. We have abandoned the ghetto because of its moral distance.

It is quite simply another country.

Act Three: The War against Black Men

Det. Thomas Hauk:	Fuck the paperwork. Collect bodies, split heads.
Det. Ellis Carver:	Split 'em wide.
Det. Thomas Hauk:	The Western District way.
Det. Ellis Carver:	A'ight.
Shakima Greggs:	You rogue motherfuckers kill me. Fighting the war on drugs, one brutality case at a time.
Det. Ellis Carver:	You can't even call this shit a war.
Det. Thomas Hauk:	Why not?
Det. Ellis Carver:	Wars end.[97]

In *The Prison Notebooks,* Antonio Gramsci noted that "when the State tottered, a sturdy structure of civil society was at once revealed. The State was just a forward trench, behind which there stood a powerful system of fortresses and emplacements; more or less numerous from one state to the next."[98]

Thus, the problem Gramsci discovered in his struggle against the authoritarian Italian government was not merely its coercive power, but the ideology on which it rested: the many thoughts and beliefs that limit its ability to "even imagine that life could be different."[99]

Segregation was as much an authoritarian regime as any that existed in Europe. The goal of the Italian fascist regime was to divide people into an economic hierarchy of different classes. In segregation, race is transposed for class. The racial hierarchy of segregation was maintained physically by violence: lynching, the coercive force of Jim Crow laws.

Behind the outer ditch of those laws was a sturdy structure of ideas and beliefs that the racial hierarchy imposed by coercive practices was natural and inevitable. In this era, the dominant narrative was that blacks were intellectually inferior. The flip side of this narrative of inferiority was a narrative of whiteness as inherently superior. This narrative was anchored by an interlocking set of laws and customs privileging even the poorest whites.

> They were given public deference . . . because they were white. They were admitted freely, with all classes of white people to public functions [and]—public parks. . . . The police were drawn from their ranks and the courts, dependent on their votes, treated them with leniency. . . . Their votes selected public officials and while this had small effect upon the economic situation, it had great effect upon their personal treatment . . . White schoolhouses were the best in the community, and conspicuously placed, and cost anywhere from twice to ten times colored schools.[100]

This system of white privilege defined whiteness. Tragically, Southern whites embraced not only the illicit privileges of the Southern caste system but the ideology that went with it.

> It was bad enough to have the consequences of [racist] thought fall upon colored people the world over; but in the end it was even worse when one considers what this attitude did to the white worker. His aim and his ideal were distorted . . . he began to want not comfort for

all men but power over all men . . . he did not love humanity . . . he hated niggers.[101]

Du Bois argues that Southern whites embraced this notion of whiteness as a kind of capital or property. Thus, even when whites received a low monetary wage, they were compensated in part by a "psychological and public wage."[102]

While the civil rights movement swept away the laws and all official government support for segregation, the ideological structure on which segregation rested remained intact.

Segregation was a caste system. Whites saw the privileges they had under the caste system and the subordination of blacks as natural. This racial hierarchy was "the way it was supposed to be" in the moral universe of the Jim Crow era. This is the meaning of white supremacy. The significance of civil rights laws was that officially blacks were full-fledged citizens. This new civil freedom for blacks threatened white privilege in fundamental ways. Blacks were trying to take "what was rightfully theirs." While civil rights was officially canonized by equal opportunity laws, privately there was gnashing of teeth by many whites, particularly white males.

Yet this call for massive, structural reform coincided with a broadening anti-civil rights backlash. No longer a southern phenomenon, resistance to civil rights reform took hold across the nation.

The response to unrest would not be along the lines of the Kerner commission report. What was to some a rebellion against unjust conditions was to others simply a matter of "crime in the streets." "Law and order, not social change, was demanded by many Americans. Into this new political cauldron stepped Richard Nixon. The republican presidential nominee would be particularly effective at tapping into backlash politics and marshalling the law and order rhetoric that now appealed to so many voters . . . just as Vietnam has eclipsed civil rights as a defining issue affecting U.S., prestige abroad, law and order had eclipsed social justice as a politically popular response to racial conflict."[103]

Similarly, Michelle Alexander writes, "Proponents of racial hierarchy found they could install a new racial caste system without violating the law of the new limits of acceptable political discourse, by demanding 'law and order,' rather than 'segregation forever'."[104]

Law and order was dog-whistle racism. It was a code word for the need to "keep blacks in their place." Veiled verbal cues can effectively express unseemly messages without social penalty; they can endow an offensive subtext with political and cultural legitimacy.

These code words became part of the public discourse through the machinations of political leaders who used them to gain influence and power.

The strategy was to link calls for equal rights to images of urban violence. On the floor of Congress, Southern politicians tried to forge an explicit link between claims of blacks for equality and urban violence.

> Fair housing legislation was defeated in 1966 in part because whites were shocked by racial violence and afraid their neighborhoods would be overrun and devalued by black residents. When fair housing measures did become law in 1968, it was accompanied by an anti-rioting provision.[105]

Similarly, George Wallace's third-party candidacy riled up voters by appealing to their visceral reactions to urban violence and their sense that the federal government had given blacks too much.[106]

But the master of this approach was Richard Nixon. Nixon famously stated "Doubling the conviction rate in this country would do more to cure crime in America than quadrupling the funds for [the] war on poverty."[107] Nixon wove law and order into a fear-mongering narrative in which American civilization was under siege.

> We live in a deeply troubled and profoundly unsettling time. Drugs and crime . . . racial discord . . . on every hand we find standards violated, old values discarded, old precepts ignored. . . . As a result all of our institutions in America today are undergoing what may be the severest challenge in our history.[108]

The answer was, once again, "law and order."

Whites were recruited to police repression of the black community by a sense that law and order meant "racial order." Law and order would return America to a place were "[s]treets were safe, whites went unchallenged, young people obeyed, work was valued. . . ."[109]

Of course, whites had no economic interest in targeting blacks for arrest and incarceration. But Nixon appealed to the deep psychological need of whites to feel superior to blacks, a need implicit in the concept of being white.

Repression of blacks was made to seem natural because there was an underlying narrative making blacks the scapegoats for "everything that was wrong in America."

As Haldeman wrote in his diary, "The president emphasized that the whole problem is really the blacks. The key is to devise a system that recognized this while not appearing to."[110] A corollary to this narrative was that crime really meant "black crime." As Robert Perkinson wrote, "Crime then was not about fear but racial fear. Emphasizing it enabled Nixon to tap visceral prejudices that had divided Americans before the birth of the republic."[111]

Nixon is remembered as an icon of the Vietnam era. He was the authoritarian figure we rallied against at demonstrations against the war. But

Richard M. Nixon, 37th president of the United States. (Library of Congress)

Nixon's most lasting legacy was that he was the first to declare war on drugs.

> Drugs are among the modern curse of youth, just like the plagues and epidemics of former years. And they are decimating a generation of Americans. My administration will accelerate the development of tools and weapons . . . to fight illegal drugs . . . more federal drug agents and massive assistance to local police.[112]

By 1971, drugs had become "public enemy number one." According to Nixon, "drug traffic is public enemy number one domestically in the United States today and we must wage a total offensive, worldwide, nationwide."[113]

Fueled by the moral panic Nixon had created about drugs as a menace to American civilization, massive amounts of funds and resources were recruited for the new war. Spending on drug enforcement alone climbed from $3 million in 1971 to $321 million in 1975. Nixon consolidated a toothless, moribund drug fighting apparatus into one agency called the Drug Enforcement Agency (DEA).

Ironically, this moral panic was whipped up in large part by false or misleading information. Nixon grossly exaggerated the dangerousness of drugs.

> Despite Nixon's assertion to the pre-election Disneyland crowd that drugs [we are] "decimating a generation of Americans," drugs were so tiny a public health problem that they were statistically insignificant: far more Americans choked to death on food or died falling down stairs as died from illegal drugs.[114]

At the same time, he exaggerated the numbers of people who were addicted. "The white house dramatically overestimated the heroin addiction problem. (Reporting a ten-fold increase in the number of addict users from 1969 to 1971.)"[115]

Nixon knotted together blacks, drugs, and crime—metaphorically "sin, drugs, and the ghetto"—in one demonic image. He did so to create a scapegoat for America's social problems for which he had no real answer.

Ronald Reagan went further than Nixon. He declared a war on drugs on October 14, 1982.[116]

Reagan's stated goal was to "shrink government." But he really meant he wanted to shift spending away from social programs to first "the arms race" with the Soviet Union and second to his newly declared "war against drugs." To facilitate this tectonic shift in national priorities, he had to dismantle federal entitlement programs, taking away the social safety net from minorities and the poor. For Reagan, yoking blacks and drugs together was part of a larger project of disinvestment in the underclass.

By 1986, in the second year of his last term, Reagan massively increased the funding for "the war." Reagan signed an enormous omnibus drug bill, the Anti-Drug Abuse Act of 1986, which appropriated $1.7 billion to fight the drug crisis.

Officially, the federal drug war budget has grown from $1.7 billion to $15.5 billion in 2011.[117] This does not include the amounts spent for incarcerating prisoners, building prisons, and buying new equipment—helicopters, planes, boats and the like.

States will likely spend another $30 billion in direct costs.[118] Since the inception of the war on drugs in 1980, there have been more than 31 million arrests for drug offenses in the United States.[119] We arrest 1.2 million people on drug-related offenses every year.[120]

Overall, between 1980 and 2003, the number of drug offenders in prison or jail increased by 1100 percent from 41,100 in 1980 to 493,800 in 2003. This massive effort could be likened to damming a river. At one point, a river of resources flowed to social programs for minorities and the disadvantaged; now that river was dammed.

> Programs and research that had for many years been directed at the social and structural sources of social problems were systematically defunded in the federal budget and delegitimated in discourse. . . . People in trouble were reconceptualized as people who make trouble; social control replaced social welfare.[121]

The impact on education was particularly significant.

From 1950 to 1980, the share of state and local government budgets spent on higher education doubled, while the share spent on corrections remained level. From 1980 to 2000, the share spent on education decreased 21%, while the share spent on corrections increased 104%.[122]

Reagan's policies operated like a self-fulfilling prophecy. By taking money away from the needy, social disorganization increased which led to more crime and potentially more drug use. Correspondingly, and not surprisingly, "urban ills . . . increased markedly under the Reagan administration."

The cause of these urban ills was structural: Drugs were and are essentially an opportunistic infection of a population weakened by structural disadvantage.

> In recent history, intellectuals . . . have noted that the crushing impact of poverty leads to low self-esteem. Consequently, when a whole community faces this condition social deterioration becomes inevitable. Alienation shatters the spirit and destroys the ability to love oneself and others.[123]

The narrative of black deviance allowed Reagan to make an effect appear to be a cause. The cause was dehumanizing urban conditions. Problems of drug within a community of low-income inner city residents—who experienced these conditions—was its effect. The narrative of black deviance denies this cause-and-effect relationship. It is a way of blaming the victim, denying the role of urban conditions as a source of dysfunction.

At the same time, as Reagan ramped up the drug war, heroin was being replaced by crack. This created a new generation of drug myths and stereotypes.

> The drug problem represented by crack was "an all-purpose scapegoat with which they could blame an array of social problems on the deviance of the individuals who suffered them" while upholding family values and ignoring their own policies' part in America's social problems.[124]

Within this new-yet old-set of narratives, racism, although thinly veiled, wore a mask. Reagan retained "plausible deniability."

> By focusing on crack as the cause of America's social ills, "Reagan and [G.H.W.] Bush appeared tough on crime and concerned about domestic issues" as they covertly "blamed social ills on minorities without communicating a sense of racism to white constituents."

During this era the fear-mongering reached a feverish pitch.

> Politicians . . . warned that an entire generation—consistently portrayed, as a frightening "biological underclass" of mainly black urban youth—would be born addicted and diseased. Much of that alarmist reporting, however, was based on shoddy or incorrect scientific research; later research which showed that the risk was not nearly so great as was feared was not widely reported.[125]

and

> In a study of network television news in 1990 and 1991, all stories concerning illegal drugs were analyzed. The study found a consistent "us against them" frame was used in the news stories, with "us" being White Suburban America and "them" being Black Americans and the few exceptional corrupted Whites.[126]

Consistent with this narrative of scapegoating blacks, Ronald Reagan deliberately targeted low-income communities in urban areas. Although the significant adverse impact of this was predictable, the astonishing level of disparity was not.

> The United States Public Health Service has estimated that in 1992 76% of illicit drug users were white, 14% were black, and 8% were Hispanic—figures that approximate the racial and ethnic composition of the United States. Yet African-Americans account for 35% of all drug arrests, 55% of all drug convictions, and 74% of all drug sentences.[127]

In some states the racial disparity is even worse. In Maryland, for example, blacks make up 25 percent of the population. Bear in mind that blacks and whites abuse drugs at statistically insignificant rates. Blacks make up 68 percent of those arrested and 90 percent of those incarcerated.

As the Sentencing Project noted, one of every three black males, aged 20–29, is in prison, on probation, or parole.[128] In some cities, the disparity has become extreme.[129]

In 1992, the National Centre on Institutions and Alternative Studies conducted a survey of young African males in Washington, D.C.'s criminal justice system. It found that on an average day in 1991, more than four in ten of all African-American males (18–35) residing in the District of Columbia were in jail, in prison, on probation or parole, out on bond or being sought on arrest warrants. This one day count suggested that approximately three out of four young black male residents of the city would be arrested and jailed before reaching the age of 35. . . . [T]he lifetime risk hovered between 80 and 90 percent.

A few months later, NCIA replicated the study in Baltimore, Maryland—finding that 60,715 African-American males aged 18 to 35, then living in that city, 34,025 (56 percent) fell under the onus of criminal justice (that is in prison, jail, probation, parole, out on bail, or being sought on an outstanding arrest warrant).[130]

The drug war had its origins in an us-versus-them narrative that scapegoated urban blacks as the source of American's ills especially crime. That stereotyping is the context in which we must understand the astonishing disproportion of black men arrested and jailed.

If arrest records are any barometers by which to measure crime, Blacks commit aggravated assault at a rate three times that of whites. On the other hand if victim surveys are the barometer the rate is virtually identical: 32 in 1000 for blacks and 31 in 1000 for whites.[131]

As Elliott Curie writes, "Under the impact of the drug war, indeed the correctional system has become our principal agency for disadvantaged young men, their chief source of publicly supported housing and one of the most important sources of nutrition and medical care."[132]

This narrative of blacks as the source of the problem of drugs and the outrageous pattern of disproportionate incarceration are mutually reinforcing.

While the facts show that the majority of drug users and profiteers are white, the nation and the world are bombarded with images of black males who are handcuffed, lying on the ground dead, or herded behind prison walls—all due to trafficking or abuse of drugs. The racist myth is that most inner city young black males are gun toting, crack smoking criminals in waiting.[133]

The same racialized moral panic that produced this system in the 1980s gave birth to new "get tough" policies in the 1990s. George Bush, with the support of the black caucus, introduced mandatory minimum legislation.

In a further demonstration of the government's "get-tough" stance on drugs, President George Bush authorized a "zero-tolerance" policy, calling for mandatory penalties for first-time drug offenders and a shift in prosecutorial focus from suppliers and dealers to small-time drug users. Congress also created the United States Sentencing Commission to develop "mandatory minimums"—laws designed to limit the discretion of judges by creating statutorily required sentence ranges for most federal crimes, particularly drug-related offenses.[134]

Using a perverse analogy between incapacitation and striking out in baseball, 24 states created three strikes laws. These laws were driven by the image that drug users were superpredators whose fiendish desire for a high had created an urban crime wave of possession. John Dilulio, a Princeton, wrote: "[W]hat is really frightening everyone from D.A.s to demographers, old cops to old convicts, is not what's happening now but what's just around the corner—namely, a sharp increase in the number of super crime-prone young males."[135]

What defined them as superpredators was their sociopathic disposition.

We're talking about elementary school youngsters who pack guns instead of lunches. We're talking about kids who have absolutely no respect for human life and no sense of the future. . . . They fear neither the stigma of arrest nor the pain of imprisonment. They live by the meanest code of the meanest streets, a code that reinforces rather than restrains their violent, hair-trigger mentality. In prison or out, the things that super-predators get by their criminal behavior—sex, drugs, money— are their own immediate rewards. Nothing else matters to them. So for as long as their youthful energies hold out, they will do what comes "naturally": murder, rape, rob, assault, burglarize, deal deadly drugs, and get high.[136]

Drug use became the apotheosis of criminal menace. Thus crack cocaine was punished at 100 times the rate of powdered cocaine.[137]

The willingness to sentence someone to life in prison for drug-related crimes—some of which were quite petty—signifies the extent to which the metaphor of war has crystallized into a militaristic mind-set about urban crime.

Between the drug war itself and the culture of maximum punishment was a rate of incarceration for black men which is astounding.

> The rate at which black men are incarcerated is astonishing. Nationwide, blacks are incarcerated at 8.2 times the rate of whites. That is, a black person is 8.2 times more likely to be in prison than a white person. Among individual states, there are even more extraordinary racial disparities in incarceration rates. . . . In seven states—Connecticut, Illinois, Iowa, Minnesota, New Jersey, Pennsylvania, and Wisconsin—blacks are incarcerated at more than 13 times the rate of whites. Minnesota has by far the highest disparity—blacks in that state are incarcerated at 23 times the rate of whites. In the District of Columbia, blacks are incarcerated at 34 times the rate of whites.[138]

Going to prison is no longer an unusual event for black men in poor urban neighborhoods.[139] It is virtually a rite of passage, a marker of coming of age in the postindustrial ghetto. "For [young black males] incarceration has been normalized."[140] For virtually an entire generation of black males in the inner city, incarceration is a routine experience.[141]

"For the first time in national history, African Americans make up a majority of those entering into prison gates every year."[142] According to Mark Mauer of the National Prison Project, "A black person born today has a one in three chance of spending at least a year in prison before they are 35."[143]

The drug war has stalled in large part because the mainstream has framed it as a debate about crime and punishment. But these patterns cannot be understood solely from the perspective of crime and punishment. As a war against crime it is a catastrophe.[144]

Tonry argues that the racial disparity happened because of indifference to the massively discriminatory impact the war has had on the incarceration of black men. As he tells the story it is accidental. This reading is ahistorical and acontextual. The astonishing disproportionate incarceration of black men is not accidental. It can be understood only against the background of history that Tonry leaves out. The drug war originated as a backlash against the civil right movement. Hard won racial progress in the 1960s implicitly threatened white privilege. The drug war was launched nominally as a campaign for law and order but implicitly to restore a racial order that equal opportunity has upended. It was escalated based on an us-versus-them narrative pioneered by Nixon and operationalized by Reagan—the great communicator.

It is not in historical context a war against drugs at all. It has become, as David Simon has argued, a war against the black underclass.[145] It is a war targeting a community that has been made a scapegoat for all that is wrong in America. I would modify this by focusing on the elephant in the room that David Simon tiptoes around. It is not the entire black underclass that is primarily targeted: it is black men.

Wacquant has powerfully noted that as a result of the drug war, the ghetto has become like the prison and the prison like the ghetto. But the most important point is one that has yet to be made. Racism like social identity has become local. The black underclass has become the new racial other. They are the new niggers. At the same time, because racism has been spatialized—inner city versus suburbs—it is difficult to call it simply racism. How does one name this oppression?

This is the context, which black urban youth must deal. They are the targets of a $40-billion program that results every year in putting massive numbers of them behind bars. They have been stereotyped as superpredators. They live in a ghetto that has become like a prison.

It is against this background that we must understand Gangsta rap. If it is noise, it is an answer to the deafening silence by judges and lawyers, and law schools, about the new apartheid that the war on drugs represents.

Notes

1. August Wilson, *Joe Turner's Come and Gone* (New York: Samuel French, Inc. 1990).
2. Alperstein Harrison, *Black Exodus: The Great Migration from the American South* (Jackson: University Press of Mississippi, 1992), 192.
3. W.E.B. Du Bois, *The Souls of Black Folk* (Rockville, MD: Arc Manor Reprints, 2008), 87.
4. Donna L. Franklin, *Ensuring Inequality: The Structural Transformation of the African-American Family* (New York: Oxford University Press, 1997).

5. Jacob Lawrence, *The Migration of the Negro*, panel 15 (1940–1941).

6. Robert Jefferson Norrell, *The House I Live In: Race in the American Century* (New York: Oxford University Press, 2005), 77.

7. Lawrence, *The Migration of the Negro.*

8. Walter White, *Rope and Faggot: A Biography of Judge Lynch* (Notre Dame, IN: University of Notre Dame Press, 2002).

9. White, *Rope and Faggot.*

10. White, *Rope and Faggot.*

11. See Stewart Emory Tolnay and Elworth Meredith Beck, *A Festival of Violence: An Analysis of Southern Lynchings, 1882–1930* (1995).

12. Norrell, *The House I Live In*, 24.

13. St. Clair Drake and Horace Roscoe Cayton, *Black Metropolis: A Study of Negro Life in a Northern City* (Chicago: University of Chicago Press, 1993), xxi.

14. Drake and Cayton, *Black Metropolis.*

15. Drake and Cayton, *Black Metropolis.*

16. August Meir and Eliot Rudwick, *From Plantation to Ghetto* (London: Macmillan, 1976).

17. Paul L. Wachtel, *Race in the Mind of America: Breaking the Vicious Circle Between Blacks and Whites* (New York: Routledge, 1999), 223.

18. Richard Wright, *12 Million Black Voices* (New York: Thundermouth Press, 1941), x.

19. James Carr and Nandinee K. Nutty, *Segregation and the Rising Cost for America* (London: Routledge Press, 2008), 53.

20. Douglas Massey and Nancy Denton, *American Apartheid: Segregation and the Making of the Black Underclass* (Cambridge, MA: Harvard University Press, 1993), 35.

21. Norrell, *The House I Live In*, 88.

22. Massey and Denton, *American Apartheid*, 30.

23. Lorraine Hansberry, *A Raisin in the Sun: The Unfilmed Original Screenplay* (New York: Signet Books, 1995).

24. Hansberry, *A Raisin in the Sun* (Statement of Mr. Linder), 164.

25. Brandon Colas, "Lorraine Hansberry, A Raisin in the Sun: The Ghetto Trap," http://www.literature-study-online.com/essays/hansberry.html.

26. Massey and Denton, *American Apartheid*, 38; Carr and Cutty, *Segregation and the Rising Costs for America*, 56.

27. Massey and Denton, *American Apartheid*, 36.

28. Jack Saltzman, David L. Smith, and Cornel West, *Encyclopedia of African-American Culture and History* (New York: Macmillan Library Reference, 1996), 1310.

29. Massey and Denton, *American Apartheid*, 37.

30. Massey and Denton, *American Apartheid*, 37.

31. Richard T. Schaefer, *Encyclopedia of Race, Ethnicity and Society*, vol. 1 (New York: Sage Publications, 2008).

32. Massey and Denton, *American Apartheid*, 37.

33. W. E. B. Dubois, *The Philadelphia Negro* (Philadelphia, PA: University of Pennsylvania Press, 1899), 81.

34. Norrell, *The House I Live In*, 87.

35. Oliver Zunz, *The Changing Face of Inequality: Urbanization, Industrial Development and Immigrants in Detroit* (Chicago: University of Chicago Press, 1982), 377.

36. Zunz, *The Changing Face of Inequality*.

37. Edward M. Pavlic, *Crossroads Modernism: Descent and Emergence in African-American Literary Culture* (Minneapolis: University of Minnesota Press, 2002), 56.

38. Alain LeRoy Locke, *The New Negro* (New York: Touchstone Press, an imprint of Simon and Schuster, 1925), 7.

39. Drake and Clayton, *Black Metropolis*, 431.

40. Kenneth L. Kusmer and Joe William Trotter, *African American Urban History since World War II* (Chicago: University of Chicago Press, 2009).

41. *Shaft*, directed by Gordon Parks (Los Angeles: Metro-Goldwyn-Mayer, 1971). DVD (Warner Brothers, June 6, 2000).

42. *Superfly*, directed by Gordon Parks (1972) DVD (Burbank, CA: Warner Brothers, January 13, 2004).

43. *Foxy Brown*, directed by Jack Hill, Los Angeles, CA: American International Pictures, 1974) DVD (Los Angeles: Metro-Goldwyn-Mayer, January 9, 2001).

44. *Across 100th Street*, directed by Barry Shear (Los Angeles: United Artists, 1972) DVD (Los Angeles, CA: Metro-Goldwyn-Meyer, October 16, 2001).

45. See Kusmer and Trotter, *African American History after World War II*, 38.

46. Formisiano, 45.

47. Formisiano, 45.

48. Marissa Chapel, *The War on Welfare: Family, Poverty, and Politics in Modern America* (Philadelphia: University of Pennsylvania Press, 2009), 204.

49. Steve Macek, *Urban Nightmares: The Media, the Right, and the Moral Panic over the City* (Minneapolis: University of Minnesota Press, 2006), 26.

50. Macek, *Urban Nightmares.*

51. Macek, *Urban Nightmares.*

52. Michael K. Brown, *Race, Money and the Welfare State* (Ithaca, NY: Cornell University Press, 1999), 285.

53. William Julius Wilson, *Bridge over the Racial Divide: Rising Inequality and Coalition Politics* (Berkeley: University of California Press, 2009).

54. Phyllis Moen, Donna Dempster-McClain, and Henry A. Walker, *A Nation Divided: Diversity, Inequality and Community in American Society* (Ithaca, NY: Cornell University Press, 1999).

55. George Lipsitz, *Footsteps in the Dark Hidden Histories of Popular Music* (Minneapolis: University of Minnesota Press, 2007).

56. Lipsitz, *Footsteps in the Dark Hidden Histories of Popular Music.*

57. Lipsitz, *Footsteps in the Dark Hidden Histories of Popular Music.*

58. Macek, *Urban Nightmares*, 18.

59. Murray Forman, *The Hood Comes First: Race, Space and Place in Rap and Hip-Hop* (Middletown: Wesleyan University Press, 2002), 46.

60. Tricia Rose, *Black Noise* (Middletown, CT: Wesleyan University Press, 1994), 29.

61. Eithne Quinn, *Nuthin' but a "G" Thang: The Culture and Commerce of Gangsta Rap* (New York: Columbia University Press, 2005), 43.

62. Michelle Hollander, *Unemployment in New York City during the Recession and Early Recovery: Young Black Men Hit the Hardest* (Community Service Society of New York, December 2010), http://www.cssny.org/userimages/downloads/OnlyOneInFourYoungBlackMenIn NYCHaveaJobDec2010.pdf

63. Black Buffalo, http://ppg-buffalo.wikispaces.com/file/view/Black_ Bflo_Profile_Table_2%5B1%5D.pdf

64. Mark V. Levine, *The Crisis Deepens: Black Male Joblessness in Milwaukee* (Center for Economic Development, University of Wisconsin, October 2010), http://www4.uwm.edu/ced/publications/blackjobless ness_2010.pdf; last accessed February 2, 2010.

65. Levine, *The Crisis Deepens*, 3.

66. Levine, *The Crisis Deepens*, 3.

67. Levine, *The Crisis Deepens*, 3.

68. *Brown v. Board of Education*, 347 U.S. 483 (1954).

69. *Plessy v. Ferguson, 163 U.S. 537 (1896), Overruled by, Brown* v. *Board of Educ.*, 347 U.S. 483 (1954).

70. Mary L. Dudziak, "Desegregation as a Cold War Imperative," *Stanford Law Review* 41 (1988): 100.

71. *Brown I*, 347 U.S., 494, 495.

72. "[W]ith all deliberate speed" is of course an oxymoron. Websters New World Dictionary says "deliberate" means "to consider carefully" and "unhurried." The source of the phrase underscores the contradiction. It derives from a poem by Francis Thompson, "The Hound of Heaven," who states "with unhurrying chase/and unperturbed pace/*deliberate speed*." [Italics added]. "The phrase was deliberately contradictory. In *Brown I*—which decides the question of whether U.S. law countenances segregation—the audience is the world. Here the court was affirming, for the world, the principles of equal justice and democracy which was the U.S. "brand". In *Brown II,* the audience is "the South"—the Judges, Lawyers, scholars of the south who would read the decision. The vagueness of the standard by which school desegregation would be paced was welcome to Southerners who favored either gradual change or none at all.

73. Gary Orfield, *Dismantling Desegregation: The Quiet Reversal of Brown v. Board of Education* (New York: The New Press, 1997), 53.

74. D. Marvin Jones, "The Original Meaning of Brown: Seattle, Segregation and the Rewriting of History (For Michael Lee and Dukwon)," 63 *University of Miami Law Review* 629 (2009): 651.

75. Julienne Malveux, "Ever Left Behind: Black Male Students," *USA Today*, September 10, 2010, 13a.

76. The Blind Boys of Alabama, *"Way Down in the Hole," and All the Pieces Matter, Five Years of Music from "The Wire."* MP3 (New York City: Nonesuch Record Label, January 8, 2008).

77. Forman, *The Hood Comes First*, 42.

78. Dirk De Meyer et al., *The Urban Condition: Space, Community, and Self in the Contemporary Metropolis* (Rotterdam, The Netherlands: 010 Publishers, 1999), 268.

79. Herman S. Gray, *Watching Race: Television and the Struggle for Blackness* (Minneapolis: University of Minnesota Press, 2004), 39.

80. Robert Entman, "Representation and Reality in the Portrayal of Blacks on Network and Television News," *Journalism Quarterly* 71, no. 3 (1994): 511–12.

81. Entman, "Representation and Reality."

82. Entman, "Representation and Reality."

83. Macek, *Urban Nightmares*, 213.

84. *Judgment Night*, directed by Stephen Hopkins (Universal City: California Universal Pictures, 1993).

85. Macek, *Urban Nightmares*, 213.

86. *Tresspass*, directed by Walter Hill (Universal City: California Universal Pictures, 1992).

87. *Tresspass*, 213.

88. *Tresspass*.

89. Tom Wolfe, *Bonfire of the Vanities* (London: MacMillan, 2008).

90. *Training Day*, directed by Antoine Fuqua (Burbank: California Warner Bros., 2001).

91. David Leonard, *Screens Fade to Black: Contemporary African-American Cinema* (Westport, CT: Praeger, 2006), 57.

92. Leonard, *Screens Fade to Black*, 60.

93. *Crash*, directed by Paul Haggis (Santa Monica, CA: Lionsgate, 1996).

94. Henry A. Giroux, *Fugitive Cultures: Race, Violence and Youth* (London: Routledge, 1996), 69.

95. Spike Lee, Do the Right Thing, Universal City: Universal Studios, 1989.

96. Robert Entman and Kimberly A. Gross, "Race, to Judgment: Stereotyping Media and Criminal Defendants," *Law and Contemporary Problems* 71 (Autumn, 2008): 93.

97. "The Target" (#1.1), *The Wire*, DVD, directed by Clark Johnson (2002; Los Angeles: HBO Studios, 2004).

98. Antonio Gramsci, *Prison Notebooks*, Vol. 3 (New York: Columbia University Press; Joseph A. Buttigieg, 2010), 169.

99. Robert Gordon, "New Developments in Legal Theory," in *The Politics of Law: A Progressive Critique*, ed. David Kairys (New York: Basic Books, 1998), 287.

100. W.E.B. Dubois, *Black Reconstruction in America: 1860–1880* (New York: Free Press; David Levering Lewis, ed., 1999), 700.

101. W.E.B. Dubois, cited in David Roediger, *The Wages of Whiteness: Race in the Making of White America* (Brooklyn: Verso Books, 1999), 6.

102. Roediger, *The Wages of Whiteness*.

103. Mary L. Dudziak, *Cold War Civil Rights: Race and the Image of American Democracy* (Princeton, NJ: University of Princeton Press, 2002), 248.

104. Michelle Alexander, *The New Jim Crow* (New York: The New Press, 2010), 40.

105. Garth E. Pauley, *The Modern Presidency & Civil Rights: Rhetoric on Race from Roosevelt to Nixon* 200 (College Station, TX: TAMU Press, 2001).

106. Pauley, *The Modern Presidency*, 201.

107. Kevin L. Yuill, *Richard Nixon and the Rise of Affirmative Action: The Pursuit of Racial Equality in an Era of Limits* (Lanham, MD: Rowman and Little Field, 2006), 220.

108. Yuill, *Richard Nixon and the Rise of Affirmative Action*, 100.

109. Paul Rutherford, *Endless Propaganda: The Advertising of Public Goods* (Toronto: University of Toronto Press, 2000), 60.

110. Richard Reeves, *President Nixon: Alone in the White House* (New York: Simon and Schuster, 2002), 110.

111. Robert Perkinson, *Texas Tough: The Rise of America's Prison Empire* (London: McMillan, 2009), 297.

112. Rudolph Joseph, *Legalizing Marijuana: Drug Policy Reform and Prohibition Politics* (Westport, CT: Praeger, 2008), 21.

113. Eva Bertram, *Drug War Politics: The Price of Denial* (Berkeley: University of California Press, 1996), 106.

114. Dan Baum, *Smoke and Mirrors: The War on Drugs and the Politics of Failure* (New York: Little Brown, 1996), xi.

115. Bertram, *Drug War Politics*.

116. John A. Powell and Eileen B. Hershenov, "Hostage to the Drug War: The National Purse, the Constitution and the Black Community," *University of California at Davis Law Review* 24 (1991): 557, 557 (citing President Reagan's Radio Address to the Nation, *Weekly Compilation of Presidential Documents* 18 (October 2, 1982): 1249, 1249); see also Alfred W. McCoy & Alan A. Block, eds., U.S. "Narcotics Policy: An Anatomy of Failure," in *War on Drugs: Studies in the Failure of U.S. Narcotics Policy* (Boulder, CO: Westview Press, 1992), 1 (claiming that drug war is really war on cocaine).

117. National Drug control Strategy, 1, http://www.whitehousedrugpolicy.gov/publications/policy/11budget/fy11budget.pdf.

118. Michael D. Lyman and Gary W. (CON) Potter, *Drugs in Society: Causes, Concepts and Control* (Burlington, MA: Anderson Publishing), 10. In 1998, states spent 39.7 billion for adult and juvenile corrections and their court systems; 77 percent of those expenditures were directly related to the war on drugs.

119. Kenneth Nunn, "Race, Crime and the Pool of Surplus Criminality: Or Why the 'War on Drugs?' Was a 'War on Blacks,'" *The Journal of Gender, Race and Justice* 6 (2002): 381.

120. Gary L. Fisher and Nancy Roget, *Encyclopedia of Substance Abuse Prevention, Treatment, and Recovery* (Thousand Oaks, CA: Sage Publications, 2009), 255.

121. Craig Reinarman and Harry Gene Levine, *Crack in America: Demon Drugs and Social Justice* (Berkeley: University of California Press, 1997), 560–61.

122. Justice Policy Inst., *Cellblocks or Classrooms? The Funding of Higher Education and Corrections and Its Impact on African Ameri-*

can Men, http://www.prisonpolicy.org/scans/jpi/coc.pdf (last visited December 24, 2002).

123. Charles Lusanne, *Pipe Dream Blues*, 26.

124. Reinarman and Levine, *Crack in America*.

125. Bryony J. Gagan, "Ferguson v. City of Charleston, South Carolina: 'Fetal Abuse,' Drug Testing, and the Fourth Amendment," *Stanford Law Review* 53 (2000): 491, 496.

126. David Jernigan and Lori Dorman, "Visualizing America's Drug Problems: An Ethnographic Content Analysis of Illegal Drug Stories on the Nightly News," *Contemporary Drug Problems* 23 (1996): 169, 174.

127. See Marc Mauer and Tracy Huling, *Young Black Americans and the Criminal Justice System: Five Years Later* (Washington, DC: The Sentencing Project, 1995), 12. Not surprisingly, given these statistics, African Americans are six times more likely than whites to enter prison, with the vast majority of the associated convictions being drug related. See Thomas P. Bonczar, *Lifetime Likelihood of Going to State or Federal Prison* (Washington, DC: Bureau of Justice Statistics, U.S. Dep't of Justice, 1997), 1.

128. Mauer and Huling, *Young Black Americans and the Criminal Justice System*, http://www.sentencingproject.org/doc/publications/rd_youngblack_5yrslater.pdf; Ronald Ostrow, "Sentencing Study Sees Race Disparity," *Los Angeles Times*, October 5, 1995, a1.

129. Jerome G. Miller, *Search and Destroy: African-American Males in the Criminal Justice System* (Cambridge: Cambridge University Press, 2011), 7.

130. Miller, *Search and Destroy*.

131. Lusanne, *Pipe Dream Blues*.

132. Elliott Currie, *Reckoning: Drugs, the Cities, and the American Future* (Boston, MA: South End Press, 1991).

133. Lusanne, *Pipe Dream Blues*, 25.

134. "Winning the War on Drugs: A Second Chance for Non-violent 'Offenders,'" *Harvard Law Reviews* 113 (2000): 1485.

135. John J. Dilulio, "The Coming of the Super-Predators," *The Weekly Standard* (Washington, DC), November 27, 1995, 23.

136. Dilulio, "The Coming of the Super-Predators."

137. Under the Fair Sentencing Act of 2010 (Public Law 111–220) the disparity was reduced from 100 to 1 to 18 to 1. There is a debate now about whether the law should be retroactive. See Charlie Savage, "Retroactive Reductions Sought in Crack Penalties," *The New York Times*, June 1, 2011, http://www.nytimes.com/2011/06/02/us/02cocaine.html

138. Jamie Fellner, *Punishment and Prejudice: The Racial Disparities in the War on Drugs* (New York City: Human Rights Watch, 2000).

139. Fellner, *Punishment and Prejudice*, 3.

140. David Garland, *Mass Imprisonment: Social Causes and Consequences* (Thousand Oaks, CA: Sage Press, 2001), 2.

141. D. Marvin Jones, *Race, Sex, and Suspicion: The Myth of the Black Male* (Westport, CT: Greenwood, 2005).

142. Loic Wacquant, *Deadly Symbiosis: When Ghetto and Prison Meet and Mesh* (Hoboken, NJ: John Wiley and Sons, 2001).

143. Timothy Davis, Kevin R. Johnson, and George A. Martínez, *A Reader on Race, Civil Rights, and American Law: A Multiracial Approach* (Durham, NC: Carolina Academic Press, 2001).

144. As William Chambliss stated,

> The war on drugs is a failure by any objective measure. It has not reduced drug consumption, the presence of drug selling gangs, the production of new products for consumers or the volume for drugs flowing into the United States. It has been successful, however, in legitimating the creation of a virtual police state in the ghettoes of our cities.

William Chambliss, *Drug War Politics: Racism, Corruption, and Alienation, in Crime Control and Social Justice: The Delicate Balance* (Westport, CT: Greenwood, Darnell F. Hawkins et al., eds., 2003), 315.

145. Ian Rothkerch, "What Drugs Have Not Destroyed, the War on Them Has," *Salon Magazine* (San Francisco, CA), Saturday, June 29, 2002. "I don't buy that in the drug war. I think it may have begun nobly enough as this crusade against dangerous drugs, but it's become a war on the underclass."

2

Thinking with the Nigga

David Banner, rapper and organic hip-hop intellectual, took the stand to portray the artistry at the soul of the music. From the looks on the faces of Congressman Bobby Rush and his aides, this music is less an art form than the scene of a crime. The atmosphere of indignation and the verbal finger waving would have been no different than if David Banner had been O. J. Simpson. Rush shouted, "You can't justify the word nigga to me because that's what the slave master called my grandmother before he raped her!"

Wow . . .

In *Godfather I,* after Sonny had been brutally machine-gunned, the Godfather asked tearfully, "How did we get this far?" That was my question. The end of politics is always war. I am witness to the war on drugs and the war on terror; now it seems the politics of race has led us to a culture war against hip-hop.

The dominant culture has always received black art as spectacle—an exhibit in the tent of native culture, a virtual three-ring event. The black caucus was not content in the role of spectator; they had created a circus of their own. Is this the congressional black caucus or the Christian right? Is this really Congressman Bobby Rush or Bill Cosby in disguise?

Then I fell asleep. In the dream my soul took flight. I flew out over the rusting, postindustrial inner city, past the closed plants, the street corners teeming with black men jobless without hope. I heard the staccato of automatic rifle fire above the din of rattling subways. I flew over abandoned houses boarded up, past row houses with ramps for those who had been disabled by gunfire, I heard babies crying, smelled trash that wasn't picked up, smelled the pungent odor of urine in the hallways of housing projects in Harlem, Bedford-Stuyvesant, and Park Heights in West Baltimore.

I saw the prison buses unload one after another, hour after hour, and most of the ones getting off the bus in this army of the lost were black kids.

Was this America or was it our valley of dry bones?

Hip-hop samples this dream. The images are simply digitized into the rhyme and flow.

Thinking with the Nigga

From the pulpit to the lectern, from the television news desk to the op-ed pages of the leading papers, the general consensus is the nigga is deadly dangerous. It is this nigga who gang bangs, who is destroying the fabric of society.-Ronald R. T. Judy[1]

The state of emergency is a state of emergence.—Homi Babha[2]

The television show, *The Wire,* captures the facts of life in the inner city. Everyone is a suspect. As the show comes on telephoto, lenses snap pictures of youth standing on corners as helicopters circle overhead, and each lamppost mounted with a constantly blinking sensor is a one-eyed informant for the police.

Congress has extended this panoptical surveillance into the realm of urban cultural production.[3] Let me say it plain: The congressional hearings on hip-hop are yet another level of surveillance and control for urban populations. It is a policing not of people but of culture.

There are three states in civil society: the state of war, state of peace, and when an emergency justifies it—a state of siege. In a state of siege, civil liberties are suspended. Reagan explicitly called for this in the war on drugs.

The mainstream media has declared a state of siege in the realm of urban culture. The sense of emergency is rooted in two key narratives: one Eurocentric and mainstream and one Afrocentric, led by aging civil rights warriors.

Narrative One: Culture as Contamination— The View from CNN

Fanon argued that for the colonialist the native was always threatening to contaminate the modern world with his primitiveness and so had to be controlled. The mainstream view of hip-hop expresses this same suspicion.

If you were to construct an image of rap music via accounts of rap in the established press, you would (besides betraying limited critical instincts about popular culture) probably perceive rap to reflect the violent, brutal, sexist reality of a pack of wilding Willie Hortons.[4]

Suspected of glamorizing criminal styles, gangsterism, and violence, it is frequently analogized to poison. It is something brought in from the ghetto threatening to poison the minds of innocent white youth, contaminating society.

Listen to Paula Zahn

Tonight, we're going to explore the question: Is hip-hop art or poison?

[Officer Andy Harris, Charlotte, North Carolina, Police Department:]

There's no work ethic. It's the easy money of robbing, stealing, and selling cocaine.

[Catherine Montsinger, Criminology Professor, Johnson C. Smith University:]

Watch a hip-hop video, and people aren't just wearing expensive items. They're literally flashing cash in their hands. To emulate their idols, some kids, too young and immature to make better decisions, break the law.[5]

No less than the threat of drugs, hip-hop is corrosive to the moral fabric of America. Listen to William Bennett, leader of Empower America. "I think that nothing less is at stake than preservation of civilization. This stuff by itself won't bring down civilization but it doesn't help."[6]

From the pulpit Rev. Calvin Butts joins in, "unless we speak against this rap music it will creep into our society and destroy the morals of our children."[7]

The narrative of hip-hop as a moral corrosive can be historicized: black music from jazz to blues has been demonized as the devil's music. The prominence of the attacks reflects how deeply Gangsta rap has penetrated into the mainstream: 80 percent of the listeners of hip-hop are white. Underlying the claim that hip-hop is a set of toxic images and rhymes is a fear of cultural amalgamation. The objection is, at the end of the day, like the objection to interracial dating. The notion is that blackness would infect the gene pool. In a similar vein, the Gangstas must not be allowed to mongrelize or debase American pop culture with its primitiveness. The high sales are driven by precisely the same sense of opening the door to the primitive, which makes it exotic and sought after. White audiences come to Gangsta rap as whites in another age came to Harlem, slumming, to see something risqué, forbidden, to rub shoulders with the natives, but from a distance.

Narrative 2: Gangsta Rap as Black-on-Black Crime

For mainstream media, Gangsta rap is analogized to the pollution in the stream of civilization. For its black critics, Gangsta rap is the scene of a crime. Like the drug dealers the Gangstas are selling death to kids.

> It was without question one of the cruelest ironies in the rise and transformation of hip-hop, the fact that livelihood—indeed its very survival as a pop juggernauht—rested almost entirely on its ability to sell black death. The embrace of guns, gangsterism, and ghetto authenticity brought an aura of celebrity and glamour to the grim but fabulously hyped portraits of ghetto life.[8]

> It not only expresses illicit criminal values; it causes crime.

> I can see now that the murder and killings are coming from the same hands that make the beats and rhymes; how is living in hip-hop any different than living in the dysfunctional black family?[9]

It is also a kind of abuse, something degrading and injurious reminiscent of the abuse blacks suffered during the slave regime. "You can't justify to me the use of the word nigger because my slavemaster used it. . . . [T]here is no justification at all. My slavemaster raped my mama and my ancestors. I am not going to buy into that . . .; I can't condone that at all. I have to deny that approach."[10] By representing themselves as Niggas, thugs, and pimps, the Gangsta has traded places with old Massa. When I debated Reverend Al Sharpton about this in Detroit, he went one better. He said, to thunderous applause, that by calling each other "Nigga" this was the equivalent of "spitting on the grave of ancestors who died to make us free."

The image of hip-hop as actually causing harm is rooted equally in the image of the minstrel show. From the old-school perspective, Gangsta rap performances are no different for the black middle class from the strutting blackface performers of the 19th century.

Every person using broken English, strutting in saggy pants, extolling violence and gangsterism is a walking stereotype. He represents the very animalistic criminal that has been used to stigmatize blacks.

This criticism of hip-hop as a perpetuation of racial stereotypes is deeply rooted in the civil rights narrative.

The raison d' être of the civil rights movement was to fight against barriers to opportunity. The perpetuation of stereotypes is the classic instance of a racial barrier.

The perpetuation of stereotypes collides as well with decades of black studies, with what is understood as the Afrocentric perspective. This perspective posits an authentic blackness that is transnational and transhistorical. Afrocentric scholars are irreconcilably at war with dehumanizing images of black people.

Thus, academic critics add their voice to the cry of alarm,

> Why has the Gangsta, pimp, ho trinity been the vehicle for hip-hop's greatest sales and market status? Why did a substyle based on hustling, crime, sexual domination and drug dealing become rap's cultural and economic calling card?[11]

(They join in the indictment but reduce the charges: the Gangsta rappers are merely corner boys, the corporations, which commodify the stereotypes, are portrayed as the kingpins.)

The Gangsta as Ghetto Primitive

To the image of the gangster as criminal, there is a linked image of the gangster as a backward, ghetto child: in order to be successful, the Gangsta must grow up, learn discipline, and join the team—by crossing over from the values of the hood to those of middle-class society. This theme is developed in local laws against saggy pants and by numerous films. *Drumline* is a classic example. In *Drumline*,[12] hip-hop represents lack of discipline, immaturity, and illiteracy (pathologies of the ghetto). Consequently, they are incapable of functioning as part of a team (representing the idea that Gangstas are bad citizens).

In *Drumline,* the generational and class conflict is personified by the struggle between Devon, the most talented performer in the band and Dr. Lee, the band leader. Devon feels that because of his extraordinary talent and virtuoso ability to play he should be on the front line. Dr. Lee says that is not enough:

Dr. Lee: You lied on your application; you lied at your audition when you played the required piece, and you lied to me.
Devon: I didn't think it was a big deal.
Dr. Lee: [Tossing sheet music in his direction] Play that. That's the musical text for the next game and you can't read it. As far as I'm concerned that is a big deal. I'm enrolling you in the percussions course.
Devon: That gives me five classes.
Dr. Lee: Damn right. Ought to be ten, especially if you plan on getting on line soon.
Devon: What do you mean getting back on line?
Dr. Lee: If you can't read music you can't be on my field.
Devon: You can't take me off the line. I'm the best drummer you got. Ain't no class gonna teach me how to do me.
Dr. Lee: Excuse me.
Devon: Doin me is what got me here in the first place.
Dr. Lee: No, lyin' is what got you here in the first place. And if you don't have the honor and discipline to learn your craft, quite frankly you don't deserve to be here.[13]

Devon represents the dysfunctional individualism of the hip-hop generation in which to be free, they wear their pants hanging down, use improper English, and refuse to conform. This sums up the middle-class view of hip-hop's dysfunctional underlying themes. Dr. Lee represents sophistication, learning, and discipline.

This threat to the success of the race (the team) is a key aspect of the emergency and supplies an explanation as to why ghetto children are failing in school, why they are unemployed.

But "the state of emergency is also always a state of emergence." Both the European perspective and the black middle-class perspective have the ambition of a God's eye view. They are not. They are both views from a cruel distance defined by both class and space. There is a third perspective which has yet to be understood.

Pushing Back: The Ghettocentric Perspective

The third perspective arises from the Fanonian dilemma.

Look! A Negro! It was an example of an external stimulus that flickers over me as I passed by. I made a tight smile.
"Look, a Negro!" The circle was drawing a bit tighter. I made no secret of my amusement. Mama, see the Negro; I am frightened.[14]

This is the power of the gaze. Fanon goes on to write,

The girl's gaze returns to her mother in the recognition of disavowal of the Negroid type; the black child turns away from himself, his race, his total identification with the positivity of whiteness. . . . In the act of disavowal and fixation the colonial subject is returned to the narcissism of the imaginary and its identification of an ideal subject that it's white and whole.[15]

Baldwin captured the resilience of the animalistic trope when he said that growing up, "we had to wrest our identity from the clutches of Tarzan." After the Obama Chimpanzee cartoon, the reference to Michelle Obama as a gorilla, or the reference to Harvard Professor Henry Louis Gates as a jungle monkey, no one can argue that even today we are still troped as beasts. Today's generation slips the trope only through a claim of exceptionalism.

Now, however, with the huge influx of a poor and Spanish-speaking population . . . there is a new candidate for the bottom position, and accordingly, America's blacks are being prepped to assimilate upwards. . . . The hidden message is that blacks will be welcomed into majority America if they are willing to reject identification with the poor, the oppressed and the downtrodden, and if they are willing to give up any and all traditional expressions of black identity.[16]

Does the black middle-class critique of Gangsta rap rest on an authentic grasp of black identity or is it at least in part of an act of disavowal?

Those who call themselves Niggas are still in the gaze; they are the ones who are disavowed. They are a rejected class, a rejected culture; their cultural productions are received as waste, as pollution; their language, their way of speaking is so full of ignorance and vulgarity. The claim to be a Nigga challenges the cultural authority of the rejection and claims itself to be the locus of cultural authority.

The nihilism expressed in Gangsta rap music is deceptive. A much-celebrated element of resistance in Gangsta rap, for instance, is the appropriation of the term "nigga". Gangsta rappers effectively have recoded the social meaning of this term. In public discourse its use is taboo although what the term connotes is a reiteration of daily newscasts of crime and violence. On a news program nightline, Ice T, a popular Gangsta rapper engaged in a long drawn out debate with Harvard professor Alvin Puissant. . . . Ice T drove home the point . . . by capping on Poussaint's view with the signifying expression "nigga please." When used in black vernacular culture such a reversal of meaning allows the term to function as a source of pride rather than denigration.[17]

In the story, the gaze is perpetrated by the stereotypical perspective of the little girl. In our contemporary postindustrial urban context, a thousand eyes watching from lampposts and a thousand telephoto lens mounted throughout the ghetto, project the gaze. In essence this is the jungle. "You must be watched because you are dangerous, like beasts."

The Nigga as a social identity expresses the attitude of turning back the gaze. The Negro tries to make himself acceptable, to straighten his hair, get a job, go to law school. The Nigga does not try to conform, he simply says in effect, "I don't give a f***."

The dominant perspective of the whites who hate/love hip-hop as a kind of ghetto porn on display is Eurocentric. The civil rights narrative which views this commodification of stereotypes as self-hating racism—or nihilism—is Afrocentric. The Nigga is ghettocentric.

The construction of the ghetto as a living nightmare and the Gangstas as products of that nightmare has given rise to what I call a new
"ghettocentric" identity in which the specific class, race and gendered experiences in late capitalist urban centers coalesce to create a
new identity—Nigga.

The Nigga cannot be reduced to nihilism any more than a Martin
Scorsese film can be reduced to the realm of profane violence. What vali-
dates the film is not its content but its perspective. What we get from the
film is not emptiness—nihilism is morally empty—but an opening up; it
opens us up to experiencing a raw side of life. The challenge is not so
much to analyze, but to feel, not to think about but to think with and feel
with the characters. As R.A.T. Judy writes,

> Thinking about the significance of hard-core rap in terms of its sig-
> nificance for African society is a way of disposing of it, unless we
> are willing to think it with . . . the nigga. Thinking with the nigga is
> to become concerned with an emergent utterance—which does not
> work according to the purpose of liberal knowledge.[18]

Nor can the Nigga accept the civil rights narrative. This civil rights vision left the masses of blacks still marooned in the inner city. The civil rights
narrative posits that black people are united across time and across space.
The Nigga pushes back. He will not accept this universalism. The identity
of the Nigga is local. The Nigga does not belong to America, or to the civil
rights movement, or to the black cultural Diaspora; he belongs to the hood.
He rejects also the moral constraints of the society that has rejected him—
constraints like don't steal, and don't use violence. He becomes an outlaw.

This ghettocentric perspective is linked to an outsider narrative. This
must be understood against two axes of inquiry. The first is historical. During the 1960s, the outsider narrative was divided between the narrative of
revolution and the narrative of blacks as Africans not Americans. As we
historicize the outlaw narrative, we find it is much older. It traces back to
the outlaw narratives of slave folklore. But the Nigga in Gangsta rap is not
simply a continuation of a folk tradition; though he is that, he is as Barry Ki-
tana notes, the product of new economic and technological conditions. A set
of extreme positives and extreme negatives has given rise to "new patterns

of race, class and gender oppression in urban America."[19] Perhaps the most profound negative is homicidal nature of inner city life. Nelson George attributes the emergence of Gangsta rap largely to the emergence of epidemics of crack addiction. I attribute it more to the violence associated with the drug culture. The extreme positive is the tantalizing cornucopia of wealth that appears to flow constantly around but just out of the reach of the urban poor. The Nigga is the identity which pushes back against the twin threats of death and devaluation. He combines the hardness necessary to deal with the violence with a Tony Montana–like desire to get a piece of the pie.

The Nigga As Outlaw

> Almost every law and method of ingenuity that could be devised was employed by the legislatures to reduce the negroes to serfdom, to make them slaves of the state, if not of individuals. . . . [T]he Negro is coming more and more to look upon law and justice, not as protecting safeguards but as sources of humiliation and oppression.[20]

The same spaces of peril are held by Gangsta rap to be the ground zero epicenter of the black experience.

Rap music takes the [inner] city and its multiple spaces as the foundation of its cultural production.[21] This is a hypersegregated space.

Loic Wacquant of Berkeley writes that this hypersegregation is the legacy of slavery. In the iconography of hip-hop, prefiguring Wacquant's writings, the ghetto is the plantation. It is the place where the blacks are confined. Simultaneously in hip-hop, the ghetto is the site of authentic African American culture[22] or the "blackest culture."[23] The Nigga embraces the authentic, unadulterated essence of the ghetto and in doing so opposes the fake culture of the suburban bourgeoisie. Malcolm X personified this split within black political consciousness through the figures of the field nigger and the house nigger.

> If the master's house caught on fire, the house Negro would fight harder to put the blaze out than the master would. If the master got sick, the house Negro would say, "What's the matter, boss, we sick?". . . . And if you came to the house Negro and said, "Let's escape, let's separate," the house Negro would look at you and say, "Man, you crazy. What you mean, separate?"[24]

And

On that same plantation, there was the field Negro. The field Negroes—those were the masses. There were always more Negroes in the field than there were Negroes in the house. The Negro in the field caught hell. The field Negro was beaten from morning to night; he lived in a shack, in a hut; he wore old, castoff clothes. . . . If someone came to the field Negro and said, "Let's separate, let's run," he didn't say, "Where we going?" He'd say, "Any place is better than here."[25]

Ice T uses Malcolm's plantation metaphor as a point of demarcation. For him, the black underclasses, whom he refers to as the field niggers, are his niggers. Ice T proclaims: "I'm proud to be a nigger."

> *Yes I was born in America too.*
> *But does South Central look like America to you?*[26]

The stereotype of a black man is that he is a beast. This has two aspects: One is an expression of hate and degraded ethnicity. The other is an expression of hypermasculinity and ultimately fear. The Nigga anchors him in this latter metaphorical mooring.

> *Nightmare, that's what I am, America's nightmare,*
> *I am what you made me, the hate and evil that you gave me.*[27]

The Nigga of course recognizes the oppressiveness of life in the ghetto, but like Camus' Sisyphus, although he cannot change his circumstances he can choose his attitude toward it.

It is an identity but not by color. . . . Niggas know whom niggas are . . . my opinion is that nigga is street smart, rebellious, able to keep composure in all situations, true to themselves and others, strong willed and wild hearted. Not all black males are this therefore they aren't niggers.[28]

Like Milton's Satan, he makes a heaven of a hell. His survival, and more importantly, his coolness in the face of daunting conditions set him apart. They make him hard, and his hard masculinity is part of what makes him real.

> *Just in case a nigga want to act out*
> *I just black out and blow they motherfuckin' back out*
> *That's a real nigga.*[29]

He has not been and is not protected by society's laws. He is economically if not politically disenfranchised. Not being a part of the larger society, he is not contaminated by having to bow to its rules. He develops a kind of outlaw mentality.

Just as there is a split within black political thought between assimilation and rejection of American values, there has historically been a split in how blacks have viewed their outlaws. Malcolm's field nigger image mirrors the earlier bad nigger of black folklore, an embodiment of the slave who would not obey the white man's laws, or accept his rules of morality.

Characterized by his absolute rejection of established authority figures—Ole Massa, the Sheriff, the Judge and his assertion of his own power and authority. . . . [His goal is] to attack and destroy all that [white] authority holds dear, including its work ethic, its political principles, its moral values.[30]

Similarly, Grier and Cobbs wrote,

The man who fought when threatened and lived to tell the tale became a man among men who held his manhood dear and though his life was likely to be brief he had laid hold of the essential task of men and particularly black men—survival and opposition to the foe.[31]

What takes place in hip-hop, as in antebellum slave culture, is moral inversion. As Brearly noted in his famous 1939 essay, the very qualities that made the bad nigger bad made him a hero as well. Dundes explains,

The point of being labeled bad by Southern plantation owners in the sense of being dangerous, obstreperous and the like indicated to black people that the individual in question was unwilling to submit passively to the oppression of slavery. Thus bad niggers were Negroes who were willing to fight the system. Bad didn't mean evil at all . . . thus the whites meant -to be -insulting epithet of "bad nigger" became virtually a badge of honor in the black community. If the white slave owner deemed one to be a "bad nigger" that was high praise indeed.[32]

This has much to do with how and why criminal lifestyles are glamorized in Gangsta rap.

"Criminal acts are turned into brilliant capers."[33] White fear of black male violence, anathema to the black middle class, becomes a way of expressing the Gangsta's power.

The historic construction of blackness in opposition to whiteness, in which blackness is demonized, has become part of the art form's consciousness. Whereas previous generations of black Americans utilized various means to establish a self-definition that negated the construction of blackness as demonic or depraved, many members of the hip-hop generation have chosen instead to appropriate and exploit those constructions as metaphoric tools for expressing power. Because this gesture is ultimately aggressive the black community does not perceive these acts as those of self-hating traitors.[34]

Among historical figures Nat Turner, Denmark Vesey, Gabriel Prosser, Cinque of the Amistad and in the Caribbean Toussaint L'Ouverture, Dessalines, Christophe, Clairveaux, Mccandal, the Maroons, the heroes of Palmares and all other slave rebels and conspirators, these are archetypal "bad niggers."[35]

In folklore, the bad nigger blends into the bad man of black folklore. These black archetypes include Railroad Bill, a feared train robber.

Railroad bill was a mighty sport,
    Shot all the buttons of the high sheriff's coat.[36]

Perhaps the most famous was Stagolee.

> *Stagolee throw seven,*
> *Billy swore that he throwed eight.*
> *Stagolee told Billy,*
> *"I can't let you go with that;*
> *You have won my money*
> *And my brand new Stetson hat."*
> . . .

Stagolee found Billy,
"Oh please don't take my life!
I got three little children,
And a very sick little wife."
Stagolee shot Billy,
Oh he shot that boy so fas'
That the bullet came through him,
And broke my window glass.[37]

More recently it includes the Dolemite figure popularized in the 1960s by Rudy Ray Moore. Dolomite "had a job in Africa kickin' lions in the ass."[38]

So Dolemite was thirteen; he say "let me try my luck on the sea."
He got a job in Africa kicking lions in the ass.
He got run out of South America for fucking steers
He fucked a she elephant till she broke down in tears.
Till finally the roll was called
So they took him down to the grave, and Dolemite was dead, but
his dick was still hard.
And the preacher said, [solemn tone] Ashes to ashes
Dust to dust
I'm glad this bad nigger is no longer with us.[39]

Both the field Negro of Malcolm's oratory and the bad nigger of black folklore coalesce in the figure of hip-hop's Nigga. The Nigga became the embodiment of black defiance against all comers through a highly masculinist imagery, where the Nigga was strong when he wasn't a punk, bitch, or pussy.[40]

Can one be both dangerous outlaw and decent man, both gentleman and savage, natural and morally constrained? In the study of folklore, John W. Roberts[41] attempts to distinguish between the bad nigger and the bad man. Whereas the bad nigger fought against unjust laws, the bad man—a "Railroad Bill"—was altogether morally undisciplined. The distinction is wishful thinking. The bad nigger and the bad man are not two separate things. The bad nigger exists for himself, placing himself beyond control of any authority other than his own autonomous will.

R.A.T. Judy states the problem this way: "The 'bad nigger' indexes a radical incommensurability. On the one hand exhibiting the individual sovereignty that forms the basis of moral order in liberal theories . . . on the other, embodying the lawlessness that morality is supposed to contain."[42]

Hip-hop's Niggas have thrown away the "shalt not" in order to be as and as *free* as the fearsome as the outlaws of black folklore. Listen to the fantasy of Big Pun, a 21st-century Railroad Bill, about a score to steal ice.

Authenticity in the black middle-class view derives from morality, while for the Nigga it derives from defiance of all authority.

> *Motherfuck the po-po's (uh-huh)*
> *. . . fuck the D.A. and P.O.'s.*[43]

"The nigger becomes the negro through moral behavior."[44] The Nigga poses the question of the compatibility of authenticity and morality, for those who live in the war zones of urban America.

> If moral and cultural correctness is seen as denial, then open representations of sexuality and grotesque carnivalesque characterizations/eroticizations of violence can be understood as potentially liberating.[45]

In a famous rap album *Ice Cube shouts,* "The world is mine" reprising and celebrating Tony Montana's famous line in Scarface.

> *Bitch I'm rich you know my name, show me the cane.*[46]

He goes on to claim "the world is mine."[47]
Similarly, Big Pun raps.

> *Here's the deal, we shatter his grill, and drill fuck him.*[48]

He goes on to openly embrace the image of himself as demonic "Far from the ghetto, a rebel of chance/the devil in pants."[49]

The Nigga As Satirical Figure

This expression of defiance of all authority is quite real, the celebration of hurting people or doing evil, the surface reading, is false.

As Keith and Pile have written, any articulation of identity formation is only momentarily complete. In art, identity is constituted by the forces that oppose it (the constitutive outside), always contingent upon surviving the contradictions that it subsumes (forces of dislocation).[50]

This is to say Gangsta rap can be understood only in context. Gangsta rap is both myth and reality, it is a serious witness, and it is creative play. It operates as a camera taking a picture both of the world as it is, and the world as it appears from the perspective of disenfranchised urban youth. It is the world in which, while they are portrayed and massively incarcerated as criminals, those on Wall Street and in the White House appear as the real gangsters. It is Russell Simmons who says Gangsta rap always tells the truth. The truth of Gangsta rap is first of all the truth of satire.

> I act like they do in the big timer, no different. There isn't a corporation that acts with morals and that ethics shit and I aren't about to either. As they say, if it's good for General Motors, it's good enough for me.[51]

And

> Instead of reacting to "culture of poverty" rhetorics by disassociating blackness from American culture, these Gangsta collectives have crowned themselves junior M.A.F.I.A., the Firm and Roc-A-Fella Records. They problematize the lines drawn between legality and illegality, morality and immorality, by articulating not the culture of poverty but mainstream American culture. The lyrics of the new Gangstas make it clear that the rhetoric of individualism pays homage to traditional mainstream values that are being used "to redistribute more income, wealth and power to classes that are already most affluent in those aspects."[52]

The Nigga and Social Conditions

Historically, the black experience was defined by slavery. The contemporary black experience is defined by the violence of the urban scene.

The role of the Nigga is to give shared meaning within these violent conditions.

This violence is not merely dehumanizing, it is racialized. In the civil rights narrative, second-class citizen referred to economic and social inequality particularized by exclusion from certain jobs and from certain schools. Second-class citizenship for the Niggas of the urban ghetto is something more urgent. Living in a ghetto means living under constant threat of violence.

Whereas white youth die primarily from accidents, black youth die primarily from homicide.[53]

The homicide death rate for young black men more than doubled from 1985 to 1993, to 167 per 100,000.[54]

In 1996, a black male was nearly seven times more likely to be a homicide victim than were his white counterparts.[55]

For most middle-class Americans, violence, death, and danger are dramatic, exceptional events. For those who live in the ghetto they are omnipresent.

Somewhere between the pervasiveness of gang culture and the constant battle for turf between rival drug crews, the ghetto has become a place where murder and death are routine.

Elijah Anderson paints a picture of this routine in a narrative journey down the mean streets of a north Philadelphia ghetto:

> Now Germantown Avenue reaches Broad Street, nearly at the intersection of Broad and Erie avenue. The triangle formed by these streets is one of the centers of the North Philadelphia ghetto. On adjacent streets, open-air drug deals occur, prostitutes ply their trade and boys shoot craps . . . here phrases like "watch your back" take on literal meaning.
>
>   . . .
>
>   In the morning and early afternoon the surrounding neighborhood seems peaceful enough, but in the evening the danger level rises . . . tensions spill over, drug deals go bad, fights materialize, seemingly out of nowhere, and the emergency room becomes a hub of activity. . . . On a back street, amid crumbling houses and abandoned stolen automobiles, whose carcasses are constantly picked at by some impoverished residents for spare parts, children "rip and run". . . .
>
>   . . .

When the boys admire someone's property they may simply try to take it; this includes a person's sneakers, jacket, hat, and other personal items. . . .

. . .

As we continue down the avenue more and more gaps in the rowhouses appear; these gaps represent places where buildings have burned down, have been torn down or simply collapsed. We pass a large building . . . gaily decorated with graffiti art, including a memorial for a young victim of street violence. The idea of a war zone springs to mind. Indeed gunshot marks on some of the buildings.[56]

These outlaw narratives are more than satire. They play the same role for the natives of the postindustrial ghetto as the church did for the generation of soul. These stories define the shared ideology of the hood; they locate the attitude necessary to survive in the peculiar space the ghetto has become. The action of the narratives is not in meaning; its meaning is the attitude toward violence. Only the hardest men survive. Niggas sometimes refer to themselves simply as G:

Hence, the adoption and recasting of "G" as a friendly form of address among African American men and to, a lesser degree, women. While the origins of "G" apparently go back to the Five Percent Nation on the East Coast where it is an abbreviation for "God" among the youth in California and elsewhere it currently stands for Gangsta.[57]

The black experience of the blues reflected the experience of urban migration; the outlaw narratives reflect the chronic confrontation with violence and death. The Nigga p ersonifies this attitude. This attitude is not strategically chosen to deal with the violence; it is one of its effects.

" 'Smoke' or 'Be Smoked' "

This determinism was summed up in a phrase. In *White Men Can't Jump,* Wesley Snipes says, it's either "smoke or be smoked." This theme of "smoke or be smoked," kill or be killed, is for me the most prominent theme in Gangsta rap.

Listen to Rasham Attica Smith, better known by his stage name, Esham (East Side Hoes and Money).

> *Kill or be killed nigga*
>
> . . .
>
> *Feel my steel nigga.*[58]

Similarly Soulja Boy raps

> *I Thought I'll Never Have To Shoot A MuthaFucka*
> *Good Thang I Was Strapped Though.*[59]

He goes on to rap, "shit, better them than me." Gangsta rap is not love poetry, it is like the poetry of the samurai: a poetry of war. In the film *Ghost Dog,* Forrest Whitaker plays a black man from the hood, who becomes a 20th-century samurai. He puts his skills to use as an assassin for the mob. In Gangsta rap, there is a deep subtext of violence as something always imminent and inevitable. Uncannily, the transition between Gangsta and samurai works is because existentially both situations are the same: they must fearlessly embrace a fate of violent death.

In *Fight Club,*[60] the author opens the book with the protagonist on top of a building wired to explode. That building is a metaphor for the urban ghetto, always ready to explode into gang violence, drug wars, and police assault.

Adapting to this imminence of danger, the Nigga develops a relationship with time. As Ellison writes,

> Once I saw a prizefighter boxing a yokel. The fighter was swift and amazingly scientific. His body was one violent flow of rapid rhythmic action. He hit the yokel a hundred times while the yokel held up his arms in stunned surprise. But suddenly the yokel, rolling about in the gale of boxing gloves, struck one blow and knocked science, speed, and footwork cold as a well digger's posterior . . . the yokel has simply stepped inside his opponents sense of time. . . .[61]

The Gangsta's move is to inhabit the now. Nowhere is this more evident than in the improvisational wizardry of the Gangstas in freestyle. The very idea of freestyle in hip-hop is captured by the hip-hop concept of battle where MCs square off on each other to see whose improvisation is more creatively aggressive. "Hip-hop is verbal offense and defense raised to high art. And both the pugilist and the MC share a common charge: 'Protect yourself at all times'."[62] In this mode the Gangsta is more like a fighter than a poet. As Jay Z states, "People compare hip-hop to other generes of music but it is more like a sport. Boxing to be exact. The stamina, the one man army, the combat aspect of it, the ring, the stage."[63]

William Jelani Cobb compares the hip-hop artist to a basketball player. "The kinesthetic genius of the NBA baller lies in his ability to construct physical freestyles, rebelling against the step-dribble-shoot simplicity of structure with an improvised use of body and time."[64]

Thus, the Nigga finds his authenticity in what he opposes. "This emphasis upon freedom of form emerges in direct relation to a group of people whose history has been defined by physical and time constraints. Free style as in the opposite of slave style—understood."[65]

What links ghetto life and "slavery" is that one is a prisoner in both situations. It is not merely that those in the ghetto disproportionately experience prison, the ghetto increasingly takes on aspects of the prison. The inevitability of the violence is "incarcerating" because even if you win a battle you are still trapped in a cycle of mayhem.[66]

> Compton 4 life
> It's the city where everybody's in prison
> Nigger's taking shit "cause ain't nobody givin"[67]

The violent conditions of the ghetto spread out in a continuum from physical brutality to the brutality of children being warehoused in schools that do not teach.

Public schools in the hyper-ghetto have similarly deteriorated to the point where they operate in the manner of institutions of confinement whose primary mission is not to educate but to ensure custody and control—to borrow the motto of many departments of corrections. . . . Like inmates, these children are herded into decaying and over-crowded facilities built like bunkers—many schools have no photocopying machines, library, science laboratory, or even functioning bathrooms. . . . The physical plant of most establishments resembles fortresses, complete with concertina wire on outside fences, bricked up window . . . and hallways patrolled by armed guards.[68]

Similarly, public housing in urban areas has become similar to high security prisons.

Get Rich or Die Tryin

The Nigga is the one who refuses to accept a life sentence in the prison of the ghetto. He is determined to get out. This impulse was captured in the title of the film, *Across a 110th Street.*[69] Harlem is separated from Morningside Heights by this imaginary dividing line of 110th street. This is the border between affluence and poverty, between greater America and the ghetto. One gets out by crossing this border. The gangster defines the border in material terms.

Ironically, the Gangsta does accept the most basic of middle-class values. He is a capitalist. He simply lacks the means. In the prison of the ghetto, a criminal lifestyle is the only avenue across the border. He is a rugged individualist, "a capitalist whose venture capital is a gun." This attitude is summed up in the Gangsta theme of *Get rich or die tryin.*

> *I'm a get rich or die tryna make it to the top*
> *Nigga I'm a keep it Gangsta.*[70]

In Spielberg's *Amistad,* the African prince-turned-slave Djmon Houston triumphs, after securing his release, by going home. We see him on the bow of the ship traveling east to Sierra Leone. The slave's journey to freedom was horizontal. The gangster's goal is to move vertically. In the cosmology of the ghetto, Sierra Leone in the east is replaced by the deluxe apartment in the sky, preferably on South Beach. He gets out by getting rich. There is then the following train—freedom = crossing into the mainstream = moving up = getting rich. The Gangsta in saying, "get rich or die tryin" is not expressing merely a personal desire but a prepolitical, prerevolutionary collective impulse to overcome oppression and spatial domination. By crossing over into the mainstream he crosses the color line itself. Freedom has become a question of money. *Get rich or die tryin*! If in the 1960s the expression was freedom by any means necessary, this is a 21st-century translation.

In this quest to change his circumstances, the Gangsta embraces the imminence of danger as normal. As 50 Cent raps in "I Run New York,"

> *I'm alive, what a beautiful feelin,'*
> *I put my vest on right after I put on my drawers,*[71]

In the outlaw narratives, even to have money you must still be ready to use violence in order to keep it. He knows of course that because of his lifestyle he has no future. "I'm a die up in these streets," he says "I got my mind made up."[72]

Art imitates life. In the film *Get Rich or Die Tryin,* which depicts the early life of 50 Cent, 50 is shot nine times by rival drug dealers. The real-life near murder of 50 Cent typifies the looming omnipresence of death for the gangster: He knows that he has no real future. So he lives only in the moment. At the point at which 50 Cent and others accept the omnipresence of death they reach the crossroads for the "sacred" and "the profane."[73] The act of making music in the face of imminent death is a kind of spiritual affirmation.[74]

Conclusion—Thinking with the Nigga

To equate the N word with racism denies the right of urban youth to name themselves. To indict hip-hop music as the cause of the violence is to scapegoat urban culture. To blame songs about pimping for the tragic relations between black males and females is to ignore ghetto conditions as the ethos in which warped notions of manhood take shape.

Ironically, the policing of urban culture, the congressional hearings, and other surveillance were designed to arrest the production of stereotypes. But, the demonization of the predominantly black male youth who make the music itself perpetuates the narrative of black deviance, denying the youth the opportunity to have a voice and stigmatizing them at the same time.

Policing culture requires a God's eye view, an objective perspective. But the policing of hip-hop occurs through the windows of race, class, and a profound lack of empathy. We must dismiss the indictment against the art form of Gangsta rap. We must stop worrying about the figures of this genre, figures like the Nigga. We must not only stop worrying about the

Nigga but we must—in the words of R.A.T. Judy— stop thinking about him altogether. We must think with him.

Notes

1. R.A.T. Judy, "On the Question of Nigga Authenticity," in *That's the Joint!: Hip-Hop Studies Reader,* ed. Murray Forman and Mark Anthony Neal (London: Routledge, 2004), 106.

2. Homi Babha, *The Location of Culture* (London: Routledge, 2004), 59.

3. Dave Goldliner, "Congress Rap Session Takes a Look at Gangsta Lyrics," *New York Daily News, Music and Arts Section*, September 26, 2007, http://www.nydailynews.com/entertainment/music-arts/congress-rap-session-takes-a-gangsta-lyrics-article-1.248303

4. Tricia Rose, "Never Trust a Big Butt and a Smile," in *That's the Joint!,* ed. Forman and Neal, 291.

5. Paula Zahn Now, "Hip-Hop: Art or Poison?," *CNN.Com*, February 21, 2007, http://transcripts.cnn.com/TRANSCRIPTS/0702/21/pzn.01.html

6. Tricia Rose, *The Hip-Hop Wars: What We Talk About When We Talk About Hip-Hop and Why It Matters* (New York: Basic Books, 2008), 95.

7. Rose, *The Hip-Hop Wars.*

8. S. Craig Watkins, *Hip-Hop Matters: Politics, Pop Culture and the Struggle for the Soul of a Movement* (Boston, MA: Beacon Press, 2005), p. 2.

9. Watkins, *Hip-Hop Matters*, 160.

10. Danny, "Congress Hears the Rap Against Rap Music," *Newstext Web-blogs*, September 30, 2007; see also "From Imus to the Industry: *The Business of Stereotypes and Degrading Images*, Hearing before the Subcommittee on Commerce, Trade and Consumer Protection of the Committee on Energy and Commerce, Washington, DC: Government Printing Office, September 25, 2007.

11. Rose, *Hip-Hop Wars*, 13.

12. *Drumline*, directed by Charles Stone (Los Angeles: 20th Century Fox, December 13, 2002).

13. David J. Leonard, *Screens Fade to Black: Contemporary African American Cinema* (Westport, CT: Praeger, 2006).

14. Frantz Fanon, *Black Skin, White Masks* (New York: Grove Press, 1952).

15. Homi K. Babha, *The Location of Culture* (New York: Psychology Press, 1994), 109.

16. Chris Sunami, "The Racial Draft," June 8, 2007, http://kitoba.com/pedia/Racial+Draft.html (last visited December 30, 2012).

17. David Theo Goldberg, *Multiculturalism: A Critical Reader* (Hoboken, NJ: Blackwell, 1994).

18. Judy, "On the Question of Nigga Authenticity," 108.

19. Judy, "On the Question of Nigga Authenticity," 22.

20. Gunnar Myrdal and Sissela Bok, *An American Dilemma: The Negro Problem and Modern Democracy*, vol. 2 (Piscatawy, NJ: Transaction Publishers, 1995), 525.

21. Murray Forman, *The Hood Comes First*, 18.

22. Phillip Brian Harper, *Are We Not Men: Masculine Anxiety and the Problem of African American Identity* (Oxford: Oxford University Press, 1998), 98.

23. Paul Gilroy, *The Black Atlantic* (Cambridge, MA: Harvard University Press, 1994), 52.

24. George Breitman, *Malcolm X Speaks: Selected Speeches and Statements* (New York: Grove Press, 1965), 10.

25. Breitman, *Malcolm X Speaks*.

26. Ice-T, "Straight Up Nigga," Original Gangster Album (Sire Records, 1991).

27. Tupac Shakur, "Young Black Male," from 2Pacalypse Now (Interscope Record 1991, Audio CD released, 1998).

28. Mary Fong and Rueyling Chang, *Communicating Ethnic and Cultural Identity* (Lanham, MD: Rowman and Littlefield, 2004).

29. Fifty Cent, "The Realest Niggaz," *24 Shots: Brand New Exclusive Material & Freestylers,* F150 Records, B000ANGFCO, *Compact Disk* (Originally released May 2003).

30. Darryl Cumber Dance, *Shucking and Jivin: Folklore from Contemporary Black Americans* (Bloomington: Indiana University Press, 1981).

31. William H. Grier and Price M. Cobbs, *Black Rage*: *Two Black Psychiatrists Reveal the Inner Conflicts and the Desperation of Black Life* (New York: Basic Books, 1992), 123–4.

32. Alan Dundes, *Mother Wit from the Laughing Barrel: Readings in the Interpretation of African-American Folklore* (Jackson: University of Mississippi Press, 1990), 581.

33. Robin D.G. Kelly, *Race, Rebels: Culture, Politics, and the Black Working Class* (New York: Free Press, 1996), 213.

34. Imani Perry, *Prophets of the Hood: Politics and Poetics in Hip-Hop* (Durham: Duke University Press, 2004).

35. *Yo Mama! New Raps, Toasts, Dozens, Jokes, and Children's Rhymes,* ed. Onwuchekwa Jemie (Philadelphia: Temple University Press, 2003).

36. Daryll Cumber Dance, *From My People: Four Hundred Years of African-Amerian Folklore* (New York: W.W. Norton Co., 2003), 491.

37. Cecil Brown, *Stagolee Shot Billy* (Cambridge, MA: Harvard University Press, 2004), 5.

38. Jemie, *Yo Mama!*.

39. Dance, *Shucking and Jivin*, 230.

40. Davarian L. Baldwin, "Black Empires, White Desires," in *That's the Joint*: *The Hip-Hop Studies Reader,* ed. Forman and Neal (New York: Psychology Press, 2004), 166.

41. John W. Roberts, *From Trickster to Badman: The Black Folk Hero in Slavery and Freedom* (Philadelphia: University of Pennsylvania Press, 1989) 171–172; see also John W. Roberts, "Railroad Bill" and the American Outlaw Tradition in Western Folklore," *Western Folklore* 40, no. 4 (October 1981).

42. Judy, "On the Question of Nigga Authenticity."

43. Trick Daddy, "I'm a Thug," *Thugs Are Us* (Atlantic Records, March 20, 2001).

44. Judy, "On the Question of Nigga Authenticity," 115.

45. Davarian Baldwin, "The Wretched of the Earth: Pleasure, Power and the Hip-Hop Bourgeoisie," in *That's the Joint*.

46. Ice Cube, "The World is Mine," Soundtrack from *Dangerous Ground*, directed by Daryll Roodt (Los Angeles: New Line Cinema, 1997).

47. Ice Cube, "The World is Mine."

48. Big Punisher, "Fast Money," *Capital Punishment*, Terror Squad/Loud Records B00000K3HL, Compact Disk, April 28, 1998.

49. Big Punisher, "Fast Money."

50. Michael Keith and Steve Pile, *Place and the Politics of Identity* (New York: Psychology Press, August 6, 2010), 27.

51. Baldwin, "Black Empires, White Desires," 166.

52. Baldwin, "Black Empires, White Desires," 169.

53. United States Department of Health and Human Services, Centers for Disease Control and Prevention, http://www.cdc.gov/men/lcod/index.htm. For black males 15–34 homicide is the number one listed cause of death; Jewelle Taylor Gibbs, *Young, Black and Male in America* (Boston, MA: Auburn House, 1988), 15.

54. Elliot Currie, *Crime and Punishment in America* (New York: Mac-Millan, 1998), 25.

55. Janice Joseph, *Black youths, Delinquency, Juvenile Justice* (Westport, CT: Greenwood Publishing, 1995), 32.

56. Elijah Anderson, *Code of the Street: Decency, Violence, and the Moral Life of the Inner City* (New York: W.W. Norton and Company, 2000).

57. Robin D.G. Kelly, "Kickin Reality, Kickin Ballistics: Gangsta Rap and Post-Industrial Los Angeles," in *Droppin Science: Critical Essays on Rap Music and Hip-Hop Culture,* ed. William Eric Perkins (Philadelphia: Temple University Press, 1996).

58. Esham, "Kill or be Killed," *Dead Flowerz* (Real Life Productions, B001H17I7O, MP3, 1996).

59. Soula Boy, "Pow," *Soulja Boy Tell Em*, Collipark Records B000V9KF0A CD (2007).

60. Chuck Palahniuk, *Fight Club* (New York: W.W. Norton, 1996).

61. Ralph Ellison, *The Invisible Man* (New York: Random House, 1995), 8.

62. William Jelani Cobb, *To the Break of Dawn: A Freestyle on the Hip-Hop Aesthetic* (New York: New York University Press, 2007), 80.

63. Cobb, *To the Break of Dawn*, 79.

64. Cobb, *To the Break of Dawn*, 78.

65. Cobb, *To the Break of Dawn*, 78.

66. Forman and Neal, *That's the Joint!*, 248.

67. Forman and Neal, *That's the Joint!*, 248.

68. Forman and Neal, *That's the Joint!*, 108.

69. *Across 110th Street* directed by Barry Shear (1972; Beverly Hills, MGM Video, 2001).

70. Yo Gotti, "Keep It Gangsta," *Gangsta Grillz* (2007).

71. 50 Cent, "I Run New York," *Bulletproof* (Mixtape) (*Independent*, 2005).

72. Yo Gotti, "Keep it Gangsta."

73. As Zanfanga writes, "While sociology's founding father Émile Durkheim asserts that religions distinguish the 'sacred' from the 'profane' and take the 'sacred' as their special concern (1915[1912]), hip-hop instead focuses on the 'profane' and sacralizes it in an attempt to invert traditional religious dichotomies;" Christina Zanfagna, "Under the Blasphemous W(RAP): Locating the "Spirit" on Hip-Hop," *Pacific Review of Ethno Musicology* 12 (Fall 2006), See http://www.ethnomusic.ucla.edu/pre/Vol12/Vol12html/V12Zanfagna.html.

74. Zanfagna, "Under the Blasphemous W(RAP)."

3

The Beauty Shop

Every time I hear a brother call a girl a bitch or a ho. . . . You know all of that gots to go.[1]

—Queen Latifah, U.N.I.T.Y.

The air conditioner in the salon is broken. The door is open to let in the cool summer breeze. A black teen, in saggy pants, passes by with a boom box in hand. The music blares with a catchy beat,

> *Let's get rich so quick, you the ho, I'm the pimp*
> *Together we'll never be broke again.*[2]

College Professor:	Rap music was built on the backs of women![3] It's a hot ghetto mess.
Middle-Class Female:	Never in the history of popular culture has a race of people so degraded themselves.
Tyrone:	But the song is just a mirror of reality. How is this harmful?
Professor:	Rap music exercises tremendous influence on youth culture, it is a powerful cultural force. It contributes to a climate in which real black women are treated as bitches.
Birthinia:	What did it for me was Nelly's video in tip drill.

> *It ain't no fun*
> *Unless we all get some*
> *I need a Tip Drill.*[4]

Every negative stereotype for black women was on display. When he slid that credit card down the crack of a woman's butt, it was the ultimate degradation. It reduces women to "hot pussy for sale."[5]

A youth outside plays another CD. It is a song by 50 Cent.

> *Come on mamma and get cha something braid it up pimpin*
> *I make a shy cryin bitch start swimming.*[6]

Birthinia:	Yeah, What did it for me is the violence of the songs. I remember Ice T's song, "6 in the Mornin'." In the song a woman insults Ice T calling him and his posse "punk pussies." Ice T responds "As we walked over to here ho continued to speak / So we beat the bitch down in the god damn street."[7]
Black Male Hairdresser:	Yeah but while some rappers may be a little wild, you can't lump all rappers together. N.W.A was pretty progressive.
College Professor:	The same group who rapped "fight the power" wrote A Bitch is a Bitch:

> *You're thru' without a BMW*
> *That's why a bitch is a bitch.*[8]

Birthinia:	They seem to see black women as the enemy. Ice T once proclaimed himself as the "bitch killa" and the "cop killa" as if both equally deserve street cred. Taking a cue from Ice-T, a hip-hop artist named "X-Raided" raps,

> *So the chase was on, I started running*
> *I said "You'd better stop, cause if you don't I'm gonna be gunning."*[9]

He goes on to describe how he chases a woman down the street and executes her in a way that was gruesome, eroticizing the brutality he used against the woman.

College Professor: In this fantasy of rebellion there is no distinction between black women and the racially oppressive police force.

It's bad because it is to hip-hop that so many black men look for models of black manhood, it is not just music it is their teacher.

And it's bad because hip-hop supposedly represents the downtrodden. The pimp-player ho thing that knots together sexism and authenticity, manhood, and using women as playthings.

This cultural pollution would not be tolerated if it were not a billion dollar industry. The ghetto rappers are like corner boys. The real culprits are the industry executives.

Birthinia: I blame the artists. They peddle poison the same as the dope dealer. They are both bottom dwellers. It's not about art, it's just about money. What does Too Short say,

Too short—Long time ago I couldn't use the word bitch without being looked down on by the community but now I can use the term and get paid.[10]

Cultural Crossings: Pimps, Playas, and the Sexual Politics of Hip-Hop

I just feel if you wanna get the roots out of your grass, don't cut it at the top. Dig down; you know what I'm saying? Dig down deep and pull it from the bottom if you really wanna get the problem resolved.[11]

—Nelly

Gangsta rap does not appear in a cultural vacuum, but, rather, is expressive of the cultural crossing, mixings, and engagement of black youth culture with the values, attitudes, and concerns of the white majority. . . . The sexist, misogynist, patriarchal ways of thinking and behaving that are glorified in Gangsta rap are a reflection of the pre-vailing values in our society, values created and sustained by white supremacist capitalist patriarchy.[12]

Gangsta rap is clearly a site in which demeaning, hurtful images are pro-duced. It is also a place where those images are contested, debated, and sometimes appropriated in a kind of iconic turnabout.

What verdict should we reach? I'm not trying to go there. My purpose is to provide a context. Here I provide two different frames of reference. The first is to ask the question: What is the source of negative images in hip-hop? I offer no defense; rather, I try to trace the negative images of women in hip-hop back to their source.

Root versus Branch

Negative images of women in Gangsta rap do not occur in a vacuum. Gangsta rap is less the root from which grows the tree of black female degradation than merely one of its branches.

The root of the problem is larger ideological structures in society. "Young black males are forced to take the 'heat' for encouraging, via their music, the hatred of and violence against women that is a central core of patriarchy."[13] Those structures are the plantation in which both black men and black women labor.

It is useful to think of misogyny as a field that must be labored in and maintained not only to sustain patriarchy but also to serve as an ideological anti-feminist backlash. And what better group to labor on this "plantation" than young black men.[14]

Part versus Whole

Sexism is a serious issue in hip-hop. But it is false—and quite racist—to reduce hip-hop to hate or sexism. This is a kind of Willie Hortonizing. Wil-lie Horton was a Massachusetts prisoner serving a life sentence, without the possibility of parole, for the 1975 stabbing death of a teenager.[15] Hor-ton was released on "a furlough" and tragically committed a murder and a rape.[16] He was a bad person, no doubt. But while black men commit only a fraction of violent crime, his face, a black male face, became the face of violent crime. A similar metonymy takes place when hip-hop's sexism is not put in perspective.

In *New Jack City,*[17] Nino Brown is the ruthless leader of the notorious Cash Money Boys, a gang of drug dealers based in Harlem. Nino is accused, among other things, of eliminating rival drug dealers with automatic weapons. The prosecutor, Ms. Hawkins, expresses moral indignation at Nino's bloody crimes. Nino demurs and says, "Lets kick the ballistics here, there are no Uzi's made in Harlem!" As we have noted, the drug war targeted young black males in low-income neighborhoods who used automatic weapons, but not the major players who produced them. Labeling Gangsta rappers as the problem is like labeling the Cash Money Boys in New Jack as the source of automatic weapons—or drugs—in Harlem.

This Willie Hortonizing is part of a larger scapegoating narrative about black men and black underclass culture.

One of the elements of this scapegoating narrative of black deviance is the construction of essentialist notion of black urban youth culture as fundamentally hateful of women. It is as if, "black males are writing their lyrics off in the 'jungle,' away from the impact of mainstream socialization and desire."[18] I thus adopt the bell hooks critique of the narrative of black underclass deviance, which attempts to make the Gangsta the root rather than the branch, or the whole when it is part of a larger, deeper problem. But I add an insight. These degrading images of women in Gangsta rap are accepted so easily by black underclass youth because of the Gangsta image itself. In black folklore, the Gangsta—or outlaw—and the pimp figure are deeply intertwined.

Words versus Meaning

The second frame I want to explore is the interface between words and meaning. Gangsta rap is a site of contestation and struggle over meaning and identity. Many of hip-hop's sexy MCs define their agency in sexual terms. As the traditional toasts showed, as Michael Jackson showed— I'm bad, I'm bad, I'm really, really bad could mean good—bitch could signify self-determination and power. The issue of interpretation is intertwined with competing strategies of resistance. The black middle class seeks to reject stereotypes, while the strategy of Gangsta rap is to embrace them.

The second question is then how do we interpret images whose meanings are within the genre of hip-hop itself as deeply contested as the meaning of race. We will start with the first question.

"How Far Will You Go to Get It?": The Seduction of the B'Boys

The Seduction

The pimp-player image which abounds in rap is a composite figure. He represents the fusing of folk traditions within the crucible of ghetto conditions. He combines the tradition of the Cagney style gangster and the trickster figure which was the alter ego of the bad nigger in urban folklore. His appeal comes from the fact that for black males society has closed off traditional avenues to power and respect. He is thus partly the creation of Western culture, partly a satirical figure, and partly a reflection of black male yearning, from a position of socioeconomic lack, for recognition.

In the film *Juice,* the characters are Bishop (Tupac), Q (Omar Epps), Raheem (Khalil Kain), and Steel (Jermaine "Huggy" Hopkins). Until now, they have been truant from school and guilty of minor crimes but have yet to become remorseless criminals like the gang that harasses them daily.

In one of the most telling scenes,

> [B]ishop is just kickin' it in a friend's living room watching television and mulling lunch. The 1949 Gangster classic, *White Heat,* flickers on the television screen, as Bishop looks on. Cagney, a tough guy who loves his mom, climbs atop an oil tank and sets himself ablaze rather than give himself up to the police. "Made it ma—to the top of the world"—is spoken simultaneously by Bishop. As Cagney burns Bishop launches into a passionate diatribe about courage and risks, yelling at his baffled friends. "That motherfucker took his destiny in his own hands. You've got to be ready to stand up and die for shit if you want juice!" Bishop, until now, has cowered his head in the face of local gangsta bullies, passively accepting the poverty of

his family and neighborhood. No longer. Now Bishop is transformed into a trigger-happy madman who "doesn't give a fuck" about his friends, his freedom, or his life.[19]

This is a story of seduction. The Cagney style gangster is an image that was created to appeal to dispossessed immigrant groups. It spoke to Bishop because of its poverty, and lack of future. The gangster ideal represents a way to make it to the top. No diploma required, no applications to fill out. All Bishop needed was the ability to throw away his fear, his moral scruples, and his love for his friends. He embraced an inhuman, nihilistic icon. It was a Faustian bargain. No sane person would take it. But it was maddening being harassed by hoodlums, being poor, having no way out. Nihilistic and inhuman though it was, it signified defiance, self-possession, power, and the respect that comes from being feared.

The gangster figure that Bishop—and Gangsta rap—embraces has two aspects: one is hypermaterialism, the other is hypermasculinity.

Hypermaterialism

Hip-hop's love affair with bling reflects a "seismic" shift in the values of hip-hop generation youth compared to their predecessors in the civil rights era.

As Marcus Reeves writes,

The goals of African-Americans under thirty five are collectively less radical and more individualistic . . . the aim of young black America—disillusioned by the old belief that political power would solve everything—was to work the system . . . for their own personal advantage. After all "why attack America's contradiction when you can make them work for you?". . . . The desire to achieve not only financial security but also millionaire status is the driving force of this generation's work ethic.[20]

This shift, from rap music as an expression of black angst, black nationalism—collective struggle—to the hardcore gangster style—individualism and bling—is chronicled in the history of hip-hop itself. Avery goes on to chronicle this history—for me the history of a seduction—of the shift from "honestly representing" in the days of Afrika Bambaataa (and as late as NWA in the 1990s) and "chasing the almighty dollar."[21]

> In 1974, the waning spirit of black power would come to be anchored within hip-hop by way of Afrika Bambaataa, a DJ and former gang member. . . . The components of hip-hop may have initially come together within the jams (or parties) thrown by Herc, but it was Bambaataa who incorporated the spirit of black power . . . into hip-hop.[22]

A great deal of hip-hop's oral style was in fact inspired by 1960s' political leaders, "Much of their metered speech and tall tales were rooted in black oral traditions of African griots [but] not surprisingly . . . rappers drew most of their poetic technique, inspired by the rapping virtuosity of figures like Muhammad Ali, James Brown, H. Rap Brown . . . and the last Poets."[23]

By the late 1970s and early 1980s, a convergence of forces produced a more commercial version of rap in which the urban poets "spoke straight from the heart of life's immediate needs and wants."[24] A key factor was the collapse of the civil rights movement heralded by cases like *Bakke v Board of Regents*.[25] This was the end of the second reconstruction and the era of racial reform. With this massive retreat by the court came also an increasing exhaustion of the civil rights generation. A second factor was that hip-hop was a victim of its own success. As hip-hop became more successful, and rappers chased mainstream dollars, corporate power infiltrated the content and the direction of the music itself. Corporations wanted to mainstream the music to white audiences, which dictated a dilution of any black nationalist or collectivist themes. Music became less concerned with verbal skill and more with finding a formula for rap music that conformed more to popular (read dance) music. The Sugarhill Gang and Kurtis Blow were the beginnings of cultural crossing that signified the shift from being about a political agenda and making money in the mainstream.[26]

By the turn of the millennium, "there was a reduced concern for shouting down social injustice, the primary focus of rap stars was reciting a laundry list of possessions (my car, my jewels, my clothes, my women, and most importantly, nigga, my money)."[27]

The rise and increasing corporate control of hip-hop coincides with "the rise of the amazing pornosphere." Increasingly corporations used sex to sell shoes, cigarettes, and of course music. The hip-hop–porn merger was inevitable once porn became increasingly pervasive. In 1972 porn accounted for 10 million in sales. Now it is 8–10 billion. "Hip-hop porn reflected the spread of sexual themes and imagery in American pop and youth culture."[28] Race and sex have always been intertwined. Corporate powers marketed explicit sexuality as a way "to bolster hip-hop's claims of ghetto authenticity." As Craig Watkins writes, "the proliferation of players, hustlers in commercial hip-hop implied a connection to the real and gritty world of black street culture."[29]

The strain of porn in hip-hop merged seamlessly with the deeper strands of hypermaterialism and gangsterism. The seduction was complete. "[R]appers lived like kings. Mixed along with the ocean-view villas, poolside mansions, luxury cars, Cuban cigars, yachts, and bottles of fine spirits were the women."[30] I have spent 20 years studying race. I noted in an earlier piece how to the colonial eye the native became part of the flora and fauna. They were exotic, colorful, and part of the landscape. Something similar happens in commercial hip-hop. Women in hip-hop videos are like that, part of the luscious scenery and background.

Hypermasculinity

In Gangsta rap, the flip side of the Nigga as thug is the Nigga as pimp. Thus, Digital Underground in a song called "Good Thing We're Rappin" easily combines the moves of a hardcore gangster and a pimp. He begins by describing how he deals with an insult. Lyrically, he describes the sudden and ruthless way he snuffs out anyone who offends him or his people.

He then moves easily from raps about being a tough street fighter to being a pimp: "We roll from city to city like kids playn' hookie. Later that night I knock a bitch named Cookie."[31]

The theme that connects the gangster and the pimp is a Faustian, cold-blooded attitude toward getting money.[32] He describes how he "counts my monies" at the same time as he reads the "funnies" in the newspaper.

Most people listening to this give it a normative spin: "they are advocating this!" Are they? Hazel Carby notes that the blues was not merely entertainment but sometimes reflected real historical events. Undeniably, the Gangsta tropes on real events, that is, it recounts lived experience which is not only their own but representative of ghetto life.

Irresponsibility and Invisibility

In Digital Underground's rap what is implicit in his character is a lack of status or recognition in society.

Rap music abounds with images of black men stepping out of and into limousines and Lamborghinis, fur coat–wearing Macs with beautiful women at their side or in bed with them, or gun toting Gangstas grimacing through lyrics proclaiming their sexual potency, their prowess in earning money, or beating down their opponents.

These performances, for all their supermasculinity, are intended at a deep level as counter-narratives, as resistance in the context of a marginalized people attempting to represent themselves as potent, large, and in charge, predators rather than victims in a society where they have found themselves jobless, powerless, social victims languishing on street corners and in jails. This does not justify the cruelty; it explains why the cruel gangster/pimp image is received as cool.

These are badmen. They get money, power, and respect. It does not matter how they get it. In the inversion of values that is basic to the ghetto perspective what is bad becomes good. Bad is being hypermasculine-hard and getting the money however you can get it.

Judge Toler in her show, *Divorce Court*, expressed best our collective angst about the destructiveness of this exaggerated masculinity. A black male in a misguided effort to portray his manhood proudly announced that for him all women were like a doorknob, "everyone gets a turn." Heartbroken at the inhumanity of this, Judge Toler eloquently asks,

> Is the game over? Have we lost, is manhood something that is torn up, bumped in. There was a time when being a man meant something, it meant responsibility, the ability to stand up and take care of your family. Is this what it's come to? Is this all we have left of our "culture"?[33]

But what Judge Toler attributes to lack of personal responsibility, the inability to grow up, which is a huge dimension of the problem, indeed leaves out the critical element of social agency. As Ellison states, "Irresponsibility is part of my invisibility . . . to whom can I be responsible when you refuse to see me? Responsibility rests on recognition. And recognition is a form of agreement."

What Ellison is getting at is that to be fully constituted as a person you need agency, the ability to deal. But the black male in urban areas is locked out: "All the big dogs understand that agency calls for representation, yet black had no public agency. If you are outside the economy, you are free to play any card in the deck."[34] I am not trying to excuse the lyrics, but to explain it in terms of cause and effect.

Black men seize upon this exaggerated masculinity, this power they derive from the game precisely because society has denied them all power, all agency, all value in any other realm.

He takes refuge in his masculinity and to compensate exaggerates it. This hypermasculinity in turn signifies true blackness. "[A]n exaggerated and amplified masculinity has become . . . [the] special symbol of the difference race makes."[35]

As Nelson George writes,

In a warped and unhealthy way the pimp's ability to control his environment (i.e. his stable of women) has always been viewed as a rare example of black male authority over his domain. Despite decades of moral censure from church leaders and those incensed by his exploitation of women, the pimp endures as an antihero among young black males.[36]

It is the lack of power (the ability to get a job is power, for example), the lack of legitimate means to wealth which defines the pimp far more than his alligator shoes. In fact as Iceberg Slim famously wrote, "the sexy part of pimping is not the sex, it's the control." So in pimping the black male gets the agency. In the social real the pimp does so in a crude imitation of the slave master: the pimp in his indifference to the degradation of his women replicates the relation between slave and master. He accepts it because "a priori the consolidation of power happens—with or without your consent." Pimp theory says, "We being an intelligent people, we knew that it was happening any way so we had to benefit from it."[37] This philosophy comes close to Willie Harris's soliloquy in *Raisin in the Sun*.

Mama, it's all divided up. Life is. Sure enough. Between the takers and the taken. We get to lookin round for right and wrong; and we worry about it and cry about it and stay up nights he'll find himself sitting in a dungeon, locked in forever and the takers have the key![38]

I would say to Judge Lynn Toler there is a crime here to be heart-broken about. This collapse of many black males into a predatory mind-set, into the lose/lose philosophy of dog eat dog, "the takers and the taken,"[39] is troubling. But there is an underlying crime which goes unspoken. It is the condition of powerlessness and the devaluation of black life—both male and female—which is the root cause of the collapse.

Neither the Gangsta rapper nor the pimp figure is the culprit in the crime of ghetto conditions. He is their witness, their interpreter.

As Henry Louis Gates has noted, interpretation requires moving between two different planes of consciousness.[40] One must move between the plane of human experience and the plane of truth, between the profane and sometimes ugly aspects of life and sublime understanding. Thus, in the scriptures Joseph speaks of "interpretation" as something divine. "And they said unto him, 'We have dreamed a dream, and there is no inter-preter of it.' And Joseph said unto them, 'Do not interpretations belong to God.'".[41] The prophet—or poet—who interprets is simply a messenger from God. In the Greek cosmology Hermes was represented by a God with wings on his feet with which he travelled between Heaven and Earth. In his role as an urban Hermes, the black poet moves between the deadly streets of the social real to the cultural imaginary on wings of rhyme. This linkage is illustrated classically in the song Stagolee. In Stagolee, the song chronicles events dating back to 1895.[42] It tells the story of a senseless murder in which the protagonist, Stagolee, loses at cards, comes back, and shoots the man who won his money:

> It was Stagolee and Billy,
> Two men who gamble' late,
> Stagolee throw seven,
> Billy swore that he throwed eight.
> Stagolee told Billy,
> "I can't let you go with that;
> You have won my money

And my brand new Stetson hat." Stagolee went home,
And got his forty-four

. . .

Stagolee went to the bar room,
Stood four feet from the door
Didn't nobody know when he
Pulled his forty-four.
Stagolee found Billy,
"Oh please don't take my life!
I got three little children,
And a very sick little wife."
Stagolee shot Billy,
Oh he shot that boy so fas'
That the bullet came through him,
And broke my window glass.[43]

Cecil Brown, a historian of black folklore says that "as chanted in the form of a toast by my Uncle Lindsey, Stagolee was a young god of virility . . . impulsive, as vulgar, as daring."[44] As in the tradition of the Stagolee toasts, the Gangsta—the prophet of the hood[45]—is about chronicling actual conditions and creating myths out of them.

That role of myth in hip-hop as in the toasts involves fashioning and celebrating icons of opposition:

The traces of the past that pervade the popular music of the present amount to more than mere chance: they are into simply juxtapositions of incompatible realities. They reflect a dialogic process, one embedded in a collective history and nurtured by the ingenuity of artists interested in fashioning icons of opposition.[46]

In hip-hop the pimp is a reflection of reality-social conditions, but he is also metaphorical. Metaphorically, he does not represent the oppressor; he represents the ability to use the knowledge of the game, to be able to transform his situation through his skills.

The pimp figure in Gangsta rap represents the passing of a cultural baton between the hustler tradition and the new cultural figure of the rapper and MC. This effort to link the two traces back to the beginning of hip-hop. Listen to "Rapper's Delight," one of the earliest hip-hop pieces.

> *I'm imp the dimp the ladies pimp*
> *Women fight for my delight.*[47]

The celebration of the pimp is linked not only to the gangster icon but also to a more traditional celebration of the hypermasculinity of negritude. This traces back deep into black folklore to the Dolemite to figure.[48]

Dolemite is a "bad man or outlaw." But in turn Dolemite, Stagolee, and other outlaws are descendants of the trickster figure of African folklore.[49] John Willie Roberts explains this transformation from Trickster to bad man as cultural adaptation.[50]

In North Carolina or Virginia a person could be sent to the penitentiary for stealing a chicken. And under Mississippi's "pig law" the theft of a pig or cow was punishable by five years in prison. . . . The impact of white manipulations of the law on the economic and social life of African Americans transformed their conception of the trickster to create the badman as an outlaw hero.[51]

The "outlaw" figure in black folklore reflects the impact of white manipulations of the law on the economic and social life of African Americans.

From the perspective of the ghetto, all these figures are indissolubly linked—the trickster and the bad man, the pimp and the bad nigger, the pimp and the struggle of oppressed people—to empower themselves.

Both the badman and the trickster embody a challenge to virtually all authority which makes sense to people to whom justice is a rare thing, creates an imaginary upside down world where the oppressed are powerful, and it reveals to listeners the pleasures and price of reckless abandon. And in a world where male public powerlessness is often turned inward on women and children, misogyny and stories of sexual conflict are very old examples of the "price" of being bad.[52]

This knotting together of the pimp and the bad nigger was expressly the theme of the famous 1960s films like *Superfly, The Mack,* and *Willie Dynamite.* In *Superfly,* the story line shows the corrupt police chief, Commissioner Reardon, as actually running or supervising drug dealing. Priest has to confront him in order to win his freedom from the game. In a famous scene, Priest uses his karate skills to beat down Reardon for nationwide audiences of cheering black fans. Goldie—played by Max Julien—in *The Mack* takes revenge on the killers of his mother. In *Willie Dynamite*—"Ain't nobody mess with Willie D"—Willie is the one who stands up to an unholy alliance of police and pimps who try to run him out of the city. Willie loses but not before displaying the defiance of authority which defines his archetype.

Hip-Hop's Bad Women and the B Word

Despite the rare visibility of a Dorothy Dandridge or Lena Horne in selected movies over the course of most of the twentieth century, black women have never been positioned as objects of beauty and desire in popular media. . . . Hip-Hop, however, as a post-black power articulation of black identity, pleasure, machismo, and agency has positioned black women as the objects of desire. . . .[53]

As Stephanie Dunn writes, since Josephine Baker wowed Parisian audiences with a provocative display exotic of primitive black female sexuality—on and offstage—the boundary between liberated woman and whore has been contested.

In 1971, Jo Freeman wrote "The Bitch Manifesto,"[54] confiscating the word *bitch* as a call to a transgressive sisterhood.

Bitches are aggressive, assertive, domineering, overbearing, strong-minded, spiteful, hostile, direct, blunt, candid, obnoxious, thick-skinned, hard-headed, vicious, dogmatic, competent, competitive, pushy, loud-mouthed, independent, stubborn, demanding, manipulative, egoistic, driven, achieving, overwhelming, threatening, scary, ambitious, tough, brassy, masculine, boisterous, and turbulent among other things. A Bitch occupies a lot of psychological space. You always know she is around. A Bitch takes shit from no one. You may not like her, but you cannot ignore her.[55]

Rap music is an art form in which male MCs have exploited stereotypes of black women as Playettes, Hustlas, and hos. But it is also a place where "sexy" female MCs appropriate and exploit those same stereotypes "to either assert control over the representations or at least reap the benefits of it."[56]

Many black female MCs deliberately portray themselves as sexually available and licentious to enhance their commercial appeal. Still others change the meaning of the images. "In rap music culture, bitch has also been revised . . . to signify hardcore woman who makes money and proudly flaunts her sexual libido and sexuality."

As Patricia Hill Collins noted,

All women can potentially be bitches with a small "b". This is the negative evaluation of the term bitch. But the students also identified with a positive valuation of bitch and argued . . . that only African American woman can be bitches with a capital "B" . . . [I]n their language black bitches are super-tough, super-strong women who are often celebrated . . . bitch links the historical constructions of black female wildness, whereas bitch suggests a woman who controls her own sexuality manipulating it to her advantage.[57]

If black male MCs portray the bad Nigga his counterpart is the bad bitch, a "black woman who goes beyond the boundaries of gender in the patriarchal domain and plays the game successfully as the boys."

Thus, in *Da Baddest Bitch* Trina raps,

> *I'm representin' for the bitches*
> *All eyes on your riches.*[58]

She goes on to say she has no time for "little dicks" because the "bigger the dick" the "bigger the bank." Similarly, Lil' Kim begins her famous *Queen Bitch* by reclaiming what has been an extreme pejorative for all women.

I am a diamond cluster hustler
Queen bitch supreme bitch.[59]

Thus, while the mainstream posits the figure of woman's sexuality as a source of vulnerability and the explicit portrayal of her sexuality as exploitation, here that same sexuality is represented as a source of power.

The same theme is developed in Foxy Brown's lyrics. She says in effect, if you get the money, they have to respect you: "From a straight broke-ass to a baller-bitch / They got no other choice but to call you rich."[60]

The Bitch or Ho then is trickster figure as well. Like the male pimp it tropes on the deadly reality that for many women they must use their sexuality to climb out of poverty. The song has a double meaning. It can be understood literally as the idea that trading sexual capital for money is cool—"use what you got to get what you need."

Cause it's much more better than all world scenes
Bitch, open up your eyes, it's a poor girl's dream.[61]

Read literally, this is the female rapper living up to or becoming the stereotype. In *The Continuing Devaluation of Black Women,* bell hooks notes that "black women have always been seen by the white public as sexually permissive, as available and eager for the sexual assaults of any man, Black or White."[62] The designation of all black women as sexually depraved, immoral, or loose has its roots in the slave system. This literal interpretation that Lil' Kim is simply proclaiming a lack of sexual inhibition for its own sake reduces her literally, and uncritically, to a typical ghetto girl, or worse a video ho.

But I don't think that is what this is. This is not really about sex at all, this is about bringing wreck to stereotypes. "Bringing wreck . . . has meant reshaping the public gaze in such a way as to be recognized as human beings—as functioning worthwhile members of society.[63] In this case it is to wreck or disrupt negative images of black women that trace back to slavery.

In the Location of culture Homi Bhabha describes colonial mimicry of the colonizer by the colonized as a disruption of the colonizer's sense of superiority. . . . "Hip-hop engages in [a] form of mimicry, one which offers a social critique and a disruption of white supremacist authority. This would be 'thug mimicry,' of becoming or turning into black American stereotypes." [I]t dislocates the authority for defining the black underworld. . . . The artist might mirror the stereotype of the black assailant or criminal and subvert the stereotype . . . [by] giving voice to the stereotypical figure.[64]

By giving voice to the thug, or criminal, they can call attention to the conditions which gave rise to the behavior which is being stereotyped. Here the bad bitch adopts the strategy of the nigga. By becoming the ho she can now call attention to the reasons why women act the way they do, shifting the focus away from cultural pathology to economic realities and choices.

Imani Perry argues "here thugs [or ho's] themselves have the authority to explain their actions" in terms of ghetto conditions or "tragic formative experiences."

> *Ask mommy every day, when daddy gon' come?*
> *But he never showed up.*[65]

I would modify this. I think the female MCs are saying black women do not owe white society an explanation at all. Thus, Lil' Kim states in *My Life,* "Have you been where I've been?"[66] Another dimension to this is to call attention to a double standard: "But if I was a dude, they all be amused . . ."[67]

The categories of "bitch" and "ho" while presented as neutral moral categories are quintessentially gendered. That is men who engage in sex promiscuously, James Bond for example, are generally not thought of in negative terms. They are simply, "cool." Similarly, the gangsters like Snoop Dogg, 50 Cent, and the many other players are seen by rap fans and themselves as large and in charge *because* they have access to dozens of beautiful women. Lil' Kim, Trina, and others "appropriate the male space of the player."[68]

In the era of the sexy female MC, many women are visually looking femme, but somehow occupy male spaces linguistically. Lil' Kim, for example, acts out the role of the bad woman. In "Player Anthem," a song in which a variety of MC's from Junior Mafia (Biggie Smalls's crew) rhyme, Lil' Kim appropriates the male space of the player, one analogous to Pam Grier in the Blaxploitation era, she becomes a Foxy Brown . . . a Cleopatra Jones.[69]

"No shame to their game," hip-hop's badwomen coolly present their sexuality as a way of turning the tables on men. Gwendolyn Pough suggests this is a postfeminist agenda: black women are taking back control over their lives, although in ways that challenge traditional feminist conceptions of womanhood. Gwendolyn Pough writes,

Their boldness does exhibit a kind of freedom. . . . Ironically, it is this same freedom that exposes myths surrounding feminism. Now that black women are no longer bound by gender expectations there will be those who will make some less than womanist choices . . . and they are free to do so. . . . What these rappers offer is the opportunity to embrace the sexuality of the self . . . after years of the black woman being read as super-sexual—or asexual in the case of the mammy stereotype—the lyrics of these women rappers offer the black women a chance to be proud of—and indeed flaunt—their sexuality. And after the image of the black bitch that has stilted assertiveness of black women, it's almost nice to have a line such as, "I'm a stay that bitch." It does create a certain amount of agency.[70]

Conclusion

At one level, the negative images of black women portrayed by black male rappers are a product of hip-hop's seduction by the gangster. The gangster and the pimp are two sides of one coin.

In turn, the seduction by this gangster/pimp figure comes as a result of the undeniable sense of emasculation which defines being a black male in America. Hip-hop pimps and Mac daddy figures strut about in the cultural imaginary, as reflections of the fact that young black males have few avenues to respectability and power in the social real. Like the black women they portray as video hos, Bishop, and the black male youth who buy these images are victims themselves. This cannot absolve hip-hop of responsibility for perpetuating dangerous stereotypes but it puts in context. It is not the source or origin of the problem, and like corner boys caught in an economic vise in which they choose selling drugs as an alternative to working for McDonalds, the sins of hop must be understood not as cause but effect.

At a deeper level, it is also essential to understand that the project of hip-hop is to bring wreck. Hip-hop lyrics cannot be understood literally but part of a signifying tradition which is about challenging hierarchy. Taking the baton from the toasts of the 19th century, the pimp is the alter ego of the bad nigger, the mac the alter ego of Stagolee. Together both do metaphorical work troping on the notion of an exaggerated masculinity as the edge black men must play in a world in which they have been otherwise denied recognition and respect. It is a way—in the imagery of hip-hop—of urban poets challenging the supremacy of white men, of those at the bottom representing themselves as being at the top.

Like the black men who embrace the identity of a Nigga, the female badmen of hip-hop also embrace and seek to reclaim the image of the bitch.

Hip-hop is a space where men who have been emasculated and women who have been and are being scarred by life experiences in the ghetto are reimagining themselves, and finding their voice.

The fact that this art form is voiced by blacks, that it allows for autobiographical narratives that center their experience, that these narratives call attention to ghetto conditions is the defining and authentic essence of the dialogue that is taking place. Those who attempt to reduce hip-hop to misogyny—to say that's all it is—or to scapegoat black men as *the* reason why black women are disrespected may have read the lyrics but they have not heard those voices. It is only when we have understood the reality of those conditions and experiences, when we can "go where they go" and stand with the badmen and badwomen of hip-hop, can we actually understand the stories that the bad niggas and badwomen are trying to tell.

Notes

1. Queen Latifah, "U.N.I.T.Y.," *Black Reign*, Motown Records, B000W00HGA, November 16, MP3, 1993.
2. Daz Dillinger, "Bitch Bitch Make Me Rich," *This Is the Life I Lead*, D.P.G. records, MP3 Albums, B0019A6SJ2, 2002.

3. S. Craig Watkins, ed., "Fear of a White Planet," in *Hip-HOP Matters, Politics, Pop-culture and the Struggle for the Soul of a Movement* (Boston, MA: Beacon Press, 2005), 85.

4. Nelly, "Tip Drill," *Da Derrty Versions: The Reinvention*, Universal Records, B000V697W0, 2003.

5. T. Sharpley-Whiting, *Pimps Up Ho's Down: Hip-Hop's Hold on Young Black Women* (New York: New York University Press, 2007), 4, See also Noreaga, "Don't Love No Bitches," *Melvin Flynt–Da Hustler* (Penalty Records, 1999). Using similar imagery.

6. Mystikel, "Pussy Crook," *Tarantula* (Explicit), Jive Records, MP3 Albums, B00138H5YC, 2001.

7. Ice-T, "Rhyme Pays," *6 in the Mornin*, Warner Brothers, MP3 Albums, B001A83H6K, 1987.

8. N.W.A., "A Bitch Is a Bitch," *Straight Outta Compton* (Vinyl), Ruthless Records, 1988.

9. X-Raided, *"Bitch Killa," Psycho-Active*, Black Market Records, MP3 Albums, B000QQKT2C, 1992.

10. Cheryl Lynette Keyes, *Rap Music and Street Consciousness* (Urbana-Champaign: University of Illinois Press, 2002).

11. Tricia Rose, *The Hip-Hop Wars: What We Talk about When We Talk about Hip-Hop and Why It Matters* (New York: Basic Books, 2008), 158.

12. Paul Chatterton and Robert Hollands, *Urban Nightscapes: Youth Cultures, Pleasure Spaces and Corporate Power* (New York: Psychology Press, 2003), 191.

13. bell hooks, "Sexism and Misogyny, Gangsta Rap, and the Piano," *Z Magazine* (Woods Hole, MA, 1994).

14. hooks, "Misogyny, Gangsta rap, and the Piano."

15. Andrew H. McCollum, "Prison at a Crossroads: To Punish or to Counsel?" *National Desk, The New York Times* (New York, 1988), 12.

16. See Murray Kempton, "Bush Tactics Turn Ugly," *Newsday*, October 30, 1988, 7. "During one of his weekends free from the prison, Horton held a Maryland couple captive for several hours, raping the wife and stabbing the husband. The Bush campaign latched onto this tragic incident and ran numerous ads throughout the country, effectively transforming Governor Dukakis' allegedly weak position on crime enforcement into the Achilles heel of his campaign."

17. *New Jack City*, directed by Mario Van Peebles and Warner Brothers, 1991.

18. hooks, "Misogyny, Gangsta rap, and the Piano."

19. Danzy Senna, "Violence Is Golden: The Tupac Shakur Story," *Spin Magazine*, 1994, 43.

20. Marcus Reeves, *Somebody Scream!: Rap Music's Rise to Prominence in the Aftershock of Black Power* (London: Faber and Faber, Inc., 2009).

21. Reeves, *Somebody Scream!*, ix.

22. Reeves, *Somebody Scream!*, 17.

23. Reeves, *Somebody Scream!*

24. Reeves, *Somebody Scream!*

25. *Bakke v. Board of Regents*, 438 U.S. 265 (1978).

26. Reeves, *Somebody Scream!*, 30.

27. Reeves, *Somebody Scream!*, 220.

28. Watkins, *Hip-Hop Matters*, 209.

29. Watkins, *Hip-Hop Matters*, 109.

30. Watkins, *Hip-Hop Matters*, 215.

31. Digital Underground, "Good thing We're Rappin," *Sons of the P* (1991).

32. 50 Cent, "P.I.M.P," *Get Rich or Die Tryin'* (2003).

33. Divorce Court, *Don Ware v. Tiffany Brown*, September 16, 2009. Ware called himself, "Don Juan the Pimpin Son!" http://divorcecourting. blogspot.com/2009_09_01_archive.html.

34. Greg Tate, *Everything but the Burden: What White People Are Taking from Black Culture* (New York: Broadway Books, 2003), 80.

35. Tate, *Everything but the Burden*, 85.

36. Nelson George, *Hip-Hop America* (London: Penguin Books, 2005), 36.

37. Beth Coleman, "Pimp Notes on Autonomy," in *Everything but the Burden*, 79.

38. Lorraine Hansberry, *Raisin in the Sun* (New York: Samuel French, Inc., 1984), 143.

39. Hansberry, *Raisin in the Sun*.

40. Henry Louis Gates, *The Signifying Monkey: A Theory of African American Literary Criticism* (1989), 8.

41. The Holy Bible, Genesis 40:8, King James Version.

42. According to Cecil Brown, it recounts the story of Lee Shelton, a 31-year-old St. Louis resident who shot William Lyons. The meaning of the song comes through if one understands it as a metaphor about oppression and resistance. In this connection the most important words are "Stagolee would never let anybody touch his hat." Bobby Seale used this symbolism in the 1970s in speeches given as minister of the Black Panther Party of Self Defense.

43. Cecil Brown, *Stagolee Shot Billy* (Cambridge, MA: Harvard University Press, 2004), 6.

44. Brown, *Stagolee Shot Billy*, 1.

45. This phrase was coined by Imani Perry. See Imani Perry, *Prophets of the Hood: Politics and Poetics in Hip-Hop* (Durham, NC: Duke University Press, 2004).

46. See George Lipsitz, *Time Passages: Collective Memory and American Popular Culture* 99 (2001). See also Tricia Rose, *Black Noise* (Middletown, CT: Wesleyan University Press, 1994), 99.

    Music critics have been strangely unresponsive to the implications of Bakhtin's work for their own discipline. Popular music is nothing if not dialogic . . . Black noise: rap music and black culture in contemporary America & lrm.

47. "Rapper's Delight" from Kristen Wartman, *The Politics of the Game: Capitalism, Hip-Hop and Pimp Theory* (Santa Cruz: University of California, 2004), 5.

48. Daryl Cumber Dance, *Shucking and Jivin: Folklore from Contemporary Black Americans* (Bloomington: Indiana University Press, 1981).

49. William E. Smith, *Hip Hop as Performance and Ritual* (Bloomington: Trafford Publishing Company, 2005), 98. See also John Willie Roberts, *From Trickster to Badman: The Black Folk Hero in Slavery and Freedom* (Philadelphia: University of Pennsylvania Press, 1989), 189.

50. Smith, *Hip Hop as Performance and Ritual*; Roberts, *From Trickster to Badman*.

51. Roberts, *From Trickster to Badman*, 189.

52. Robin D. G. Kelley, *Race Rebels: Culture, Politics and the Black Working Class* (New York: Simon and Schuster, 1994), 187.

53. Jeffrey O.G. Ogbar, *Hip-Hop Revolution: The Culture and Politics of Rap* (Kansas: University of Kansas Press, 2009), 95.

54. Jo Freeman, "The Bitch Manifesto," in *Notes from the Second Year, Women's Liberation: Major Writings of the Radical Feminists*, ed. Shulamith Firestone and Anne Koedt (Santa Barbara: ABC-CLIO, 2011).

55. Freeman, "The Bitch Manifesto."

56. Stephanie Dunn, *"Baad Bitches" and Sassy Supermamas: Black Power Action Films* (Urbana-Champaign: University of Illinois Press, 2008).

57. Dunn, *"Baad Bitches" and Sassy Supermamas*, 26.

58. Trina, "Da Baddest Bitch," *Da Baddest Bitch*, Atlantic Records B00004R8Q5, Audio CD, 2000.

59. Lil' Kim, "Queen Bitch," *Hard Core*, Big Beat, B000000112, Audio CD, 1996.

60. Foxy Brown, "Queen Bitch," *Chyna Doll*, Album, 1999.

61. Brown, "Queen Bitch."

62. bell hooks, *Ain't I a Woman: Black Women and Feminism* (Brooklyn, NY: South End Press, 2007), 51.

63. Gwendolyn D. Pough, *Check It While I Wreck It* (Lebanon, NH: University Press of New England, 2004), 17.

64. Perry, *Prophets of the Hood*, 109.

65. Foxy Brown, "My Life," from *Chyna Doll*, Album, 1999.

66. Brown, "My Life."

67. Brown, "My Life."

68. Perry, *Prophets of the Hood*, 157.

69. Perry, *Prophets of the Hood*, 157.

70. Pough, *Check It While I Wreck It*, 188.

Part II

Family Affairs

"Brothers and sisters, my text this morning is the 'blackness' of 'blackness'"

And a congregation of voices answered: "That blackness is most black, brother, most black . . . "

"In the beginning . . . "

"At the very start," they cried.

" . . . There was blackness . . . "[. . .]

"Now black . . . " the preacher shouted.

"Bloody . . . "

"I said black is . . . "

"Preach it, brother . . . "

" . . . an' black ain't . . . "[. . .]

"Black will git you . . . "

"Yes, it will . . . "

" . . . an' black won't . . . "

"Naw, it won't!"

"It do, Lawd . . . "

" . . . an' it don't."

"Halleluiah . . . "

" . . . It'll put you, glory, glory, oh my L'awd, in the whale's belly."

" . . . an' make you tempt . . . "

"Good God a-mighty!"[1]

Of course there is no such thing as blackness. As Baldwin stated, "We had to be black so that they could be white, so that we could be used as no white person could be used."[2] But the caste system of slavery and segregation rested on color. So color became the basis on which the oppressed defined their kinship. It was a kinship of blood. Not blood as common ancestry only, but blood shed because of racism: the blood of slaves, the blood of lynching, the blood of martyrs. At the root of slavery and segregation was the notion that blackness was a badge of inferiority. Claiming the badge of blackness was an act of a people holding their heads up in the midst of hostility and disrespect.

Blackness is the sign of a family bound together by history and blood. But there is a schism within the family.

One of the most famous cases in legal history was *Plessy v. Ferguson*.[3] Homer Plessy was seven-eighths Caucasian. He looked "White: the mixture of colored blood was not discernible in him."[4] Plessy was arrested for sitting in a car reserved for whites. Plessy's actions were not random but strategic. Plessy wanted to be arrested so he, and other mulattos, could challenge the constitutionality of racially segregated trains. While Plessy lost before the Supreme Court, he remains an iconic symbol of an old and pervasive strategy used by light skin blacks to deal with the problem of racial caste: try to pass, to blend in. Plessy had passed. So successfully he felt he had a reputation as a white person. Segregation laws were wrong because it took away from him his white reputation and stigmatized him as black. Plessy in his aspiration to assimilate rejected any and all solidarity with other blacks. Blackness, in Plessy's mind, was not a tie that bound him.

My generation resoundingly rejected Plessy's choice. We embraced our blackness. We demanded and got separate dorms, we sat by ourselves at lunch and dinner. The white students referred to this as self-segregation. But this was about common cultural identity. It was also about power. Wayne Glasker writes, "The purpose . . . is not to withdraw from society . . . but rather to organize a power base from which to enter the mainstream. Nor is this so different from the ethnic associations one finds at [many] universities."[5] White fraternities were in reality, at least then if not now, "ethnocentric comfort zones."[6] We substituted race for ethnicity in a struggle not merely for success as individuals but for power as a group. Homer Plessy by trying to pass expressed the idea in Ellison's vernacular that "black ain't." At bottom what we were saying was "Black is."

That black identity that we performed and affirmed is an identity in crisis. An identity crisis occurs when the truth that defines that identity among a group becomes unstable. For us it was undisputed truth that blackness represented a bond of common struggle. Despite its contradictions at a deep level, hip-hop still witnesses that truth. Whether one listens to "The Roots" who declare it "ain't plastic, it's pro-blackness" or Gangsta rap, there is a shared sense of blackness as "we" or "us." It is certainly a local sense of blackness—the hood comes first. But in hip-hop black still is.

On the other hand, the same generation that demanded the black dorms has become stock brokers, doctors, lawyers. Many of them want to change the channel: collectivist thinking does not often survive the ethos of individualism that defines professional life.

It is against this background that the debate about hip-hop is taking place.

On the surface the debate within the black community is about profanity, lyrics that glorify crime, and images that degrade black women. Cut through the stereotypes. Hip-hop poses the question to black middle class of who is really black. It is a debate about what choices are authentic and what choices are fake. This struggle over authentic blackness is not abstract; it is a battle between competing sets of ideas. It is a debate waged between different generations, fathers versus sons, brothers, and sisters; it is a debate between black elites and their cousins from the inner city. It is a family affair.

Notes

1. Ralph Ellison, *The Invisible Man* (New York: Random House, 1995), 9.
2. Speech by James Baldwin, Morgan State College, 1978.
3. 163 U.S., 537, 538 (1896).
4. 163 U.S., 541.
5. Wayne Glasker, *Black Students in the Ivory Tower: African-American Student Activism at the University of Pennsylvania* (Amherst, MA: University of Massachusetts Press, 2009), 14.
6. Barrett Seman, *Binge: What Your College Student Won't Tell You* (New York: John Wiley and Sons, 2005), 167.

4

Souls on Ice

Here, then, is the dilemma, and it is a puzzling one, I admit. No Negro who has given earnest thought to the situation of his people in America has failed, at some time in life, to find himself at these cross-roads; has failed to ask himself at some time: What, after all, am I? Am I an American or am I a Negro? Can I be both? Or is it my duty to cease to be a Negro as soon as possible and be an American? If I strive as a Negro, am I not perpetuating the very cleft that threatens and separates Black and White America?[1]

—W.E.B. Du Bois

If you had a choice of colors which one would it be my brother. If it could be day or night which would you prefer to be right?[2]

—Curtis Mayfield

We were the generation of "Soul." We grew up with The Temptations, Diana Ross, The O'Jays, The Four Tops, and segregation.

Du Bois described segregation as a

Wall strait and stubborn to the whitest, but relentlessly narrow, tall, and unscalable to sons of night who must plod darkly on in resignation, or beat unavailing palms against the stone, or helplessly watch the streak of blue above.[3]

On the surface, the wall that Du Bois referred to was a system of laws, which dictated what schools one could go to, what swimming pools, what theatres. But behind this wall of law was a system of thought that depicted us as an inferior order of human life.

> I remember shows like Tarzan, Jack Benny, and Amos 'n' Andy por-
> traying the Negro variously as a native, as a childlike butler, or as
> a con man long on ambition but short on talent, trying to bilk his
> friends. . . . From behind the wall I would call my parents to the liv-
> ing room whenever a miracle would happen, as they did from time
> to time—when a Negro would be shown, not as a native with a spear
> or a con man or a servant, but in a respectable job, perhaps as a high
> school teacher.[4]

Aunt Jemima beamed from the pancake box, Uncle Ben from boxes of rice. "Flesh colored band-aids" were sold at stores—but they were pink. The official story of segregation portrays its violence through pic-tures of blacks being knocked down by water hoses or bitten by police dogs. This was only the external manifestation. It was the ideology of segregation itself, which was the height of its violence. This ideology was hegemonic.

Let me explain what I mean by hegemonic. The pictures of "Negroes" being beaten and bitten by police dogs are heart-wrenching scenes of human cruelty. But the camera cannot capture the violence of the images of us as depicted in television, history books, and film. The difference between a lie and ideology is that when someone tells a lie, they are con-scious of it.[5] The mythology of race that we consumed daily was part of our culture, so deeply ingrained that we accepted these images as facts of life. We received these images as natural, normal, and inevitable. We ingested them much the same as we ate our oatmeal and rice. But on the inside they tore us apart. As Fanon wrote,

> I could no longer laugh, because I already knew that there were
> legends, stories, history, and above all *historicity*. [. . .] Then, as-
> sailed at various points, the corporeal schema crumbled, . . . I was
> responsible at the same time for my body, for my race, for my an-
> cestors. I subjected myself to an objective examination, I discov-
> ered my blackness, my ethnic characteristics; and I was battered
> down by tom-toms, cannibalism, intellectual deficiency, fetishism,
> racial defects, slave-ships, and above all else, above all: "Show'
> good eatin'."[6]

Blackness was bad, very bad. When I was growing up, when you wanted to insult someone you called him or her a "black nigger." The "black" amplified the insult. One of the most common expressions of this internalized inferiority was a common saying at the time, "niggers ain't shit," almost always followed by laughter. Clearly, in order for us to say this we had to distance ourselves from this racial other who was stigmatized. "I took myself far off from my own presence, far indeed, and made myself an object. What else could it be for me but an amputation, an excision, a hemorrhage that spattered my whole body with black blood?"[7]

During this time Ebony magazine advertised skin lighteners. "Process" hairstyles, with men putting lye in their hair to straighten it, were common. My own choices reflected this racial cross-dressing. When I went to high school, between 1966 and 1969, I always wore a shirt and tie. The tie was a clip on. I read my mother's catalogue and saw clothes, nice sweaters, and slacks like those worn by Ward and Beaver Cleaver on television. I wanted to look like them and ordered regularly from the catalogue. Going a step further, I never hung out with the guys in my neighborhood whom I considered thugs. I went to the library after school and read. I was ridiculed for this. This social identity that I was constructing for myself was not strategically chosen; deep inside I wanted to rise and instinctively I sought to absorb this European essence through books.

Aunt Jemima and Uncle Tom are dead, their places taken by a group of amazingly well-adjusted young men and women, almost as dark, but ferociously literate, well-dressed and scrubbed, who are never laughed at, who are not likely ever to set foot in a cotton or tobacco field or in any but the most modern of kitchens.[8]

In this assimilationist mode we accepted segregation as a fact of life.

It was as if issues of abuse had nothing to do with us, that only white people were worthy of naming abuse. Suffering and systematic abuse in communities of color was so normalized. We often didn't even know we were oppressed. Some of us thought suffering was just part of being black.[9]

The music we listened to mirrored this identity politics. One of my favorite songs was "The Tracks of My Tears." The song is a story, which portrays a man wearing his smile as a mask.

> *So take a good look at my face*
> *You'll see my smile looks out of place.*[10]

Underneath the smile, it's easy "to trace" the "tracks of my tears." The smile is his masquerade for the world. His true face—his true feelings: his pain, his vulnerability—are for the woman he loves. Smokey's poetic lyrics expressed a worshipful attitude toward love. The number one song "My Girl"[11] by the Temptations used similar imagery.

In "My Girl" the weather can be overcast but for the protagonist in the song the sun is always shining: "I got sunshine on a cloud day." He doesn't mind the cold; the temperature can fall but he still "has the month of May." The song recalls American country music, "Got spurs on my boots, but I don't give a hoot, cause I got me a pretty woman's love."[12] It portrays a love that is innocent, pure, and which gives him a happiness inside which is impervious to what is going on outside.

Soul music has been described as a cross between rhythm and blues and gospel. As Professor Gena Caponi writes, "the feelings experienced by the audience in listening to these songs results from the subtle use of aesthetic principles associated with gospel music."[13] Like gospel it took us away from the segregated squalid neighborhoods we lived in, from degrading, race-coded jobs as busboys, maids, day laborers, garbage men, and cooks, to a heaven of romantic ideals which were universal. It was a way, through the lyrical imagination, to get over the wall between our contaminated places as Negroes to another place, one of racial anonymity.

There was no sex, no violence, and none of the machismo, gamesmanship, or women as a sexual playground imagery that populated real relations between black men and their women. The songs with their innocent, squeaky-clean lyrics thematized our desire to cross over and blend in. Fittingly, David Ruffin sings *My Girl*, wearing a processed hairdo.

The psychological impulse to assimilate found political expression in what was then a movement for equal rights. In our music we expressed our transhistorical longing for freedom through a celebration of romance and love. Politically we sought it through a struggle for full citizenship.

Our destiny is bound up with the destiny of America—we built it for two centuries without wages, we made cotton king, we built our homes and homes for our masters and suffered injustice and humiliation—but ours of a bottomless vitality continued to live and grow. If the inexpressible cruelties of slavery could not extinguish our existence, the opposition we now face will surely fall. We feel that we are the conscience of America—we are its troubled soul.[14]

King's message was a redemptive retelling to both blacks and whites of America's story of origins. The same founding fathers that signed the Declaration of Independence—"We hold these truths self-evident that all men are created equal" went on to define black slaves as three-fifths of a person. From the beginning, America was conflicted, torn between values it professed and those it practiced.[15]

As King retold the story, America is no longer "a house divided," it becomes a table of brotherhood in which all could sit. King told whites we marched not against America, but for America.

Our aim must never be to defeat or humiliate the white man, but to win his friendship and understanding. And it said to blacks we are "heirs"; America's own ideals have chartered our struggle. If we are

Dr. Martin Luther King. (Library of Congress)

wrong the Supreme Court is wrong. We simply need to get America to remove the scales from its eyes. It must rise up to see "the true meaning of its creed."[16]

In appropriating and revising America's story of origins in this way, King invited everyone to a kind of second founding, to help build a new society in which the last could be first, and that which is crooked is finally made straight. This was a conservative social gospel. It said our salvation would come through reform, not revolution, and it was syrupy sweet. But it resonated with all classes. I said Amen too.

But we were children of two fathers: if one was Dr. King, the other was the African revolution. I did not fully understand all the forces that were twisting, pulling, and shaping me.

Like the bird fighting its way out of the egg, Africans on the continent broke out of the colonial arrangements. Hands broken by European domination began to straighten themselves out. Voices stilled by subjugation cried "freedom!" Led by Kwame Nkrumah, Ghana achieved complete independence by 1961. Kenya, after years of bloody insurrection by the Mau Mau, achieved independence by 1963. The struggle for African independence profoundly uplifted the self-esteem of American Negroes. I saw an explosion of dashikis, Afros, and a new generation of Negro sports heroes—like Muhammad Ali in boxing[17] and John Carlos in track and field. Everyone in my generation remembers the black power salute that Carlos gave as he stood on the pedestal to receive his Olympic medal in the 1968 Olympics.[18]

A new ethos was born. We saw ourselves as no longer Negroes. James Brown screamed,

> *Say it loud,*
> *I'm black and I'm proud . . . huh.*[19]

People like Stokely Carmichael added a political dimension. I still remember his chant of beep, beep bang bang oongawa black power. Stokely's call for black power awakened a different historical longing,

Paul Robeson, Richard Wright, and Adam Clayton Powell had used the term just as the activism of Malcolm X, Robert Williams, and

Gloria Richardson had embodied the phrase, even before its wide-spread use. The writings of Lorraine Hansberry and Harold Cruse, the music of Nina Simone, Abbey Lincoln, and Max Roach and the traveling urban pageants of the African Jazz arts society also reflected the movement's diverse cultural forebears.[20]

To whites this was militancy, to us this was self-discovery. We discovered a common struggle, that we were a nation within a nation. We discovered a connectedness that linked us through history and across space.

This notion of a black diaspora was handed down to us by Marcus Garvey. Garvey personified the notion that America was fundamentally "a white man's country" and would never accept black people. Standing on the shoulders of Garvey, Malcolm X took the separation a step further, beyond merely rejecting cultural values, to rejecting American identity. At the extreme the message was that we were aliens in the country of our birth. It was common for us to give ourselves African names, some went further to not merely embrace the African within, but to reject that we were American at all. Malcolm captured this outsider strand of the black consciousness that emerged in the1960s.

Malcolm X in thought. (Library of Congress)

I'm not going to sit at your table and watch you eat, with nothing on my plate, and call myself a diner. Sitting at the table doesn't make you a diner, unless you eat some of what's on that plate. Being here in America doesn't make you an American. Being born here in America doesn't make you an American. Why, if birth made you American, you wouldn't need any legislation, you wouldn't need any amendments to the Constitution, you wouldn't be faced with civil-rights filibustering in Washington, D.C., right now. . . . No, I'm not an American. I'm one of the 22 million black people who are the victims of Americanism. One of the 22 million black people who are the victims of democracy, nothing but disguised hypocrisy.[21]

This outsider narrative was even more strongly articulated by Imamu Baraka. "To be an American one must be a murderer of Black people. A white murderer of colored people."[22] As Komozi Woodard has written, by that logic for Negroes to qualify as Americans they first had to murder themselves.[23] Blacks flirted with the idea that freedom meant separation, in a brief moment that included groups like the Republic of New Afrika, the Congress of African People, and the songs of Nina Simone.

While cultural nationalists searched for an authentic black identity based on African traditions, Huey Newton and the Black Panther party for self-defense sought a political resolution. Moved by the assassination of Malcolm X in February 1965, Huey began the party in 1966. Combining elements of nationalism and Marxism, Huey modeled the struggle of blacks on the struggle of their African counterparts against colonialism. The relationship between the black communities was the same as the relationship between the colony and the mother country. Newton's internal colonialism thesis was later adopted by Berkeley sociologist Robert Blauner, "It is the experience of colonization that Afro-Americans share with many of the non-white people of the world."[24] For a time, I read every Black Panther newspaper. Each paper published their 10-point program and Newton beamed from every paper sitting in a wicker chair, which we associated with Africa, holding a spear.

Huey took the symbol of the panther from a Southern voting rights group. It "had been used effectively by the short-lived voting rights group the Lowndes, County (Alabama) Freedom Organization."[25] Both Baraka and Huey agreed on one point—that blacks constituted "a nation within a nation."[26] They were both disciples of Malcolm, who in turn stood on the broad shoulders of Garvey.[27]

You hear an echo of this outsider narrative in the words of Rev. Jeremiah Wright.

> The government gives them the drugs, builds bigger prisons, passes a three-strike law and then wants us to sing "God bless America"? No, no, no. Not God bless America, God damn America. That's in the Bible for killing innocent people. God damn America for treating her citizens as less than human.[28]

The call to separate, "come out from among them," resonated in the cadences of the Old Testament. America was Egypt and we were in bondage. Garvey was our Moses, and Malcolm was our Jeremiah.

We vacillated between notions of separation and assimilation. As Du Bois wrote,

> Here, then, is the dilemma, and it is a puzzling one, I admit. No Negro who has given earnest thought to the situation of his people in America has failed, at some time in life, to find himself at these crossroads; has failed to ask himself at some time: What, after all, am I? Am I an American or am I a Negro? Can I be both? Or is it my duty to cease to be a Negro as soon as possible and be an American? If I strive as a Negro, am I not perpetuating the very cleft that threatens and separates Black and White America?[29]

We answered Du Bois's question by saying we can be both. With posters of Angela and Malcolm on our walls we chose to be doctors, lawyers, and corporate executives. We chose lives that would lead us away from the hood not merely spatially, but culturally, politically, and spiritually. We chose assimilation. We—I—betrayed Malcolm. We betrayed Angela, and ultimately Du Bois.

The movement zigged and zagged through momentary expressions of rage and rebellion. But the chants of black power died down. We were defeated, not by water hoses, police dogs, or raids on our headquarters by police, but by material success.

The term affirmative action comes from the Wagner Act of 1935, when Congress prohibited certain unfair labor practices. Employers who had engaged in such practices were required to take affirmative action. Roosevelt in 1941 under threat of black demonstrations passed an executive order, which had no teeth, nominally desegregating work on defense contracts. In 1961, Kennedy issued an executive order requiring affirmative action for defense contracts. All this nibbled at the edges of the problem of race. But in 1965 Johnson made a speech that opened the door.

> You do not take a person who for years has been hobbled by chains, liberate him, bring him to the starting line and then say, you are free to compete with the others.[30]

The hallmark of this era was that corporations and schools recruited blacks that could not have gained admission under normal standards. The biblical prophecy that "the last shall be first" came true for the talented tenth. America opened the doors to this talented tenth to obtain degrees from Ivy League schools, to enter professional sports, and to move from the street to the corporate suite.

As conservatives have pointed out, demands for affirmative action were originally associated with "the black power movement," which largely began in 1966. This movement that began as the civil rights demonstrations, formally, was bearing fruit.[31] Shelby Steele attributes the backlash against affirmative action to a natural white reaction: affirmative action was an expression of "black power," an effort not achievable by equality—equal opportunity laws provided that he seems to imply—but special rights, not equality but black privilege. It was, from Steele's perspective, a manipulation of white guilt: "It tries to make black weakness profitable by selling it as white guilt."[32] Steele goes on to suggest that it is blacks' own claims of "victimization" that have crippled them and led to their social isolation.

What is outrageous about this is that it makes the effect—that blacks feel victimized—the cause. Let's historicize this to see what came first. Affirmative action, despite the high-blown rhetoric, was a remedy for the talented tenth; it was in a word tokenism. In other words the isolation was already in place. Thus, low black self esteem could perhaps contribute to the social marginalization of blacks. But low black self esteem did not create the marginalization. Segregation did that.

Had the black community remained intact, what we refer to as 1960s' activism—against ghetto conditions—might have continued. The chief effect of affirmative action was to suburbanize the intellectuals, to in effect split the black community. The green shoots of black militancy quickly dried up.

By 1975, the struggle for civil rights could be defined as a struggle for economic progress. This shift was reflected in a new TV show featuring George Jefferson. George's theme song captured the zeitgeist or spirit of the last quarter of the 20th century for my generation.

> *Took whole lot a tryin'*
> *But we finally made it up that hill.*[33]

The piece of the pie becomes the deluxe apartment in the sky.

Henry Ford had a ceremony in which he had immigrants walk through a large melting pot. When they began the journey they were dressed in costumes of their native country. When they come out of the pot they are dressed in an American business suit. They are no longer foreign. They have new identities.

So did we. We began by wearing our business suits as suits of armor to protect us as we made the transition from citizen of the urban ghetto to citizen of the suburbs and greater America. The credentials we had attained were not just achievements: they were proof that we did not fit the stereotype. The house in the suburbs was not just a place to live in for proof; exhibit no. 1, of our exceptionalism. Soon we began to wear the business suit on the inside. We answered Du Bois's question—Am I an American or a Negro?—by saying we could be both. The elements of African culture, which may be displayed occasionally in February as a costume to wear to church, have largely disappeared. The elements of militancy, which were popular in the 1960s, have faded, fists have un-clenched, and Afros have been cut down. Many have become republicans. We drank the Kool-Aid.

Dyson in his book *"Is Bill Cosby Right? Or Has the Black Middle Class lost its Mind?"* fittingly refers to the new black middle class, most of whom climbed the ladder up from the ghetto like myself, as the Afris-tocracy—"composed of lawyers, physicians, intellectuals, bankers and the like." This segment of the black middle class is not a monolith. But there is an overwhelming tendency within this group to rail in private about the pernicious tendencies of the black poor.

When they do so it is their own hard-won respectability this Afristocracy defends when they denounce saggy pants, the N word, and the hot ghetto mess of ungrammatical names. In *A Soldier's Play,* Sgt. Waters connives to imprison one C. J. Memphis because he is a geechie. A geechie is someone culturally backward, who is in the way of Negro progress. The sergeant had a God's eye view of what progress is. While Sarge knows C. J. is innocent of a crime, his incarceration is just because this is where people like C. J. belong. Listen to Sarge as he explains C. J.'s fate to him while he (C. J.) sits incredulously behind bars:

> Them Nazis ain't all crazy. Whole lot of people just can't seem to fit in to where things seem to be going. Like you, C.J. See, the Black race can't afford you no more. There used to be a time, we'd see someone like you singin,' clownin,' yassuh-bossin' . . . and we wouldn't do anything. Folks liked that. You were good. Homey kind of nigger. When they needed somebody to mistreat, call a name or two, they paraded you. Reminded them of the good old days. Not no more. The day of the Geechee is gone, boy. And you're going with it.[34]

Sarge and Bill Cosby tell the same story. The cruel distance between Sgt. Waters and C.J. is symbolic of that between the black middle class and the hip-hoppers. There is the same God's eye view of how black people should carry themselves and what is necessary for blacks to move ahead. If the black underclass is overwhelmingly incarcerated they are at the end of the day where they belong. As Bill Cosby states,

> They cry when their son is standing there in an orange suit. . . . Where were you when he was two? Where were you when he was twelve? Where were you when he was eighteen, and how come you didn't know he had a pistol? And where is his father?[35]

Sarge and Bill Cosby tell the same story.

Consciously the black middle class is not expressing hatred of people but of values which in their experience are self-destructive. The ghetto poor are demonized as ignorant and in jail because of their ignorance. On the surface this is a narrative about choices and personal responsibility. But as the black middle class joins the mainstream chorus about the pathology of ghetto, dysfunctional black families inevitably rely on a notion of black inferiority. We have simply substituted cultural inferiority for racial inferiority. Let me say it plain. This is racism. Black-on-black racism.

In demonizing their underclass cousins, the black neoconservative is operating with the prejudice that qualitatively is no different from that expressed by Europeans toward the indigenous natives of Africa. Like new immigrants from the colonies they have simply adopted the values and perspectives of the mother country. Once one accepts citizenship in Greater America, one renounces identification with the ghetto, its culture, and its people. The black underclass is as foreign to many members of the black middle class as the natives were to the Europeans.

This is a classic phenomenon that psychologists analyze under the optimal distinctiveness theory. The immigrants who have entered the mother country and become accultured still experience at best marginal acceptance. The unassimilated, by association, threaten the limited acceptance of the new immigrants. Charles Silverman documents this phenomenon with the Irish. Foner documents this with second generation Indians. In his hostility and rage—in a sense toward his own origins—Sarge is attempting to protect his own marginal acceptance. The hostility of Sarge is a reaction to this threat of in-group acceptance. Would it matter if C.J. were his father, cousin, or brother?

Houston Baker in his book accounts for the transformation I am describing—the alienation of large segments of the black middle class from their poorer cousins in terms of a conversion. In the Bible, man must move from a fallen state of slavery to his own desires, to a higher state through spiritual awakening.

What is it that the black middle class has awakened to? Two things. The first is the good life. The good life is a mix of cultural style, personal wealth, and the accumulation of the trappings of success. In our post-Fordian era, success is represented by such iconic symbols as J.D., M.B.A., and BMW.

A mix of hard work, refusing to be denied, and the adaptation of street smarts make the good life possible in part by choices—to the task of climbing the corporate ladder.

The second thing they have awaken to is the imperative of distancing themselves from values associated with the ghetto. In the 1970s, Moynihan and others famously ascribed the problem of ghetto as a problem of culture. He called it a tangle of pathology. At the time, Moynihan's report was denounced as racism. What in the 1970s was denounced as racism has become the middle-class gospel.

The gospel is that we, the black middle class, made it because we had the right values, and the ghetto folks have not because they remain stuck in time, mired in pathological cultural patterns.

> Conversionist's discourses, whether they are motivated by religion, science, or politics, always underestimate culture or regard it as pathological. Conversionists, whether they are politicians or religious leaders, appeal to their audiences by blaming the culture of the people they are trying to convert. They always expect people to come to a . . . spiritual awakening, and walk out of their culture, shedding it like a shell or cracked skin.[36]

This gospel is not new—the Cosby critique of inner city blacks, the attack on hip-hop culture, all follow an arc tracing back to Moynihan's original neoconservative campaign. But part of the price of becoming neoconservatives is that the black middle class had to erase—or forget—significant portions of their history. Black nationalism, or the Malcolm X period, is forgotten. Neoconservatism at its deepest imagines identity as individual. This fierce individualism rejects collectivist notions of unity with the masses of black people or any other kind of collectivism.

Listen to Shelby Steele:

> [I]t was not a matter of hating lower class blacks but a matter of hating what we did not want to be . . . it is fundamentally true that my middle class identity involved a disassociation from lower class black life and a corresponding identification with values . . . that are common to the middle class everywhere. Be an individual and a responsible citizen. . . . Hard work, education, individual initiative, stable family life, property ownership—these have been the means by which ethnic groups have moved ahead in America. Regardless of past or present victimization these laws apply absolutely to black Americans also. . . . What we need is a form of racial identity that energizes the individual.[37]

The great harm of neoconservatism is, when it is used as a total explanation for racial disparities, it is a form of denial. Part of the problem is certainly that the black underclass needs to take more personal responsibility. But as a "total" explanation the rhetoric of personal responsibility, individual choice, the culture of poverty, and the culture of failure works as political sleight of hand shifting the focus away from structural racism. It places the blame for social isolation on the victims themselves. This rhetorical sleight of hand has led, in the aftermath of the Obama election, to a new narrative of racial transcendence. Racism has disappeared or receded to insignificance. This story is the main ingredient of the Kool-Aid we mentioned earlier.

It is true, as Tricia Rose and many others have written, hip-hop has many contradictions. But whom does this disquisition or lambasting urban culture serve?

There is a war against the urban poor. It is conducted through massive incarceration, benign neglect, particularly of inner city schools, the dismantling of social safety nets, hypersegregation, and the concentration of poverty. All wars require some justification. We must rationalize the human losses. The brutal conditions of the urban poor are rationalized in the neoconservative narrative because racism has quit, and the inner city poor are to blame—through their pathological culture—for their own problems. The demonization of hip-hop is a critical component in this machinery of rationalization. It facilitates the war against the urban poor.

The New Racism: The Changing Same

What is different about the new racism is the way it is different yet *the same*: it is now urban culture versus mainstream culture and urban space versus suburban space. This is different; it replaces the color line of the past. What remains unchanged is that the oppressed black masses remain invisible.

In the aftermath of Hurricane Katrina, for example, the victims in the ninth Ward were true victims. They were recast as refugees—almost as if they were from a foreign country. Did the storm take away their citizenship as well as their homes? They were thieves, hooligans, thugs, rapists, criminals, and looters. These stereotypical images made them invisible as human beings.[38]

The rhetorical abuse of the Katrina victims prefigured and helped to justify their actual abuse, the fact that help was so long in coming. They were "still on the roof"[39] while one Bush administration official, Condoleezza Rice, attended an opera.

Instead of focusing on how the Katrina victims looked, or what they did in response to inhuman conditions, we should have focused on how we could help them. This is a parable for the hip-hop wars.

We carry water for the neoconservatives when we participate in the demonization of urban culture. We become Sarge; we become part of the new racism. Instead of focusing on the violent imagery of hip-hop we should focus on the conditions that the imagery is a response to.

The conflict within the family has a gendered aspect as well. Hip-hop music, the central institution, of urban cultural life, has been portrayed as the perpetrator of black female oppression. Michael Eric Dyson pointed out in his testimony some years ago that hip-hop did not invent hatred of women, especially black women.

In point of fact the notion that black women had a place, that black women's sexuality was a playpen for black men traces back to the black power generation. In fact the very goal of black power was to create a safe place for black men.

The Pussy Edict

Sterling Stucky has a poem about the many barriers blacks faced during the era of Jim Crow. He talks about the signs of "reserved for whites only." But we will break through, he seems to say. He says one thing they cannot stop: "The strong men comin' on, the strong men gittin' stronger!"[40]

We, as black students in the early 1970's, were the strong men of what we believed was the greatest generation of black people. We would break through the barriers that had held generations of blacks back. Strength for us was a combination of notions of both manhood and militancy, which walked hand in hand in our ideals. We romanticized ourselves as in the tradition of African kings and warriors. If the black man was the king, the black woman was the queen. She was as celebrated and prized as she could be in a movement created and defined by black men.

Part of our struggle was to empower ourselves to protect and take care of *our* women. Cedric Johnson traces this image of protector to Malcolm

X: "His (Malcolm's) rhetoric most often recalled notions of citizenship which predated the passage of the Nineteenth amendment and equated civic agency with . . . the capacity for masculine self-defense."[41] Malcolm stated,

> When I listen to Mrs. Hammer, a black woman—could be my mother, sister, or daughter—describe what they have done to her in Mississippi, I ask myself how in the world can we expect to be respected as men when we will allow something like that to be done to our women and we do nothing about it? How can you and I be looked upon as men with black women being beaten and we do nothing about it? No we don't deserve to be recognized and respected as men as long as our women can be brutalized in this manner . . . but we sit around singing "we shall overcome.[42]

bell hooks traces this protector notion back to slavery.

> Experience has taught me that nothing can be more heart-rending than for one to see a beloved mother or sister tortured, and to hear their cries and not be able to render them assistance. But such is the position the American slave occupies.[43]

Freedom was having the power to do what the slave could not. This was powerfully expressed in the film *Glory*. In the film, the struggle by black soldiers against the Southern military forces becomes a personal struggle for their own freedom. They came to terms with death in battle in terms of what the sacrifice signified. As Denzel's character expressed it, "Ain't even much a matter what happens tomorrow, 'cause we men, ain't we?[44] There was no more eloquent line in the history of American film. Our ability to do what men did defined citizenship, freedom, and manhood. They are all intertwined. What men did was to protect their women.

The ultimate goal was to build a nation, and the foundation of that nation was not merely a family but one in which the man was the head.

> We understand that it is traditional that the man is the head of the house. . . . Women cannot do the same things as men—they are made by nature to function differently. Equality of men and women is something that cannot happen even in the abstract world. Men are

not equal to other men, i.e. ability, experience, or even understanding. The value of men and women can be seen in the value of gold and silver—they are not equal but both have great value. We must realize that men and women are a complement to each other because there is no house/family without a man and his wife.[45]

In context Baraka's gendered notion of the movement was radical at the time.

[This was] intentionally sexist . . . such black male assertiveness was viewed as radical when juxtaposed against stereotypical images of black men as cowering weaklings before "the white man."

In essence the goal of freedom, citizenship, and empowerment for blacks was defined in terms of freedom, citizenship, and empowerment for black men. This conceptual linkage led unerringly to contradictions. Stokely Carmichael famously argued that sistas should service their black men in the struggle, sexually. At the time many sistas ridiculed this as the pussy edict.

Racism, as Martin Luther King noted, was wrong because it substitutes an I–it relationship, for an I–Thou relationship. We had assumed the existence as a hierarchy, I think unconsciously. Consciously we gave the sistas our utmost respect. But it was a respect entangled with the I–it patriarchy that colonized our notions of manhood. This symbolism was played out on a national stage at the Million Man march.

I got on the bus, I answered the call to go to the Million Man march, but I recognize the contradiction. The same problem was played out in countless family decisions, like that of Clarence Thomas's family. His family chose to give Clarence, the male, an elite education, but not the daughter. He became a Supreme Court Justice, she became a welfare mother.

Alasdair McIntyre talks about the people who come after, who only have the fragments of books, and science of the previous civilization. The hip-hop generation is in a similar position. The 1960s era (and much of the 1970's) is for them like a lost election campaign. After the suburbanization of the black middle class, investment, and the disappearance of jobs, the gains of the civil rights era were largely invisible. The ghetto either remained the same or worse. The oral history, the albums and CDs of Soul music played by their parents, the speeches of Martin Luther King that still take place in television documentaries— these fragments of a bygone era are all that is left. The hip-hop generation has "gathered up the fragments"[46] that remained. The music, culture, and norms of the new generation sample the norms and culture of the black power era much the same as they sample classic songs.

Today's debate about the hypermaterialism, the misogyny, of hip-hop lacks historical context. It projects onto the hip-hop generation responsibility for the weeds of sexism in that preexisted them in black community—weeds which were planted by the generation of Soul. This discussion is a prologue to a much longer one. These issues have their roots deep in black culture, and even deeper in the culture of America itself.

Notes

1. W.E.B. Du Bois, "The Conservation of the Races," in *The Souls of Black Folk*, ed. Brent Hayes Edwards (Oxford: Oxford University Press, 2007), Appendix I, 184.

2. The Impressions, "Choice of Colors," *Movin' on Up, The Music and Message of Curtis Mayfield*, DVD (Santa Monica, CA: Hip-O Records (part of Universal Music Group), 2008).

3. W.E.B. Du Bois, *The Souls of Black Folk.*

4. D. Marvin Jones, "No Time for Trumpets: Title VII, Equality, and the Fin de Siecle," *Michigan Law Review* 92 (1994): 2311, 2312.

5. It is commonplace to speak of racism as a function of individual prejudice. I think this way of thinking about racism oversimplifies a much deeper malaise. It is essential to understand that discrimination is not an individual act but a social practice driven by a widely shared negative images and ideas that function as a kind of ideology. The most important work on this is D. Marvin Jones, *Race, Sex, and Suspicion: The Myth of the Black Male* (Westport, CT: Greenwood, 2005).

6. Frantz Fanon, *Black Skin, White Masks* (New York: Grove Press, 1952), 186.

7. Fanon, *Black Skin*, 112.

8. James Baldwin, *The Price of the Ticket: Collected Nonfiction* (New York: Macmillan, 1985), 67.

9. Patricia Hill Collins, *From Black Power to Hip-Hop: Racism, Nationalism, and Feminism* (Philadelphia, PA: Temple University Press, 2006), 180.

10. Smokey Robinson, "The Tracks of My Tears," (Detroit, MI: Tamla Records, 1965) on *Motown Legends: Smokey Robinson—The Tracks of My Tears* (CD).

11. The Temptations, *"My Girl," Single (Vinyl)* (Detroit, MI: Gordy Records (Motown), 1964).

12. Fess Parker, "Wringle-Wrangle," *Walt Disney Archive Collection* (Burbank, CA: Walt Disney Productions, 1957).

13. Gena Dagel Caponi, *Signifyin(g), sanctifyin,' and Slam Dunkin* (Amherst: University of Massachusetts Press, 1999).

14. Martin Luther King Jr., "The Case against Tokenism," in *A Testament of Hope: The Essential Writings of Martin Luther King*, ed. James Melvin Washington (New York: Harper-Collins, 1991), 111.

15. See generally Gunnar Myrdhal, *An American Dilemma, the Negro Problem and Modern Democracy*, vol. 1 (Piscataway, NJ: Transaction Publishers, 1944) (Published in New Brunswick, NJ: Harper & Brothers, 1996).

16. *A Testament of Hope*, 200.

17. On the significance of Ali in shaping the spirit of the 1960s, see Miek Marqusee, *Redemption Song: Muhammad Ali and the Spirit of the Sixties* (London: Verso Books, 2005).

18. See Jeffrey Ogbar, *Black Power: Radical Politics and African-American Identity* (Baltimore, MD: Johns Hopkins University Press, 2005), 118–19.

19. James Brown, "Say It Loud—I'm Black and I'm Proud," *Say It Loud— I'm Black and I'm Proud* (Cincinnati, OH: King Records, 1968) on *Say It Loud (Best of James Brown Live)* audio CD (Cincinnati, OH: Setco Records, 2010). It is difficult to overstate the inspiration, and the feeling of a common purpose this song instilled in my generation. James Brown's influence on hip-hop music also probably cannot be overstated. More than a dozen hip-hop musicians and groups have sampled "Say It Loud—I'm Black and I'm Proud," including Eric B. and Rakim, Big Daddy Kane, LL Cool J, and 2 Live Crew.

20. Peniel Joseph, *Waiting Til the Midnight Hour: A Narrative History of Black Power* (New York: Henry Holt and Company, 2007), 147.

21. George Breitman, *Malcolm X Speaks: Selected Speeches and Statements* (New York: Grove Press, 1994), 26.

22. Amiri Baraka, "The Congress of African People and Black Power Politics from the 1961 United Nations Protest to the 1972 Gary Convention," in *The Black Power Movement: Rethinking the Black Power Era,* ed. Peniel Joseph (New York: Routledge, 2006), 55, 66.

23. Baraka, "The Congress of African People."

24. The paper was entitled "Studies of Violence," delivered in Los Angeles, June 1, 1968. The quote is from a later iteration of the same ideas in a paper by Blauner entitled "Internal Colonialism and Ghetto Revolt" in *American Sociological Review*, Summer 1969. Blauner to his credit acknowledges the debt he owes to Newton and others, "As a good colonialist I have probably restated (read stolen) more ideas from . . . such contributors to the Black Panther Party newspaper as Huey Newton [and others] . . . than I have generated myself." Kenneth L. Kusmer, *Black Communities and Urban Development in America, 1720–1990: The Ghetto Crisis of the 1960s* (New York: Garland Pub., 1991). Ironically, Newton, as a significant writer, is unknown to mainstream sociology. His ideas, despite appropriate attribution by Blauner, are known to sociology as the Blauner thesis.

25. Yvonne Bynoe, *Stand and Deliver: Political Activism, Leadership, and Hip-Hop Culture* (Berkeley, CA: Soft Skull Press, 2004), 55.

26. Komozi Woodard, *A Nation within a Nation: Amiri Baraka (LeRoi Jones) and Black Power Politics* (Chapel Hill: University of North Carolina Press, 1999), 17. Woodard attributes the statement to Martin Delaney dating back to 1852. "We are a nation within a nation; as the Poles in Russia, the Hungarians in Austria, the Welsh, Irish, and Scotch in the British Dominions." Woodard, *A Nation within a Nation.* Frederick Douglas also expressed a similar idea,

> This people, free and slave, are rapidly filling up the number of four millions. They are becoming a nation, in the midst of a nation which disowns them, and for weal or for woe this nation is united. The distinction between the slave and the free is not great, and their destiny seems one and the same. The black man is linked to his brother by indissoluble ties. The one cannot be truly free while the other is a slave. The free colored man is reminded by the ten thousand petty annoyances with which he meets every day, of his identity with an enslaved people—and that with them he is destined to fall or flourish. We are one nation . . .

27. James L. Conyers and Andrew P. Smallwood, *Malcolm X: A Historical Reader* (Chapel Hill: University of North Carolina Press, 2008), 203. Locating Malcolm "within the framework of the legacy of Marcus Garvey."

28. Diane Sawyer and Chris Cuomo, "Reverend Jeremiah Wright: Obama's Pastor Now a Campaign Liability?" *Good Morning America*, 7:07 AM EST, March 13, 2008.

29. W.E.B. Du Bois, *The Souls of Black Folk*.

30. Barbara Jordan and Elspeth D. Rostow, *The Great Society: A Twenty Year Critique* (Austin: University of Texas at Austin, 1986), 71.

31. The landmark legislation of the 20th century was the Civil Rights Act of 1964, which became effective in 1965.

32. Shelby Steele, *A Dream Deferred: The Second Betrayal of Black Freedom in America* (New York: Harper Collins, 1998), 11.

33. Ja'net Du Bois, "Movin on Up" theme song from "The Jefferson's," see Bob Lally, Oz Scott, Jack Shea, Tony Singletary, and Arlando Smith, *The Jeffersons—The Complete First Season*, DVD, Sony Pictures, August 6, 2002. The show "The Jeffersons" aired on CBS from January 18, 1975—June 25, 1985. See Ken Bloom, Frank Vlastnik, and John Lithgow, *Sitcoms: The 101 Greatest TV Comedies of All Time* (New York: Black Dog and Leventhal, 2007), 184–85.

34. Charles Fuller, *A Soldier's Play* (New York: Hill and Wang, 1981), 67.

35. Michael Eric Dyson, *Is Bill Cosby Right or Has the Black Middle Class Lost Its Mind* (New York: Basic Civitas Books, 2006), xii quoting Bill Cosby.

36. Houston A. Baker, *Betrayal: How Black Intellectuals Have Abandoned the Ideals of the Civil Rights Movement* (New York: Columbia University Press, 2008), 217.

37. Baker, *Betrayal*, 144.

38. See D. Marvin Jones, " 'Been in the Storm So Long': Katrina, Reparations, and the Original Understanding of Equal Protection," in *Hurricane Katrina: America's Unnatural Disaster*, ed. Jeremy I. Levitt and Matthew C. Whittaker (Lincoln: University of Nebraska Press, 2005).

39. See Kenneth B. Nunn, " 'Still Up on the Roof': Race, Victimology, and the Response to Hurricane Katrina," in *Katrina: America's Unnatural Disaster.*

40. Sterling A. Brown, "Strong Men," in *Making It on Broken Promises: Leading African-American Male Scholars*, ed. Lee Jones and Cornel West (Sterling, VA: Stylus Publishing, 2002), 61.

41. Cedric Johnson, *Revolutionaries to Race Leaders: Black Power and the Making of African-American Politics* (Minneapolis: University of Minnesota Press, 2007), 188.

42. George Breitman, *Malcolm X Speaks*.

43. bell hooks, *We Real Cool* (New York: Routledge, 2004), 3.

44. *Glory*, directed by Edward Zwick (1989; Culver City, CA: Sony Home Pictures Entertainment, 1998), DVD.

45. Manning Marable and Leith Mullings, *Let Nobody Turn Us Around: Voices of Resistance, Reform, and Renewal* (Plymouth, UK: Rowman and Littlefield, 2009), 505.

46. "When they were filled, he said unto his disciples, Gather up the fragments that remain, that nothing be lost," John 6:12 (King James Version).

5

Black Skin, New Masks: Hip-Hop and the New Politics of Blackness

We create race by creating ourselves.

—Ralph Ellison

So what is the veil then? Is it a barrier or a defense, a curse or a blessing? Is it a flimsy and rent fabric or a rigid, imprisoning cage? Is it a mark we wear or a role we play?

—Howard Winant

In *The Souls of Black Folk,* W.E.B. Du Bois captured the dilemma of the black experience in the concept of the veil,

> After the Egyptian and Indian, the Greek and Roman, the Teuton and Mongolian, the Negro is a sort of seventh son, born with a veil, and gifted with second-sight in this American world, a world that yields him no true self-consciousness, but only lets him see himself through the revelation of the other world. It is a peculiar sensation, this double-consciousness, this sense of always looking at one's self through the eyes of others, of measuring one's soul by the tape of a world that looks on in amused contempt and pity.[1]

The "veil" is sometimes used to refer to the color line itself: "The veil in political terms represents the harsh lines of Jim Crow segregation that contained Afri-US peoples within a system of American apartheid."[2]

But another meaning of the veil is as an impenetrable curtain that divides internally. It divides the black child's sense of herself—subjective identity—and the black child's sense of Negroness—objective identity—that is how the child is perceived. In this cultural context the veil refers to the received sense of prejudice that is so deeply associated with race. Du Bois describes this confrontation with racial identity in a moving passage in *The Souls of Black Folk.*

> When the shadow swept across me . . . in a wee wooden schoolhouse, something put in the boy's and girl's heads to buy gorgeous visiting cards . . . and exchange. The exchange was merry, 'til one girl, a tall newcomer refused my card. . . . Then it dawned on me with a certain suddenness that I was different from the others.[3]

Charles F. Peterson explains the significance of this confrontation with prejudice.

> Du Bois' discovery of the veil in that "wee schoolhouse" opens up for him an unknown world in which race as caste serves to determine his movement and position in U.S. society. Reflected in the eyes of his schoolmates was the belief that "Willie's" physical appearance completely determined his life as a "hewer of wood" and a drawer of water.[4]

To himself he is an individual with feelings, thought, ideas, and dreams but to his classmates he is an inferior order of human life.

Of course, contradictory self-awareness is part of the human condition. As Lacan's writings tell us, identity formation is intimately involved with a process of "negation"—which begins with the separation from the mother.[5] Lacan calls this "the mirror stage." What happens is that "At some point very early in the child's life she looks in the mirror and apprehends the fact that her body is a distinct and coherent entity in itself, that there are boundaries between what constitutes herself and what constitutes the other."[6]

As Hegel would state, "Only when I apprehend what I am not, does the self become objective to me."[7] This self-consciousness signifies the beginning of language the child passes from the realm of being to the symbolic realm of meaning. For blacks this process takes on a racial aspect:

"Only when I apprehend that I am not (white) does the self become objective to me." This black self becomes I/negro.[8] This is a conflicted identity because the I/negro can never be an independent subject; the Negro aspect of the self is dependant upon and a function of the perceptions of whites. As a result the child objectifies himself.

The double consciousness Du Bois referred to as a veil Fanon described through the metaphor of black skin/white masks. The mask represents the face of white power. But this is power constituted by the language, culture, and worldview of the white world. In this framework black skin signifies inferiority: it is on the wrong side of a dichotomy that separates good from bad.

Emotion versus Reason

Fanon writes, "Yes we are—we Negroes—backward, simple, free in our behavior. This is because for us the body is not something opposed to what you call the mind. *Emotion is completely Negro as reason is to Greek* (i.e. White)."[9]

Thus in films, blackness is represented by the subordination of intellect to emotion. This is a vein of thought that has fed film from *Gone with the Wind,*[10] in which blacks are portrayed as happy to be slaves, to *Soul Plane*[11] in which Snoop Dog is the pilot of an airline whose motto is, "We fly, We party, We land!" This stereotyping pervades popular culture: black men, like Herman Cain and Tiger Woods are sex obsessed,[12] black women are angry.[13]

According to this way of thinking, spontaneity naturalness, a sense of rhythm, emotion, and sensuality predominate over intellect as essentially black characteristics.[14]

Savagery versus Civilization

Barbara Smith writes,

In the Darwinist 1890s "civilization" had become a racial concept. Rather than simply meaning "the west" or "industrially advanced societies" civilization denoted a precise stage in human evolution—the one following the more primitive stages of "Savagery" or "barbarism." . . . But only whites had, as yet, advanced to the civilized stage.[15]

This 19th-century imagery continues to resonate in Fanon's description of how modern whites have knotted together blackness and primitive culture:

Black Magic, primitive mentality, animism, animal eroticism, it all floods over me. All of it is typical of peoples that have not kept pace with the evolution of the human race. Or, if one prefers they constitute third-rate humanity. . . . Yes we niggers are backward, naïve and free.[16]

Fanon anchors this through the images of Prospero and Caliban. In Shakespeare's play, *The Tempest,* Prospero represents a civilizing force and Caliban a half-human savage. When Prospero tells Caliban how much he owes him, Caliban replies "You taught me language and my profit on't is, I know how to curse."[17] In Fanon's analysis black skin is a curse in the settler's language. By internalizing this language—worldview—the black child curses himself. "As I begin to recognize that the Negro is a symbol of sin, I catch myself hating the Negro. But then I recognize I am a Negro."[18]

The curse of black skin is supremely oppressive because it is imposed from within,

It is one thing to position a subject or set of peoples as the other of a dominant discourse. It is quite another thing to subject them to that "knowledge" not only as a matter of imposed will and domination [but] by the power of inner-compulsion and subjective conformation to the norm.[19]

Let me bring this home. In *Briggs v. Elliot,*[20] Dr. Kenneth Clark testified about an experiment he conducted using two sets of dolls. Let us call Dr. Clark back to the stand, to recall his testimony five decades ago.

THE WITNESS
[Dr. Kenneth Clark]:   I made these tests on Thursday and Friday of this past week at your request, and I presented it to

children in the Scott's Branch Elementary school, concentrating particularly on the elementary group. . . . —May I read from these notes?

JUDGE WARING: You may refresh your recollection.

THE WITNESS: Thank you. I presented these dolls to them and I asked them the following questions in the following order:

"Show me the doll that you like best or that you'd like to play with," "Show me the doll that is the 'nice' doll,"

"Show me the doll that looks 'bad,'" and then the following questions also: "Give me the doll that looks like a white child,"

"Give me the doll that looks like a colored child," "Give me the doll that looks like a Negro child," and "Give me the doll that looks like you."

By MR. CARTER, Q: "Like you?"

A: "Like you." That was the final question, and you can see why. I wanted to get the child's free expression of his opinions and feelings before I had him identified with one of these two dolls. I found that of the children between the ages of six and nine whom I tested, which were a total of sixteen in number, that ten of those children chose the white doll as their preference; the doll which they liked best. Ten of them also considered the white doll a "Nice" doll. And, I think you have to keep in mind that these two dolls are absolutely identical in every respect except skin color. Eleven of these sixteen children chose the brown doll as the doll which looked "bad." This is consistent with previous results which we have obtained testing over three hundred children, and we interpret it to mean that the Negro child accepts as early as six, seven or eight the negative stereotypes about his own group . . .

By MR. CARTER, Q: Well, as a result of your tests, what conclusions have you reached, Mr. Clark, with respect to the infant plaintiffs involved in this case?

A: The conclusion which I was forced to reach was that these children in Clarendon County, like other human beings who are subjected to an obviously inferior status in the society in which they live, have been definitely harmed in the development of their personalities; that the signs of instability in their personalities are clear, and I think that every psychologist would accept and interpret these signs as such.

Q: Is that the type of injury which in your opinion would be enduring or lasting?

A: I think it is the kind of injury which would be as enduring or lasting as the situation endured, changing only in its form and in the way it manifests itself.

MR. CARTER: Thank you. Your witness.[21]

Fanon identified traced feelings of black inferiority to the machinations of the colonial regime. Dr. Clark identified the source of the inferiority as the postcolonial regime of Jim Crow. Clark confirms that the internalization of racism, and its destructive effect on the Negro child's concept of "self," leaps the outer ditch of formal labels that separate the colonial and the postcolonial experience of otherness. Consider for example that when CNN's AC360° redid the doll test 60 years later the results were chillingly similar:

Earlier this year, AC360°, with the help of a seasoned team of researchers, conducted a pilot study based on the 1940s doll test. In this pilot study, more than 130 kids were asked a series of questions about five cartoon dolls with varying skin tones. Half of the children were African-American and half were white, half were in the north and half in the south. The results were surprising: white children have an overwhelming white bias, and black children also have a bias toward white.[22]

Dr. Kenneth Clark conducting the Doll Test. (Library of Congress)

The problem of the 20th century was the color line. It was the problem of the veil. As Howard Winant has written, "In the 1950s and early 1960s [H]e (Du Bois) . . . was still saying the veil could not be lifted . . . this would only serve to expose black folk to . . . something almost worst: the bleaching of the black soul, the compulsory abandonment of black identity."[23]

Since Clark gave his history making testimony the visible elements of the veil have largely disappeared. The fact that equal opportunity is now the law means that there are no longer formal barriers separating black America and greater America.

There was a time in America when all black people regardless of class status had to occupy the same physical space. This of course had to do with legally justified segregation that pervaded the land in one form or another. At this time the idea of community was quite accurate. In that there was a stratified representation of the people who inhabited that space. But when people with the proper resources could move to other places, the only people remaining were those who could not afford to move. This is the point at which a purely black community ceased to exist, at least in a physical, racially exclusive sense.[24]

Nonetheless, the veil has not been lifted.

The fact that blacks have moved spatially and economically has not changed the cultural significance of race.

Race has simply been diffused into a spectrum of identity. Black and white remain poles separating two cultures— two groups—one powerful, one powerless; one associated with intellect, self-control, civilization building and the other with emotion, criminality, and cultural pathology.

Social identity, on the continuum between these poles of black and white, has become in part a matter of location. It is less a question of what color you are than a question of the zip code you live in. (Race has become space.) It is also a function of one's attitudes, style, where you went to school, and how much money you have. I call this cultural assimilation. (Race becomes culture.) This mutation tends to make the social identity of an individual a function of color, culture, and space. This is the continuum that Todd Boyd referred to.

The essence of blackness has been its genius at improvisation. Its genius is to take the language, the songs, and the technology of European tradition and transform them. In jazz, musicians take a Broadway song and blow it up. In hip-hop, urban artists take language from the mainstream and blow it up as well: "Friend" becomes "dog" (man's best friend); abstract qualities like honesty are visualized, straight up. The fluidity of blackness now flows into improvising identity where the old code of color and ancestry is in flux. This has led simultaneously to two cultural communities— two different styles of black identity each claiming to be authentic. But they actually represent two ends of the spectrum. Du Bois talked about double consciousness, the notion that within each black person there are "two souls, two unreconciled strivings."[25]

Here we have a social split that mirrors the internal conflict Du Bois described. This cultural chasm within the black community equally mirrors the internal division noted by Fanon: each fragment of this "split" within the black community represents a different end of the duality I would name as I/negro.

Modern Blackness

The black middle class, as they see themselves, represent modern blackness. Modern blackness is "mobile, fluid, adaptable, educated, chic and cool."[26] In *Hustle and Flow,* director Craig Brewer explores the life of Djay (played by Terrence Howard), a pimp, who has ambitions of being a rapper. As he tells Shug (Taraji P. Henson), one of his wives, "Everybody's gotta have a dream."[27] While Djay hustles to survive in the sleazy underworld of the ghetto, he sees on television an old high school buddy named Skinny Black, who has made it out of the ghetto and blown up as a Gangsta rapper. "Skinny Black" (played by Ludacris wearing a "grill of gold teeth") is coming back to his old hometown to party. Djay decides to crash the party to give his rap demo tape to Skinny Black.

Determined to make a powerful impression on Skinny, Djay dresses for the occasion. He puts on a leather jacket in the middle of summer in preparation for a meeting with his old friend. Questioned on his choice of apparel Djay says,

> I'm a step my game up
>> And get what's coming to me
>> Thank you.
>> Ain't you gonna be hot in your coat?
>> No, this is good leather, man.
>> The kind that keep you
>> At the temperature you wanna be at,[28]

This is a metaphor for modern blackness, it is always cool, whether in the street or in the suite . . .

In late capitalism this form of blackness is blackness emptied out of all potentially radical elements but which retains "stylized elements of cool that black is supposed to connote."[29] It is "a step up in game," something that adapts to changes, enabling one to fit in wherever.

Obama, Oprah, and Venus Williams embody this modern blackness. They are well heeled, well housed, and as well educated as their white counterparts. They are visible at the theater, at the Mercedes dealership, in Martha's Vineyard, some of them, and in the corporate boardroom. Never have the black middle class been so successful. But as reflected in the lives of the middle class, blackness is an identity in crisis.

Black thought has always diverged between assimilation and separation. For the generation of soul, the civil rights generation, this choice was defined by migration to the suburbs. They did so under official policies of color blindness. Color blindness recognizes that race exists but holds that one should not consider this in making decisions about who to hire or who to sell one's house to.

The 21st-century black middle class has inherited the same suburbs their parent-pioneers began to move into in the 1970s and 1980s but the political landscape has changed around them. They inhabit a postracial America. This postracial notion says if you go to the right schools and make the right choices, race no *longer matters*: the door is open, the wall of segregation has come down. This narrative defines the terms of their acceptance in greater America.

The postracial narrative has become the dominant perspective. It is the song everyone is singing. Anyone who cannot carry that tune is as welcome in corporate America as a man with a key against a chalkboard. Obama painfully discovers this when he criticized the Cambridge Police after they arrested his friend, Henry Louis Gates.

The black middle class either accepts this perspective or acts as if they do. This is simply the rule of the game.

Ralph Ellison notes that American colonists wore a racial mask, masking themselves as Indians at the Boston Tea Party.[30] The mask gave them the freedom to act. Each group wears the racial mask for the same reason. The black middle class wears the white mask—adopting the point of view of the dominant society—in order to have the freedom to move into the precincts of the mainstream.[31] But they lose the ability either to have true self-consciousness or having it to speak their minds freely.

Undeniably, also, they lose connection with the black majority in the ghetto.

Hip-hop threatens modern blackness with an older version. For the black middle class the old version represents something landlocked, segregated, and immobile.

Urban Blackness

Hip-hop represents the culture of the urban underclass for whom the veil is still unmistakably there. It is the possibility of inclusion that anchors the vision—held by the black middle class—that the veil has lifted.

But for the black majority[32] the possibility of inclusion "dangle [es] like a red cape that the bullfighters use to entice an angry bull, or better yet like a loaded crack pipe in front of a fiendin' crackhead."[33]

They seek material aspects of success of greater America but have embraced the hood as their cultural home. They refuse to assimilate. A conscious refusal to integrate with the mainstream America now characterizes those black people who willingly exist in their own world. Hip-hop is an outgrowth of this Black Nationalist sentiment, "for us, by us."

In *True to the Game,* Ice Cube denounces assimilation. "I refuse to switch, even though I could move to the snow," he says. "But you, you wanna be white and corny," "Nigger go home, spray painted on your house."[34]

Assimilation equals a kind of masquerade—trying to be white and corny—as well as a kind of betrayal. Being true to the game seems to mean something like authentic blackness. This is defined in terms of space-maintaining one's ties to the hood. Consciousness, not color, defines community. This is adumbrated with notions of hard-edged unapologetic hypermasculinity.

They embrace racial stereotypes, the stereotype of the thug or criminal, in order to embrace a ghettocentric version of black identity. From a Fanonian perspective, these ghetto-centric images represent the black skin.The black skin that the black middle class has thrown off like a garment out of fashion is one hip-hoppers pick up: to make explicit the crisis of identity that the middle class would like to deny.

Chris Rock had a skit he called "no time for fake niggas." The black middle class portrays itself as real as if authentic blackness is performed through success. Success in turn is defined by recognition (acceptance) by the dominant society—through admission to elite schools, selection by top law firms, and moving into the right neighborhoods, among other things.

For the hip-hop masses authenticity is defined in terms of recognition in the hood—the Hood comes first—according to its own values. They reject the mainstream, its perspective, and norms. On the other hand, they want the cars, the clothes, the cribs, and what money can buy.

We have a generation of black people who have decided to take what they want from the mainstream, while leaving behind what they do not embrace. Hip-hop could care less what white people have to say. As a matter of fact hip-hop more accurately wants to provoke white people and bourgie ass niggas to say something.[35]

They seek to be the new mainstream.

So who are the fake niggas? Or stated in Fanonian terms, "Who wears the mask?" The discussion of authenticity in the past has floundered on an effort to discover the relationship between hip-hop music/dress and "authentic" black culture. This is so abstract it is discursively a dead end street. What critics of hip-hop need to understand, before they can understand the lyrics of songs is the politics of the veil. As Fanon writes, confronting the stigma of race, one has two choices: "I ask others to pay attention to my skin or I ask them not be aware of it."[36] Hip-hop music is an expression of urban blackness, a form of black identity that asks others to pay attention to their skin. Skin here refers to cultural and spatial location. They are limning out a sense of collective identity, local and urban, but in a Du Boisian sense black.

Modern blackness in essence takes the other road; it asks others not to be aware of their blackness—in the past by arguing race should not matter, now by saying as a fact it does not matter.

While modern blackness exults in the individualism and freedom that comes from no longer being chained to this monolith of black identity, the freedom comes at a cost. Within the relentless individualism of modern blackness there is no room to embrace a black nationalism, or any other kind of collective strategy to deal with continuing patterns of racism. Given the terms of the Faustian bargain they have made they cannot even talk—publicly—about racism. We make this particularly clear when we examine the predicament of the first black president. Modern blackness is amphibian. If the veil has lifted, however, this archaic nationalism is no more necessary to us than gills were to the first amphibians that walked on land. If the veil has lifted the black middle-class approach makes complete sense.

But if it hasn't the critique of Ice Cube rings true. Cube focused on a claim of race treason. I have a different argument. Du Bois stated that if the veil were lifted it would result in a loss of self-consciousness—a kind of blindness. I want to spend some time explaining why I think Du Bois's prophecy has come true.

We will discuss the extent to which the black middle class is blind to the continued existence of the veil and how this represents a crisis of identity.

Bleaching Blackness

Those who can bend class and geographic position to their own purposes have the power to shape what "race" is. By reshaping race, they add to the complexity of the discourse of black identity rather than impoverishing it with "false notions."[37]

In *Dreamgirls*,[38] one of the most moving moments of the film is when Curtis Taylor (Jamie Foxx in the film) decides to replace the lead singer Effie White, played in the film by Jennifer Hudson. The group has a once in a lifetime chance to perform on television. A white television audience means that a thick, buxom black woman would not do. Jennifer Hudson's lament in the song "Heavy" was one of the breakout performances of the film.

> *You use to be so light and free. . . .*
> *Come on baba, baba lose some weight.*[39]

Although the song is sung with an upbeat exuberance the problem of being too heavy is a metaphor for being an African American woman in a world where Eurocentric standards of beauty control. Jennifer is axed despite her much greater talent, because another singer better conforms to the Eurocentric Barbie doll image of a dream girl. The episode speaks volumes not merely about how racialized America's standards of beauty are but the lengths to which blacks will go, to fit into it. Art imitates life. The Supremes, the historical referent for *Dreamgirls* was a group which performed with bouffant hairdos, long white gloves, and evening dresses—a picture of cultural assimilation, 1970s style.

DJ Run and DMC reproduced the assimilationist move of Curtis Taylor in their fusion of rap and hard rock. Run–DMC is often remembered for their 1980s act in which they appeared scowling, rapping to typical hip-hop beats. But they blew up because of their savvy use of a different musical art form.

Run–DMC gained market traction because of early appropriations of Hard Rock. Indeed they called themselves the "Kings of Rock" positioning themselves on the same level as "Elvis." Hard Rock guitar chords were layered over the beats of certain songs, including their first hit, rock box (1984). Run–DMC's Jam Master Jay (Jason-Mizell) had cut the classic breakout from "Walk this way" by Aerosmith.[40]

They became the first rap act to have their video aired on MTV, and the first rap act to appear on the cover of Rolling Stone.[41]

When Run–DMC famously performed "Walk this Way" on MTV two things happened. First they launched hip-hop into mainstream culture. But paradoxically they bowed down to the intersection of aesthetics and mainstream market reality: They had to sing a rock song, something completely removed from the black experience. This was prototypical modern blackness—the intermarriage of black ethnicity with white cultural orientation to produce a cultural hybrid.

But Curtis Taylor, Diana Ross, and Run–DMC were clearly black people trying to get over in the white world. Their imitative efforts are transparent. What modern blackness represents is the point where you are no longer pretending to fit in but you in fact have assimilated in the most intimate way. Paradoxically it involves de-racing blackness.

In *Paradise* Toni Morrison's first line is "They shoot the white girl first." In context this was artful. This is true because while there are many things important about the characters, race is not, and very little information is given about race. This sets up the mystery.

> It was important to me to demonstrate that in "Paradise," by withholding racial markers from a group of black women, among whom was one white woman, so that the reader knew everything, or almost everything, about the characters, their interior lives, their past, their faults, their strengths, except that one small piece of information which was their race. And to either care about that, like the characters, dislike them, or dismiss the characters based on the important information which was what they were really like. And if I could enforce that response in literature, it was a way of saying that race is the least important piece of information we have about another person. Forcing people to react racially to another person is to miss the whole point of humanity.[42]

Morrison's excerpt captures the spirit of modern blackness.

Whereeas the civil rights generation spoke as members of black America, the black elite today speak as individuals. The civil rights generation seemed to say we, as blacks, have a common struggle. The postracial black middle class challenges the "we." Black unity is associated with victimology. Thus, Juan Williams argues that it is the albatross of victimology that holds blacks back, not white racism.

If modern blackness has an icon it is Oprah Winfrey as its patron saint. Her show was described as "a comforting non-threatening bridge between black and white cultures."[43] Her innovation was to substitute a dialogue of rapport talk particularly between women for the masculinist report talk of then popular shows like *Donohue*. By emphasizing her identity as a woman she deemphasized her identity as a black. Through the 1970s blacks in their public discourse focused *outward* at social issues relating to the black struggle. Oprah broke with that. Using her life story of oppression as a wedge, her focus was inward at issues that were personal to women or black women—their struggles, their worries, and their dreams. In the words of the feminist slogan, "She made the personal political." Armed with stories of angels, telling countless tales about people who had turned lives around she also characteristically substituted optimism for pessimism: a sense that we had the responsibility and ability to change our lives. It was often said that Oprah transcended race. But she was still clearly a black woman albeit black now refers only to *ethnicity* not a political point of view.

Tiger Woods's famous quote about his mixed heritage was a more radical break with racial orthodoxy.

Fittingly, Woods took his stand on Oprah. Asked if it bothered him to be called an African American he replied "It does. . . . Growing up, I came up with this name: I'm a 'Cablinasian.' I'm just who I am." Woods told Oprah Winfrey, "whoever you see in front of you."[44]

Writing in online magazine Salon.com Gary Kamiya explains the acronym, "As in Caucasian-black-Indian-Asian. Woods has a black father (or to be precise, if I am interpreting Woods's reported ancestry correctly, a half-black, one-quarter American Indian, one-quarter white father) and a Thai mother (or, with the same caveat, a half-Thai, half-Chinese mother)."[45]

Soledad O'Brien, beautiful, multi-talented, fiercely intelligent host of *Black in America* updated this and expressed this idea best. When asked about her heritage, she responds with a story about the many strands of her ancestry:

My mother is black and also Latina, more specifically Cuban. She is a devout Catholic who credits the Virgin Mary with any success she's had in this country. My father was Irish and Scottish, but from

Australia, and my parents added Teresa when I was confirmed. . . .
I'm black and Cuban, Australian and Irish, and like most people in
America, I'm someone whose roots come from somewhere else.[46]

Race is no more important to her heritage than her mother's religion,
her kinky hair is relevant less as a statement of who she is than something
that she has to deal with and comb through. The host of CNN's *Black in
America*, she nonetheless never refers to black people in the first person. It
is not clear how she gets to where she is. Perhaps she sees blackness simply an aspect of ancestry. Or perhaps it is merely a construct, something
that exists only in the realm of perception, in the eye of the mind. I don't
know but what is clear is that race is not central to her identity. Her job,
what she does, defines her more than color.

Q: Who are you? How do you define yourself?
A: I would have to say what day are we talking about? Are we talk-
         ing about the days where I am dashing to school with my kids, then
         I am a mom. If I am late for a meeting in the office, then I am a work-
         ing mom. Am I out to dinner with my husband, on one of our rare
         dates alone, then I am a wife, been married 15 years to a guy I met
         in college, who has been my best friend forever. I am a journalist. If
         I am knee-deep in covering a story, like Haiti, then I am a journalist,
         a working journalist, covering breaking news. If I am doing a docu-
         mentary and on a plane, then I am a reporter working on a story that
         sometimes takes literally years to get done. So I guess I am a lot of
         things, so my identity is all based on where I am at the moment.[47]

Black is in the mix, but it is not in the core, it adds a hint of color but it
does not capture identity. They simply happen to be black, as some happen
to be tall or short.
   As Bonnie M. Davis wrote, "My father is black, and my mother is
white, but their race does not define me."[48]

The Declaration of Independence

This loosening of the knot between race and identity reflects the idea that
blackness is a box. They feel that notions of being loyal to a group or

struggle is limiting. Stephen Carter spoke for many when in a recent book he made his declaration of independence.

> To be black and intellectual in America is to live in a box. So I live in a box, not of my own making and on that box is a label, not of my own choosing. Most of those who have not met me, and many of those who have, see the box and read the label and imagine they have seen me. . . . As an intellectual struggling to escape from other's preconceptions I find development of loyalty test particularly distressing.[49]

In Carter's fiercely individualistic perspective solidarity reflects the old racial politics of victimhood, something modern blackness rejects. Similarly Randall Kennedy called the black man who achieves this attitude an ideal. "the unencumbered self."[50]

> I reject the notion of racial kinship. I do so in order to avoid its burdens and to be free to claim what the distinguished political theorist Michael Sandel labels "the unencumbered self." The unencumbered self is free and independent, "unencumbered by aims and attachments it does not choose for itself."[51]

Touré gives all this a contemporary spin. He analogizes traditional blackness to religion or belonging to a church. Many free thinking people have abandoned traditional religion. They often say "I am spiritual but not religious." Touré captures something similar with the notion that "there are 40 million ways to be black."[52]

What emerges from this declaration of independence seems to be that the individual member of black elite has no obligation to blacks in general or the black underclass in particular. At least, they have no more obligation than someone who is white.

John Ridley, an African American Huffington Post Blogger and NPR contributor made this point explicitly. He wrote, in his 2006 *Esquire Magazine Piece,* "The Manifesto of Ascendancy for the Modern American Nigger,"

> So I say this: It's time for ascended blacks to wish niggers good luck. Just as whites may be concerned with the good of all citizens but don't travel their days worrying specifically about the well being of

hillbillies from Appalachia, we need to send niggers on their way. We need to start extolling the most virtuous of ourselves. It is time to celebrate the New Black Americans—those who have sealed the Deal, who aren't beholden to liberal indulgence any more than they are to the disdain of the hard Right. It is time to praise blacks who are merely undeniable in their individuality and exemplary in their levels of achievement.[53]

Even being the wife of the president provides no cover against this class-based prejudice. When Michelle Obama was about to visit Martha's Vineyard, one anonymous member of the black elite basically turned up her nose.

[S]he's basically a ghetto girl. That's what she says—I'm just being sociological. She grew up in the same place that Jennifer Hudson did. If Mrs. Obama were light skinned with Hazel eyes maybe she would be a little more tolerable.[54]

The Bargain

If Oprah, Woods, and O'Brien are stars in the pantheon of modern blackness, Obama is the sun. In popular culture there are two stories about Obama. It is often said in the media that Obama is the first black president. This story is a narrative of ascent, about "a skinny kid with a funny name who believes that America has a place for him too."[55] Obama is often seen also as the first postracial president. He, Obama, personifies the empowerment that comes from the highest levels of achievement: for the majority of America's electorate his race simply did not matter.

We've had black presidents before. But this was only on the silver screen— Morgan Freeman in *Deep Impact*,[56] Dennis Haysbert in *24*.[57] In all cases they were portrayed as charismatic American leaders who just happened to be black. They transcended race. But they did and they didn't. They transcended it only by abandoning any conscious reference or identification with blackness. They were black in a hybrid sense. Black skin but the language, dress, the spaces they move in, the people that surround them, their pedigree, and their values are those of the dominant group. It is not that two worlds, one black and one white, no longer exist—as transcendence would truly imply. Rather their hyrbridity allows them to move between two worlds. Obama might agree with this,

> As it was I learned to slip back and forth between my black and white worlds, understanding that each possessed its own language and customs and structures of meaning, convinced that with a bit of translation on my part the two worlds would eventually cohere.[58]

But this amphibian behavior is tricky magic. In *Somewhere in Time*[59] Christopher Reeve plays a man who is able to move between two worlds as well. He finds a penny from a bygone era. He concentrates very hard visualizing that other world of long ago while holding the penny. Magically he returns to this time in the past. But if his mind returns to the world of the present—which he comes from—the spell is broken and he returns. Consider what happens when Obama made the comment about the police in the case of Henry Louis Gates. Gates was a victim in an outrageous instance of racial profiling. Gates was arrested in his own house because the policeman, who barges in and essentially accuses Gates of being a burglar, did not think that the Harvard Law Professor was deferential enough.[60] Obama in an unguarded moment of candor stated that "the police acted stupidly."[61] I cheered. I thought his word choice was excellent.

It needed to be said.

The American electorate was horrified. "[As a candidate] race transcendence was a narrative around him. So whenever he talks about race, he becomes racialized, he becomes the black candidate."[62] His race-consciousness broke the spell—his hybridity was gone. The magic was gone. Like Christopher Reeve's character, he lost his ability to move between two worlds. Obama apologized to Sgt. Crowley over his remarks on the Gates arrest, saying of both men, "[t]hose are two decent people."[63] That was not enough. The magic does not return until he convenes a "beer summit" at the White House. Said Adam Serwer, "now we know what a black man can't do—not if he's president and not if he wants to get anything done: He can't tell white people something about race they aren't willing to hear, no matter how true it is."[64]

Denial

Certain things go with the territory. July and hot days. The beach and sand. Ice and cold. What goes with the idea of modern blackness is a sense that racism in the main is past.

This idea is anchored by an accelerating, snowballing narrative of black success: The number of black elected officials exceeds 10,000; there is a sixfold increase in black–white marriages between 1960 and 2000[65]; popular culture is breaking down racial barriers, there is an explosion of black entrepreneurs, and formally we are now protected by equal opportunity laws.[66] Implicit here is the idea that success or failure is determined by individual choices and will. The black middle class—though clearly in different degrees—takes this idea very seriously.

The problem is the paradox, the duality of the racial moment we inhabit. One side of this duality is defined by the titles, credentials, suburban homes, and other trappings of success the black middle class has achieved. The other side of the duality is captured by a phenomenon described best in the words of Gramsci. After defeating 19th-century Italian fascism, Gramsci wrote "[W]hen the state trembled a sturdy structure was revealed."[67] He writes, "The state was only an outer ditch behind which stood a sturdy system of fortresses and earthworks."[68] In our case that fortress is constituted by the ideas—myths—about race that propped up slavery and alter segregation. While those institutions have passed away, notions of black inferiority are still deeply embedded in our culture.[69]

The veil is still there.

The veil in the past was quite visible, constituted as it was by laws and well-known customs of exclusion. What I speak of as the "unlifted veil" is largely invisible: it is constituted by unconscious racism or institutional practices that continue to result in systemic racial exclusion.

We have talked about "invisible" racism in the context of the black underclass. But this kind of exclusion affects the black middle class as well. My starting point here is that the black middle class is itself an oxymoron. Middle class has historically meant privileged. The black middle class is systemically less privileged than their white counterparts. There is still a separation, subtle but pervasive, between two realms of social life, one— white and one black— defined by lack of privilege or status. In the next few pages we will unflinchingly look at realities that show how real the veil still is.

The Unlifted Veil

To confront the reality I am talking about, let us begin by recalling the moment on February 17, 2009, when Obama signed the stimulus bill into law. On February 18, 2009, a *New York Post* cartoon depicting two police officers shooting a chimpanzee sparked a national controversy over Obama and race.

As the chimp lays dead the caption reads, "They'll have to find someone else to write the next stimulus bill."

The Obama Chimpanzee slur captures the duality of the black middle-class condition.[70]

It was hilariously obvious that the chimpanzee cartoon was a reference to Obama. To paraphrase Jesse Jackson "hands that have picked cotton" have indeed picked a president. And that president is portrayed in the mainstream media as a chimp. At its most benign, the cartoon suggests that the stimulus bill was so bad monkeys may as well have written it.

But through a historical lens it was not benign.

In the 19th century and well into the 20th, popular media—from movies to fiction to political cartoons—frequently portrayed blacks as more simian than human. It was an association that provided at different times cover for slavery, as well as antiblack violence. Lynchings in the United States were often justified by relying on this dehumanizing association. It surfaced in the Rodney King controversy in Los Angeles: Laurence Powell, an officer at Los Angeles Police Department, had referred to a black couple as "something right out of 'Gorillas in the Mist' "[71] moments before he was involved in the King beating. Like nooses, the N word and white sheets, referring to blacks as apelike is among the most violent and hurtful legacies of our nation's difficult racial past.

Fittingly Rev. Al Sharpton wrote,

> The cartoon in today's *New York Post* is troubling at best given the historic racist attacks of African-Americans as being synonymous with monkeys. The ape image though not explicitly racist has been so deeply associated in history with blacks that to portray a black person as an ape symbolically evokes that whole racial history.[72]

Sharpton's analysis was echoed by social scientists Jennifer Eberhardt and Phillip Goff.

Eberhardt of Stanford and University of Pennsylvania psychologist Phillip Goff did a study which found that students tested at those two schools subliminally associated blacks with apes.[73] The scientists described the study:

> In one study, for example, we exposed some participants to words such as "chimp," "gorilla" and "orangutan" flashed on a computer screen at such a rapid rate that they could not be consciously detected. Next, we asked all the participants to watch a two-minute videotape of police officers who had surrounded a suspect and were violently subduing him. Some participants were led to believe that the suspect was white; others were led to believe he was black.[74]
>   What did we find?
>   When the participants were led to believe that the suspect was white, exposing them to the ape words beforehand made no difference in their judgments about the use of force displayed in the video. However, when participants believed the suspect was black, those who were exposed to the words thought the police officers were more justified in the amount of force they used. They thought that the black suspect deserved the violence that was directed at him.[75]

Returning to the image of the chimpanzee shot dead by police, the linkage to Obama—who's going to sign the stimulus bill—it seems to say that perhaps Obama "should get his." Anthony Asadullah wrote, "prior to the deaths of Presidents Lincoln and Kennedy, and even black leaders like Malcolm and King, incendiary political cartoons made the publishing rounds suggesting they were better dead than as living advocates of unpopular social action."[76]

Given this subliminal linkage the cartoon delivers a symbolic message—it operates as code. It was calculated to have maximum effect on angry whites who have never accepted the idea of a black president. For them it operates in essence as a dog whistle. As Beau Friedlander wrote, "*The New York Post* today ran a cartoon that splashed classic dog-whistle racism (in black and white no less)."[77]

One animalistic trope deserves another: Senator Rusty Depass referred to one of Michelle Obama's ancestors as a gorilla. In a Facebook comment *regarding* a report about a gorilla escaped at a zoo, Rusty Depass wrote, "I'm sure it's just one of Michelle's ancestors—probably harmless."[78] More recently Boston police officer Justin Barret in an e-mail referred to Harvard Professor Henry Louis Gates as a "banana eating jungle monkey."[79] Barrett says of Gates, if he had been the officer he (Gates) had verbally assaulted "[L]ike a banana-eating jungle monkey, I would have sprayed him with OC."[80] OC, by the way, is pepper spray.

The generation that wanted to sing "We have overcome" now must ask instead, "How far have we come?" The black middle class goes to black tie dinners, gala balls, and eats escargot. They are George Jefferson and Weezy, moving with swag into deluxe apartments and gated estates; they are the Huxtables with doctorate degrees, and fine cars, living the dream. They've moved up, blended in, and become role models. Yet every day they must confront racism like that which oozes like sleaze from the pages of the *Daily News*.

The black middle class also continues to face covert racial tropes about black skin as something that contaminates in close quarters. Althea Wright, Director, The Creative Steps Day-Care Center, contracted to use the Valley Swim Club in Huntingdon Valley, once a week. The children ages kindergarten through the seventh grade visited the swim club on June 29, 2009. During the first visit some children said, "They heard club members asking why African-American children were there."[81] According to CNN, "One of the boys told the Philadelphia Inquirer that a woman at the club said she feared the children 'might do something' to her child."[82] A few days later the swim club returned the Creative Steps Day-Care Center's check of $1,950.00. John Dueler, president of the Swim Club, told two Philadelphia television stations that the children had changed "the complexion" and "atmosphere" of the club.[83]

This incident made headlines because of the popular perception that both geography—the suburban setting—and a sturdy structure of equal opportunity laws insulated these middle-class blacks from Jim Crow style segregation. But to paraphrase Faulkner "the past is not dead."[84] If the dividing line between the era of segregation and our postracial era is thought of as a railroad track, the blacks in the suburbs of today have moved across the tracks but yet they are still dangerously close. It doesn't run them over but it is so close to them that it rattles their windows and they can hear the shriek of the whistle real loud as the train rumbles by.

In the past, moving geographically—from the hood to the burbs—meant moving from a black area to a predominantly white one—with concomitant improvement in quality of life. A neighborhood's racial makeup is still "frequently a proxy for the things that really count—quality of schools, security, appreciating property values, political clout, and the availability of desirable amenities (like swimming pools)."[85] In black suburban enclaves living in the suburbs does not necessarily mean all that.

As Mary Pattillo-McCoy tells us, in her brilliant treatment of the lives of middle-class blacks,

> [B]lack middle class neighborhoods are often located next to predominately black areas with much higher poverty rates. As a result blacks of all socioeconomic statuses tend to be confined to limited geographic space, which is formally designated by the discriminatory practices of banks, insurance companies, and urban planners. . . . Researchers at the Rockefeller institute . . . report that 78 percent of Chicago's African Americans live in majority black tracts. . . . In all nine primary metropolitan statistical areas (PMSA's) including Atlanta, Baltimore, Chicago, Detroit, Houston, Los Angeles, New York, Philadelphia, and Washington D.C., 68 percent of black Households with annual earnings over $45,000 and 58% of black households earning over 75,000 live in majority black census tracks.[86]

Thus, for blacks the ghetto and the suburbs are not entirely distinct. As Pattillo-McCoy put it, the ghetto has its "core and periphery areas."

> Middle class blacks have attempted to leave behind their poor neighbors in ghetto areas—only to relocate to peripheral areas abutting their previous residences. In the contemporary African American ghetto there are still the best, mixed and worst areas. This situation is the result of both the continuous out-migration of middle class blacks and the racially segregated housing market they encounter in their attempts to move.[87]

Thus, the black middle class has always attempted to leave [the ghetto] but has never been able to get very far.

One problem is an expanding poverty core. In McCoy's study of a black middle-class community called Groveland, she noted from the 1970s through the 1990s increasing outmigration of the urban poor into that area. "The percentage of families with incomes below the poverty line also rose from 5 to 10 to 12 percent in 1970, 1980, and 1990 respectively."[88]

They have moved across the tracks but they can still hear the whistle and feel the rumble of the train. "Even the most affluent blacks are not able to escape from crime, for they reside in communities as crime prone as those housing the poorest whites."

So the ghetto follows blacks even as they try to flee from it. This is true on a cultural sense as well, as Henry Louis Gates discovered when he moved into his tony neighborhood at Harvard. Blacks carry their ghetto with them in their skin. This has something to do with why blacks pay more for loans.[89] During the sub-prime crisis more than half of black borrowers received sub-prime loans, while only one-fifth of white borrowers did.[90]

It also has something to do with why blacks with a college degree earn 70 cents for every dollar whites earn, possess 23 cents of every dollar of wealth owned by similarly situated whites.[91] Melvin L. Oliver and Thomas M. Shapiro write that there are really two middle classes, one white, one black. A sturdy "pillar" of wealth supports the white middle class; the black middle class lacks this pillar of support. Members of the black middle class make their homes on the ledge of affluent society always one misstep away from falling back into the ghetto.

The Tea Party's Racial Mask

Gun owners are the new niggers . . . of society.

—John Aquilino

When the American colonists revolted against Great Britain they painted themselves as Indians and threw tea into the Boston harbor. The racial mask as Ellison has called it provided something more than a mere disguise. By assuming the identity of savages it freed them from the inhibitions native to Englishmen.

The disguise freed men from the full responsibility for their deeds and perhaps too from revenge against their manhood. After all, it was mere women [or mere blacks, or indeed black women] who were acting in a disorderly way.[92]

Imagining themselves as 21st-century heirs of the Boston Tea Party, Fox News figures Sarah Palin and Glenn Beck led a backlash live in the media against Obama.

Exploiting the anger and frustration of working families who have lost jobs, homes, and dreams in the deepest recession in 70 years, the tea party spurs its followers into action with speeches about immigrants taking our jobs, and that welfare is subsidy for ghetto blacks who use the money to buy drugs. Doubling down on the politics of division, their central message is: Blacks and other minorities have made progress at white expense. The central figure in this story is of course Obama.

They are united by their unwillingness to accept a black man as president.

Today they are hunkered down in a paranoid crouch convinced their country has been stolen from them by a usurper—a man so illegitimate they believe he is not even an American citizen, much less a qualified leader . . . their militia is made up of former members of the "Patriot" movement. John Birchers, white Supremacists, "Birthers," and various other permutations of the radical fringe.[93]

Carrying signs—often misspelled—they charge variously that Obama is a socialist, an imposter, and sometimes a joker—often depicting him in greasepaint with the Joker's red disfigured lips.[94]

But it is not merely Obama who is masked; they wear a mask themselves. The tea party story, in which they depict themselves as whites dispossessed of their birthrights, is itself a mask. In essence they, as whites, switch places with blacks. In their narrative of imposition they turn the moral universe upside down. Now it is blacks who are in power. Whites are oppressed.

This narrative, like the warpaint of those who threw the tea overboard, seems to give this group the freedom from social constraints so much so that members of the tea party attacked—spit on—members of congress during the health care debate of 2009.[95]

"They were shouting the N-word," Carson said. "It was like a page out of a time machine."[96] Carson said Capitol Police surrounded the group and escorted them across the street to the Capitol. And staffers and Members reported seeing Rep. Barney Frank (D-Mass.) slurred for being a homosexual and a protester spitting on Rep. Emanuel Cleaver (D-Mo.), another African American lawmaker.[97]

This is subliminally an appropriation of blackness in two ways. First, this white riot—white noise—clearly imitates and mirrors earlier rebellions by blacks against governmental authority. Through this performance they seem to say black people have taken over their government and they—the new oppressed (the new niggers?)—will take it back, by any means necessary. Whiteness has been associated with the law and order, with authority. Blackness is associated with the object of law. In the real world blacks are powerless while whites, the dominant majority, are powerful. Upending the true order in the world, in tea party ideology, power relations are reversed—so is the meaning of black and white.

What has most clearly defined blackness in the post–civil rights era has been an aggressive masculinity, a hip thuggishness expressed in saggy pants, twisty braids, and the attitude of the MCs. The tea party in many ways out-thugs the urban gangsters. They are the first ideological thugs. Dr. Laura Schlessinger responded to a woman who called in for counseling about a husband who used racial slurs. Instead of denouncing this racism she repeated the N word over and over as if for fun.[98] It was deliberate, gratuitous, and in a real sense obscene. Sarah Palin responded to this breach of decency by saying, "Don't apologize reload!"[99]

They know little about the constitution but more importantly have no respect for constraints like equal justice under law. So they propose an Arizona Immigration Bill which implicitly calls for profiling of Mexicans. They propose to drug test welfare recipients even though there is no evidence welfare mothers abuse drugs at rates any different from those on social security.

But what is more stunning is that—as the incident in the capital shows—they—some of them—are thugs in the most literal and physical sense as when they physically attacked members of the black caucus.

It was this ignorant thuggishness which prompted a moment of unguarded honesty from Senator Byrd. Speaking of whites "Who are still opposed to civil rights," a thinly veiled reference to the tea party, Senator Byrd said, "I've seen a lot of white niggers in my time, I'm hoping to use that word."

In *The White Negro,* Norman Mailer argued that "white negroes" are outsiders to dominant society and draw much of their inspiration from "black life."[100] Mailer's white Negroes acted out "the myths and evaluations ascribed to fantasized black people long resident in the social memory of dominant culture."[101]

Perhaps the most dramatic instance of this racial masquerade takes place when Glenn Beck called a "march on Washington" dubbing it "liberty evangelism." This is first of all an appropriation of history.

Taylor branch called Glenn Beck Dr. King's latest marcher.[102] I would go further, Glenn Beck portrayed himself as a new "Reverend Dr. King" with angry, mostly white people as his audience on the mall. Beck preached a gospel of division and discrimination while at the same time portraying Obama as "a racist."[103]

Historically, conservatives have condemned the identity politics of the civil right movement as tribalism: "diversity leaders enflame their 'victim' groups to dwell on their grievances and to demand retribution. The victims must proclaim fidelity to their separate cultural or ideological tribes against the general culture."[104]

Ironically, the Tea Party Express acts precisely like a tribe of whites motivated by fears of political and cultural envelopment.

In many ways they not only appropriate the story of oppression from blacks but also appropriate elements of hip-hop. Hip-hop has been accused of minstrelsy, of being 21st-century blackface. But blackface originally was a way of crossing cultural frontiers. "For trade to occur frontiers have to be established that can be crossed, or zones created in which different peoples may come together with impunity. These sanctuaries are fire free zones, places in which difference itself, especially stylistic difference, is highly valued."[105]

W. T. Lhamon traces the origins of blackface to dances by blacks, slaves, and freedman at the Catherine Market, between Manhattan and Brooklyn.

After the Jersey Negroes had disposed of their master's produce at the "Bear Market," which sometimes was early done, and then the advantage of a late tide, they would "shin it" for the Catherine Market to enter lists with Long Islanders, and in the end an equal division of the proceeds took place. The success which attended them brought our city Negroes down there, who, after a time, even exceeded them both, and if money was not to be had "they would dance for a bunch of eels or fish.[106]

Whites laughed at them of course, but, presaging the seductiveness of modern hip-hop, they also wanted to emulate them, to be them. These marks of grace they appreciated and wanted to absorb. They wanted to overlay this black cachet on their own identities even as their own identity.

Thus, Lhamon writes,

We want to dance too. Let's shin it. Ourselves. . . . Shucking our constraints, let's admit their old, and large ambition is also ours. . . . Fascination adheres in these gestures. . . . To coin these gestures was to produce currency for exchange . . . [w]e can see their economy: the conditions of their cultural transmission. It is pretty to think that we might all share "in the proceeds." We all want those eels.[107]

The original blackface performers were black. However, whites, seeing the ability of blackface to communicate across cultures, appropriated it.

When white actors in *Vaudeville* wanted to perform as comedians they did so in blackface. Popular from 1848 to the 1960s, white blackface performers in the past used burnt cork and later greasepaint or shoe polish to blacken their skin. They exaggerated their lips, and often wore woolly wigs, gloves, tailcoats, or ragged clothes to complete the transformation. In the process they debased it, as an art form.

As Hazel Carby notes, the appropriation of black art is not new. But here we are talking about appropriation of blackness, not merely the pirating of black culture—Elvis Presley style—but the appropriation of identity itself.

In a way Sarah Palin, with her tag line—"What is the difference between a soccer mom and a pit bull? Lipstick."[108]—did something similar to the minstrelsy of *Vaudeville*. This was "gangster." She, Glenn Beck, and others are spoken word artists who appropriate the conditions of cultural transmission used by rappers—posturing as hyperaggressive performers they transgress traditional boundaries of culture. Fittingly, a conservative rapper, Lloyd Marcus, who performs the lines in staccato hip-hop style, does the tea party anthem.

Mr. President! Your stimulus is sure to bust.
It's just a socialistic scheme.
The only thing it will do, is kill the American Dream.[109]

The piano which accompanies the rap is somewhere between pop and country. But the rhythm and body motions are a poor but unmistakable version of hip-hop. All that's missing is the beat. Rap is an art form which in its rhythmic qualities traces back to African traditions. Ironically, Marcus while opportunistically choosing rap as the medium of expression says loudly in a weak voice, "I am not an African-American," I am an "Ameri-can." Like the white *Vaudeville* chameleons, who put on shoe polish to be black for the length of the performance, they wrap themselves up in this urban culture for a brief moment. It is Mike Hill who says what is at the end of white desire—is something that whiteness cannot have and still be white.[110] Baldwin talked about "The sunlit prison of the American

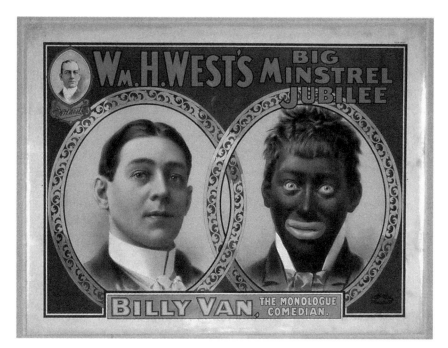

White actor in black face. (Library of Congress)

dream."[111] Culturally, whiteness is imprisoning; it is a box. This is true because there are certain modes of feeling and expression that lie beyond the precincts of whiteness.

The blackness of blackness is a deep soulfulness. Blacks express in all of their oral art forms from blues to the spoken word. So Tea Partiers briefly shin it with the black rapper to absorb blackness—in depoliticized form. At the same time they refuse to relinquish being white.

If there were any doubt about the tea party appropriating black culture, listen to rapper Polatik who put it down in classic hip-hop style, the beat is gangster,

> *I didn't know I had the power to fire officials*
> *We could break this dependency that keeps our cities cripple.*[112]

With that intro David Suacedo, Polatik as he dubs himself, launches into an attack on abortion rights—"black and Hispanic babies killed by the millions," the "evil" of raising the debt ceiling. Incredibly talented, he generates tremendous energy. He has found a way to track the tea party line that government is simply an obstacle in the way of freedom, that the democrats are not leaders but deceivers, and that the conservative ideology is not a political perspective rooted in the interests of the elite—which it is—but a popular movement.

Hip-hop grew out of anger, alienation, a yearning of urban youth for a voice. He appropriates this spirit asking, through his songs, the audience to imagine the tea party conservatives among American economic elite as a voiceless oppressed. Through the songs the crowds seem to express solidarity, a freedom from inhibition—they whoop like crowds at a hip-hop concert. Hip-hop speaks to aspiration to limn out a local identity separate from the universal of blackness—they are blacks from the hood. They share a sense of being harder and more authentic for that. There is here a sense of local identity as well. While for urban blacks it is created by their social isolation, for the tea party crowd it is as a result of their political marginalization.

It's tribal, it's "in your face Mr. President," it appeals to emotion rather than reason. It allows suburban whites to immerse themselves in black urban culture to step out of white identity momentarily. This is blackface.

Blackface is always an effort to achieve a kind of inversion. In *Inside the Minstrel's Mask,* Annemarie Bean and James Vernon Hatch link blackface to "times of radical change."[113] Barbara Babcock Abrahams has likened stage tricksters to E.J. Hobsbawm's "primitive rebels": those backward marginal antinomians who demonstrate quite literally that "oppression can be turned upside down."[114] Natalie Davis describes blackface performances as "safety valves" that deflect attention away from social reality. This fits the tea party moment like a glove.

They have turned oppression upside down. While the black majority is overwhelmingly poor, the tea party is funded by oil billionaires who don't want to be regulated. The white males of the tea party have grown up in a world in which blacks still earn three-fifths of what whites earn. As of 2011, while blacks comprise 12.1 percent of the population, they comprise 5.3 percent of the lawyers,[115], 2 percent of elected officials,[116] 5.3 percent of the physicians,[117] 5.2 percent of the architects and engineers,[118] and 6.1 of college and university professors.[119]

In this ethos they seem to say that blacks are now in power. While they brand themselves after the revolutionaries of the Boston Tea Party, their message does not resonate with the egalitarian rhetoric that defined the revolution. Jefferson in the Declaration of Independence spoke of universal ideals: "all men are created equal." Their rhetoric seems to say "just us." Their revolution is not about universal ideals, it is about race. They are less like Jeffersonian rebels than they are like white citizen groups in the South that banded together to oppose reconstruction—I'm thinking of the Jayhawkers, the White Camelias, and the Klan. Reconstruction, which lasted roughly from 1868 to 1877, was the period in which the North fastened black "suffrage" on a defeated South.[120] This new regime of rights for blacks was enforced by the encampment of Northern troops on Southern soil.

Reconstruction ended when Northern republicans—the party of Lincoln—agreed to remove the troops from the South in exchange for winning a Presidential election.[121] Once the troops left the Klan disenfranchised blacks through a variety of means ranging from the subterfuge of "Grandfather" clauses to open threats of violence.[122] This battle of Southern whites to take back their country was dramatized in the film *Birth of a Nation* in 1915. The tea party narrative—"we are going to take our country back"—could have been taken from that film. They are acting as if this is the second reconstruction and they are putting an end to it. The mask of the

Klan was a mask of bed sheets. The mask of the tea party, a racial mask, is the mask of themselves as an oppressed group.

Fusion

Beck, Palin, and Cain exploit the fluidity of racial identity. Now that race has become a continuum in which individuals choose their positions by cultural attitude and style, why can't whites get in the game? Palin and Beck, the new "Wiggers," are saying, "We want to dance too." Their smashmouth styles of rhetoric, and hyperaggressiveness—when they attack members of the black caucus; their civil rights marching; their explicit use of hip-hop form in the creation of their anthem are all part of a perverse fusion of urban cultural styles and a white political agenda.

Notes

1. W.E.B. Du Bois, "Of Our Spiritual Strivings," in *The Souls of Black Folk*, ed. John Edgar Wideman (New York: Library of America, 1990).
2. Charles F. Peterson, *Du Bois, Fanon, Cabral: The Margins of Elite and Colonial Leadership* (Plymouth, UK: Rowman & Littlefield, 2007), 14.
3. Du Bois, *The Souls of Black Folk*, 7.
4. Peterson, *Du Bois, Fanon, Cabral*, 17.
5. Charles Shepardson, *Lacan and the Limits of Language* (New York: Fordham University Press, 2008), 127.
6. Karen Coats, *Looking Glasses and Never-Lands: Lacan, Desire, and Subjectivity in Children's Literature* (Iowa City, IA: Iowa University Press, 2004), 19.
7. Peterson, *Du Bois, Fanon, Cabral*, 15.
8. Peterson, *Du Bois, Fanon, Cabral*, 15.
9. Frantz Fanon, *Black Skin, White Masks* (New York: Grove Press, 2008), 127.
10. *Gone with the Wind*, DVD, directed by George Cuckor, Victor Fleming, 1939, (Burbank, CA: Warner Home Video, 2000).

11. *Soul Plane*, DVD, directed by Jessie Terrero (Beverly Hills, CA: Metro-Goldwyn Mayer, 2004).

12. See Ellis Cose, *The Envy of the World: On Being a Black Man in America* (New York: Simon and Schuster, 2002).

13. Denene Miller, Angela Burt Murray, and Mirzi Miller, *The Angry Black Woman's Guide to Life* (New York City: Plume, 2004).

14. Ed Guerrero, *Framing Blackness: The African-American Image on Film* (Philadelphia: Temple University Press, 1993), 123.

15. Gail Bederman, " 'Civilization,' the Decline of Middle-Class Manliensss and Ida B. Wells Anti-Lynching Campaign (1892–94)," in *Radical History Review*, ed. Barbara Smith, 52 (1992): 9.

16. Fanon, *Black Skin, White Masks*, 105.

17. William Shakespeare, Burton Rafael, and Harold Bloom, *The Tempest* (New York: Infobase Publishing, 2006), xxi.

18. Fanon, *Black Skin, White Masks*, 175.

19. George Yancy, *Black Bodies, White Gazes: The Continuing Significance of Race* (Lanham, MD: Rowman-Littlefield, 2008), 86.

20. 342 U.S. 350 (1952).

21. Gordon J. Beggs, "Novel Expert Evidence in Federal Civil Rights Litigation," *The American University Law Review* 45 (1995): 2.

22. AC360°, "Doll Study Revisited, Girl Calls Her Skin Nasty," August 12, 2010, http://ac360.blogs.cnn.com/2010/08/12/ac360°-doll-study-revisited-girl-calls-her-skin-"nasty"/?iref=allsearch (lst visited January 3, 2013).

23. Howard Winant, *The New Politics of Race: Globalism, Difference, Justice* (Minneapolis: University of Minnesota Press, 2004), 28.

24. Todd Boyd, *The New HNIC: The Death of Civil Rights and the Reign of Hip-Hop* (New York: New York University Press, 2004), 35.

25. Du Bois, *The Souls of Black Folk*.

26. In an essay entitled, "It's Your Nigger Problem Not Hip-Hop's" Marc Anthony Neal divides the trope of blackness between the concept associated with the blacks of "pre-twentieth century American South" which he describes in spatial terms: it was "landlocked, entitled, and static." The more modern version the trope he describes as "mobile, fluid, and adaptable." See Marc Anthony Neal, "It's Your Nigger

Problem Not Hip-Hop's," *The New Black Magazine*, April 27, 2007, http://www.thenewblackmagazine.com/view.aspx?index=737.

27. Craig Brewer, *Hustle and Flow*, DVD (Los Angeles, CA: Paramount Pictures, 2005), B000I52LVS.

28. Brewer, *Hustle and Flow.*

29. David L. Andrews and Steven J. Jackson, *Sport Stars: The Cultural Politics of Sporting Celebrity* (New York: Psychology Press, 2001), 103.

30. Ralph Ellison, *Shadow and Act* (New York: Random House, 1995), 53–54.

31. This is of course complex. This is not an issue of authenticity. At this point in our history, color no longer reliably predicts cultural orientation. Many blacks who are culturally white are certainly being true to themselves as individuals. But there can be no question as to whether there is a dominant group in this society and that the perspective, values, and culture of this dominant group—which in Fanonian terms is the white perspective—is privileged by the media, by educational institutions, and corporate culture.

32. The official story is that the majority of blacks are middle class. I disagree.

33. Boyd, *The New HNIC.*

34. Ice Cube, "True to the Game," *Death Certificate* (Priority/Emi Records, 1991), B000003B7W, CD.

35. Boyd, *The New HNIC*, 10.

36. Fanon, *Black Skin, White Masks*, 197.

37. J. Martin Favor, *Authentic Blackness: The Folk in the New Negro Renaissance* (Durham, NC: Duke University Press, 1999), 22.

38. *Dreamgirls*, DVD, directed by Bill Condon (Universal City, CA: Dreamworks, 2006); see also, Darlene Millner and Bill Condon, *Dreamgirls* (New York: Harper-Collins, 2006).

39. Millner and Condon *Dreamgirls*, 120.

40. By Todd Souvignier, *The World of DJs and the Turntable Culture* (Milwaukee, WI: Hal Leonard Corporation, 2003).

41. Mickey Hess, *Icons of Hip Hop: An Encyclopedia of the Movement, Music, and Culture*, vol. 1 (Westport, CT: Greenwood Press, 2007), 82.

42. Kelly Lynch Reames, *Women and Race in Contemporary U.S. Writing: From Faulkner to Morrison* (New York: McMillan, 2007), 151.

43. Trystan T. Cotten and Kimberly Springer, *Stories of Oprah: The Oprahfication of American Culture* (Oxford, MS: University of Mississippi Press, 2010), 21.

44. Gary Kamika, "Cablanasian Like Me," *Salon Magazine*, April 30, 1997.

45. Kamika, "Cablanasian Like Me."

46. Soledad O'Brien, "Soledad O'Brien Explores Mixed-Race Heritage," *CNN Living*, May 13, 2010, http://www.cnn.com/2010/LIVING/05/13/soledad.obrien.heritage/index.html?iref=allsearch

47. O'Brien, "Soledad O'Brien Explores Mixed-Race Heritage."

48. Bonnie M. Davis, *The Biracial and Multiracial Student Experience: A Journal to Racial Literacy* (Thousand Oaks, CA: Corwin Press, 2009), 136.

49. Stephen Carter, *Reflections of an Affirmative Action Baby* (New York: Basic Books, 1991), 1. At a later point in the book Carter states that he embraces "racial pride" and to some degree "solidarity." "We need unity . . . in the sense of group love. Few ethnic groups have made progress . . . without the aid of temporary solidarity." In essence he argues that "self-reliance" and "solidarity" are not inconsistent. Carter, *Reflections of an Affirmative Action Baby*, 241.

50. Randall Kennedy, "My Race Problem and Ours," *The Atlantic Online*, May 1997. http://www.theatlantic.com/past/docs/issues/97may/kennedy.htm

51. Kennedy, "My Race Problem and Ours."

52. Toure, *"Who's Afraid of Post-Blackness? What It means to Be Black Now* (New York: Simon and Schuster, 2011).

53. John Ridley, "The Manifesto of Ascendency for the Modern American Nigger," *The Daily Voice*, November 30, 2006, http://thedailyvoice.com/voice/2009/06/first-lady-called-ghetto-girl-002037.php

54. John L. Reynolds, "First Lady Called Ghetto Girl by Martha's Vineyard's Elite," *The Daily Voice*, June 25, 2009, http://www.esquire.com/features/ESQ1206BLACKESSAY_108 quoting an anonymous member of Martha's Vineyard's black elite.

55. Barack Obama, "Senator Obama's Speech at the Democratic National Convention in Boston, Massachusetts on Tuesday, July 27, 2004 from, Obama's Speech," *Jet Magazine*, August 16, 2004.

56. *Deep Impact*, DVD, directed by Mimi Leder (Los Angeles, CA: Paramount Pictures, 1998).

57. "*24 Season 1*," DVD, directed by Paul Shapiro (Los Angeles, Century City: Fox Broadcasting Company, May 14, 2002). "24" was a television show that aired from November 6, 2001 until May 24, 2010. Dennis Haysbert played David Palmer. "David Palmer, J.D. was a Democratic senator from Maryland, and later the first African-American President of the United States of America." Wikimedia, "Wiki24," http://24.wikia.com/wiki/David_Palmer (last accessed January 7, 2012).

58. Barack Obama, *Dreams from My Father: A Story of Race and Inheritance* (New York: Crown Publishing Group, 2007), 82.

59. *Somewhere in Time*, DVD, directed by Jeannot Swarc (New York: NBC Universal, October 31, 2000).

60. See Charles Ogletree, *The Presumption of Guilt: The Arrest of Henry Louis Gates, Jr. and Race, Class and Crime in America* (London: McMillan Publishing Company, 2010).

61. Ogletree, *The Presumption of Guilt.*

62. Comments by Marc Lamont Hill, Don Lemon, David Mattingly, John King, Tony Harris, and Anderson Cooper, *Storm Passes, Ships Return; Who Is Shirley Sherrod?*, CNN NEWSROOM 10:00 PM EST July 24, 2010.

63. Adam Serwer, "This Is What Happens to a Black Man in America," *The American Prospect*, July 24, 2009.

64. Serwer, "This Is What Happens to a Black Man in America."

65. Dan P. McAdams, *The Redemptive Self: Stories Americans Live By* (New York: Oxford University Press, 2005), 206.

66. We have formal equality but not real equality. I devoted four years of my life to working with the Equal Employment Opportunity Commission (EEOC) as a Senior Trial Attorney litigating claims of discrimination on a daily basis. Every day I witnessed the profound gulf between the powerful moral aspiration of equal opportunity law—we

enforced, in theory Title VII of the Civil Rights Act of 1964 (42 U.S.C. 2000e et seq.)—and the actual reality faced by people of color in the workplace. The problem has to do with how discrimination is defined.

> Ironically, while Title VII retains its significance as a symbol, it has little, if any, significance as a means of helping blacks. Title VII created a context in which it was impossible to speak, in public discourse, of employment discrimination as a legitimate activity. But reciprocal to this new concept of discrimination as a public wrong, Title VII inaugurated a concept of discrimination as something extremely difficult to find.

D. Marvin Jones, "The Death of the Employer: Image, Text, and Title VII," *Vanderbilt Law Review* 45 (1992): 349, 351.

Discrimination in Title VII is understood as a problem of discrete identifiable decisions. The first step is to trace the loss of the benefit to this decision, which requires proving an employer's intent. It is a convenient fiction that proving intent is actually possible. St. Thomas Aquinas noted the impossibility of this, "[M]an, the framer of human law, is able to judge only outward acts, because man seeth those things that appear according to Kings 16.7, but God alone . . . is able to judge the movement of divine wills." Joel Samaha, *Criminal Law* (Stamford, CT: Cengage Learning, 2002), 118. Nonetheless, the law since the 19th century has routinely assumed that it is possible. "The state of a man's mind is as much a fact as the state of his digestion." *Eddington v. Fitzmaurice,* 29 Ch. Div. 459, 483 (1885). In turn, these discrete decisions must be traced to a specific harm. However, overwhelmingly most cases in the EEOC are dismissed. The conservative reading of this pattern is that this is so because so many suits are frivolous. But by what standard? I often felt that I knew that discrimination—that is, racism had occurred. But to paraphrase Denzel Washington's character in Training Day "It's not what you know, it's what you can prove."

67. Antonio Gramsci, Quintin Hoare, and Geoffrey Nowell-Smith, *Selections from the Prison Notebooks of Antonio Gramsci* (London: Lawrence and Wishart, 1971), 483.

68. Gramsci et al., *Selections from the Prison Notebooks of Antonio Gramsci.*

69. D. Marvin Jones, *Race, Sex, and Suspicion: The Myth of the Black Male* (Westport, CT: Greenwood, 2005).

70. See Sam Stein, "New York Post Cartoon Compares Stimulus Author to Dead Primate," *The Huffington Post*, March 29, 2009, http://www.huff ingtonpost.com/2009/02/18/new-york-post-chimp-carto_n_167841. html.

71. Associated Press (AP), "Judge Says Remarks on Gorillas in the Mist May be Cited in Trial on Beating," *New York Times*, June 12, 1991, http://www.nytimes.com/1991/06/12/us/judge-says-remarks-on-go rillas-may-be-cited-in-trial-on-beating.html

72. The full statement can be found at Gothamist, http://gothamist. com/2009/02/18/does_this_post_cartoon_go_too_far.php.

73. Jennifer Eberhardt and Phillip Goff, "Not Yet Human; Implicit Knowl-edge, Historical Dehumanization and Contemporary Consequences," *Journal of Personality and Social Psychology* 94, no. 2 (February 2008): 293–306; See also Dehumanization and Discrimination against Blacks Are Linked, Study Finds, http://www.medicalnewstoday.com/ articles/96734.php.

74. Eberhardt and Goff, *Not Yet Human.*

75. Eberhardt and Goff, *Not Yet Human.*

76. Anthony Asadullah, "Between the Lines: New York Post 'Chimp' Car-toon—Incendiary Satire Has a Dangerous Past," *The Black Commen-tator*, February 26, 2009, issue 313, www.laprogressive.com/rankism/ between-the-lines-new-york-post-"chimp"-caroon.

77. Beau Friedlander, "The New York Post Jumps the Shark," *The Huff-ington Post*, February 18, 2009, http://www.huffingtonpost.com/beau-friedlander/the-new-york-post-jumps-t_b_167892.html.

78. Rusty Depass, "South Carolina GOP Activist Says Escaped Gorilla Was Ancestor of Michelle Obama," *Huffington Post*, Politics Section, July 15, 2009, http://www.huffingtonpost.com/2009/06/14/rusty-de pass-south-caroli_n_215439.html.

79. Jessica Van Sack, "Cop Apologizes for Rant; Police Vow to Review Officer's Past," *The Boston Herald*, July 31, 2009.

80. Jason Kessler, "Jungle Monkey E-Mail Jeopardizes Officer's Job," *CNN*, July 29, 2009.

81. Susan Candioto and Jean Shin, "Swim Club President Denies Rac-ism in Pool Controversy," *CNN*, July 12, 2009, http://edition.cnn. com/2009/US/07/10/philly.pool.response/

82. Candioto and Shin, "Swim Club President Denies Racism in Pool Controversy."

83. Candioto and Shin, "Swim Club President Denies Racism in Pool Controversy."

84. William Faulkner, *Requiem for a Nun* (New York: Vintage International, 2012), 73.

85. Faulkner, *Requiem for a Nun*, 29.

86. Mary Pattillo-McCoy, *Black Picket Fences: Privilege and Peril among the Black Middle Class* (Chicago: University of Chicago Press, 2000), 216.

87. Pattillo-McCoy, *Black Picket Fences*, 27.

88. Pattillo-McCoy, *Black Picket Fences*, 231.

89. Ivory Johnson, "How the Sub-Prime Mortgage Crisis Is Affecting the Black Community," *Ebony Magazine*, vol. 63, January 28, 2008.

90. Center for Responsible Lending, "A Snapshot of the Sub-Prime Market," (2007), 2, http://www.responsiblelending.org/mortgage-lending/tools-resources/snapshot-of-the-subprime-market.pdf.

91. Melvin L. Oliver and Thomas M. Shapiro, *Black Wealth, White Wealth: A New Perspective on Racial Inequality* (Boca Raton, FL: CRC Press, 2006), 112–13.

92. Eric Lott, *Love and Theft: Blackface Minstrelsy and the American Working Class* (New York: Oxford University Press, 1995), 28.

93. John Amato, *Over the Cliff: How Obama Drove the American Right Insane* (Sausilito, CA: Polipoint Press, 2010), viii.

94. For example, Joanna Sloame, "Teabonics: The Most Ridiculous—and Misspelled—Tea Party Protest Signs," *The Daily News*, http://www.nydailynews.com/news/national/teabonics-ridiculous-misspelled-tea-party-protest-signs-gallery-1.1918 (accessed August 10, 2012).

95. Ellis Cose, *The End of Anger: A New Generation's Take on Race and Rage* (New York City: Harper-Collins, 2011), 37.

96. Face the Nation, "Hosted by Bob Schaffer," *CBS News Transcript*, March 21, 2010, http://www.cbsnews.com/htdocs/pdf/FTN_032110.pdf.

97. Face the Nation, "Hosted by Bob Schaffer."

98. Dr. Laura Schlesinger Apologizes for N Word Rant, *ABC News Videos*, August 13, 2010, http://abcnews.go.com/Entertainment/video/dr-laura-schlessinger-apologizes-for-n-word-rant-11391822.

99. Adam J. Rose, "Sarah Palin Supports Dr. Laura Via Twitter: 'Don't Retreat . . . Reload!,'" *Huffington Post*, August 18, 2010, http://www. huffingtonpost.com/2010/08/18/Sarah Palin Supports Dr. Laura Via Twitter: 'don't retreat . . . reload!'.

100. Norman Mailer, *The White Negro* (San Francisco, CA: City Light Books, 1970).

101. Ed Guerrero, *Framing Blackness*, 124.

102. Taylor Branch, "Dr. King's Newest Marcher," *The New York Times*, Op-Ed Pages, September 4, 2010.

103. "Fox Host Glenn Beck: Obama Is a 'Racist' (VIDEO)," *Huffington Post.com*, August 28, 2009, http://www.huffingtonpost. com/2009/07/28/fox-host-glenn-beck-obama_n_246310.html (accessed August 10, 2012).

104. William Davis Eaton, *Liberal Betrayal of America and the Tea Party Firestorm* (Oakland, OR: Elderberry Press, 2010), 205.

105. T. Lhamon, *Raising Cain: Blackface Performance from Jim Crow to Hip Hop* (Cambridge, MA: Harvard University Press, 1998), 1.

106. Lhamon, *Raising Cain.*

107. Lhamon, *Raising Cain.*

108. Myra Mendible, *Race 2008: Critical Reflections on an Historic Campaign* (Boca Raton, FL: Universal Publishers, 2010), 162.

109. Justin Sharrock, "Oath Keepers and the Age of Treason," *Motherjones.com*, 2, http://motherjones.com/politics/2010/03/oath-keepers? page=2.

110. Michael Hill, *Whiteness: A Critical Reader* (New York: New York University Press, 1997), 3.

111. James Baldwin, *The Price of the Ticket: Collected Fiction* (New York: St. Martin's Press, 1985).

112. Polatik, *The Tea Party Rapper*, http://www.poetv.com/video.php? vid=77048.

113. Annemarie Bean and James Vernon, *Inside the Minstrel Mask: Readings in Nineteenth Century Blackface Minstrelsy* (Middletown, CT: Wesleyan University Press, 1996), 15.

114. Eric Hobsbawm, *Primitive Rebels: Studies in Archaic Forms of Social Movement in the 19th Century* (Manchester: Manchester University Press, 1971), 24.

115. Unites States Department of Labor, Bureau of Labor Statistics, "Labor Force Characteristics by Race and Ethnicity, 2011," August, 2012, p. 3.

116. Steffen W. Schmidt, Mack C. Shelley, American Government and Politics Today, 2010–2011, Cengage Learning, January 1, 2010, p 99

117. See U.S. Department of Labor, supra. at page 4

118. Id at p.2

119. Warren Richey, "Affirmative Action's Evolution," *Christian Science Monitor*, March 28, 2003.

120. See generally, Eric Foner, *Reconstruction: America's Unfinished Revolution* (New York: Harper-Collins, 1988).

121. This was the infamous Hayes-Tilden compromise. Philip A. Klinkner and Rogers M. Smith, *The Unsteady March: The Rise and Decline of Racial Inequality in America* (Chicago: University of Chicago Press, 2002), 89. See also, D. Marvin Jones, "No Time for Trumpets: Title VII. Equality and the Fin de Seicle," *Michigan Law Review* 92 (1994): 2311.

122. See Klinkner and Smith, *The Unsteady March*.

6

Lessons from the Second Civil War

We want schools, not necessarily equal but separate, just schools. Those disaster factories in Harlem are not schools. .Of course that transfer of power involved millions of dollars, and that's what the battle was about.[1]

This is a struggle against educational colonization.[2]

—Rev. Glamson

The civil rights movement dreamed in all the colors of the rainbow. Summoned by the eloquence of Dr. King—"if democracy is to live, segregation must die!"[3]—they locked arms: Blacks, Jews, Hispanics, liberal whites, and Labor.[4] The federal government under Kennedy and later Johnson joined with them to form a magnificent and invincible coalition for change. (Of course, the federal government was motivated by the politics of the Cold War far more than the words of Dr. King.)[5]

This movement represented a kind of second reconstruction. Like the first, it focused on securing citizenship for blacks in the South who still sweltered under a caste system enforced both by law and private violence. We won, officially. The Southern system of *de jure* racial subjugation was dismantled. The victory is memorialized by the Civil Rights Act of 1964 and the Voting Rights Act of 1965.[6]

But by the mid-1960s, the Negro struggle for equality had turned North, and had taken on a dramatic new militancy. The civil rights movement was directed by the black middle class leading from the pulpit. But the new militancy was driven by the black underclass and led from the street. According to the Kerner Commission there were more than 100 "race riots" in 1967 alone.[7] If King's civil rights movement was animated by liberal notions of the individualism and the goal of integration, this was racial politics in its rawest form: Black Nationalism. The new black militancy was captured by a slogan coined by Stokely Carmichael in 1966: "This is the 27th time I have been arrested. I ain't goin to jail no more. The only way we gonna stop these white men from whippin us is to take over. What we go start sayin now is 'black power'."[8]

For whites in the North, the civil rights movement took place in their living rooms—on television. The era of black power knocked loudly on the door, challenging white sensibilities in a way that was quite personal. Black high flyers sought homes in the suburbs, black students sought to integrate Northern schools, and moving beyond mere civil rights they sought affirmative action, in higher education and in new voting districts.

The shift from negative rights—to be free from segregation—to integrating neighborhoods, from civil rights in the abstract and the right to live next to us was for many whites, particularly white workers and unions, a deal breaker. In essence, the new militancy threatened white privilege. But the backlash against the new black militancy was rationalized by a narrative that linked race and crime. This narrative was particularly divisive in New York City at the time.

> The city's violent crime rate had skyrocketed between 1960 and 1965. Many outer-borough Jews believed that this increase was traceable to the city's rapidly growing poor black communities. Between 1940 and 1965, New York's black population tripled, as a great wave of migrants poured in from the South. The migrants pushed out of older black neighborhoods like Harlem and Bedford-Stuyvesant and into adjoining areas, like Ocean Hill-Brownsville, from which whites, including large numbers of Jews, promptly fled.[9]

Ironically, as Podair points out, there were objective reasons why crime was higher in New York.

> Black newcomers to the city during the quarter-century following World War II were caught on the wrong side of a seismic economic shift. New York lost almost half of its unskilled and semi-skilled manufacturing jobs—jobs that had been a lifeline to white immigrants earlier in the 20th century, and which the newcomers had

hoped to obtain. They were replaced by positions in white-collar service areas—corporate, finance, real estate, insurance, law—as well as in the expanding public sector, which required education and skills the black migrants largely did not possess. This closing off of a traditional route of upward mobility, combined with the de facto housing segregation that prevailed in the city after World War II, created economically and geographically isolated ghettos.[10]

Crime in New York then was rooted in a geography of inequality. As Eric Schneider writes,

Certain urban neighborhoods concentrated the effects of poverty and ethnic discrimination. . . . These neighborhoods were the by-products of economic development and the spatial expressions of a market economy that simultaneously concentrated poverty and wealth, marginality and centrality, disadvantage and advantage, and underdevelopment and development. These spaces were not simply the containers of events; they were also their producers.[11]

This geography of inequality has much to do with Robert Moses. He wanted to keep the middle class in the inner city. He consciously chose, under the guise of urban renewal, to separate the middle class, overwhelmingly white, from the housing of the urban poor: "Moses' primary goal here was to provide housing for middle-class and middle-class-aspiring New Yorkers that was physically separated from that of the 'undeserving poor' . . . "[12] In practice, this meant de facto residential segregation, since Moses essentially viewed the first group as comprising whites, and the latter, blacks. Under Moses, "slum clearance" consisted of constructing apartments for middle-class whites through private firms and shuttling blacks into physically separated public housing projects.[13]

Residential segregation in turn led to segregated schools. By 1964, the average black student attended a school which was 90 percent white.[14]

New York Effectively Had a Dual Public School System

"In its white system, presided over by a cohort of experienced teachers, students read at or above the national average, and won a disproportionate number of National Merit and Westinghouse Science scholarships. In the 'black' system, pupils in crowded classrooms, receiving instruction from teachers who were learning on the job, read an average of two years behind the city's white students, and dropped out of school at a rate double that of the city as a whole."[15]

Although de facto black schools received equal money as whites, they suffered grievously from two things: massive overcrowding and the "worst" teachers.[16]

The dual school systems mirrored a larger schism: In essence, there were "two New Yorks."[17] There was a white New York that was upwardly mobile, educationally successful, and culturally dominant, and a black New York that was geographically isolated, economically undeveloped, and culturally marginalized.[18] In the mix with the polarization of races in New York along spatial lines were two competing narratives. Blacks rightly saw their conditions as a reflection of racism, while working class whites saw these same conditions through the window of a scapegoating narrative that attributed the problems of blacks not to inequality but to racial inferiority. The black perspective crystallized into two competing schools of thought: one school wanted integration, the other a piece of the pie, that is, empowerment (the autonomy to control their own institutions).

The white perspective crystallized into anti-busing campaigns, a law and order movement, and white flight. As the anti-integration campaign became more successful, the empowerment movement gained strength: if their efforts at integration were blocked they sought quality schools by taking over the schools they were relegated to in order to improve them. It was unprecedented and that was part of the appeal.

> The reason African American families placed such emphasis on greater community control can be attributed to two issues. First over the years educators and politicians had tried virtually every other means of raising the level of inner-city student achievement, for example, raising school expenditures, providing extra tutoring, reducing class sizes and so forth. . . . Second since the 1960s New York City's school system had become increasingly centralized to the degree that by 1967 people recognized that it had devolved into an infectious bureaucracy.[19]

In addition, while the Ocean Hill–Brownsville school system was 75 percent black with 255 Puerto Ricans, the overwhelming majority of the teachers were white.[20] A good bit of the rationale was that to improve the quality of education black teachers were needed.

Part of the idea behind community control was that students of color would perform better if local school boards hired more minority teachers as role models. Bundy—whose 1967 report on school decentralization, "Reconnection for Learning: A Community School System for New York City," laid the intellectual and political groundwork for community control—noted that 50 percent of New York City public-school students, but just 9 percent of the system's staff members, were black or Puerto Rican. While New York City schools had long been run by a single citywide school board, the Bundy report called for establishing between 30 and 60 community control boards and allowing local boards to use race as a factor in hiring and promotion. Black and Puerto Rican candidates often had special "knowledge of, and sensitivity to, the environment of pupils" and should be provided preference, the Bundy report said.[21]

What made the experiment possible was a new civil rights coalition. Mayor Lindsay, who personified a cosmopolitan humanism, urban white elites, the media, and the Ford Foundation united with blacks in support of black empowerment.[22] (Probably this support was motivated not entirely by compassion but a desire to avoid long hot summers of racial violence.)

"During the summer of 1967, the city's central Board of Education began an experiment in 'community control' of schools in the predominantly black Ocean Hill–Brownsville section of Brooklyn."[23] On August 3, 1967, Ocean Hill–Brownsville residents elected a local board to run their schools consisting of seven parents and five community leaders.[24]

The decision reflected a realism about the failure of racial integration. By 1967, it was clear that white parent resistance had succeeded in derailing the school integration movement in the city. This was an alternative: it was a redistribution of power to give blacks themselves a mechanism to provide quality education for their children. In essence, this was the New York City government voluntarily and openly embracing a form of race-conscious affirmative action at a time when King's words on affirmative action still resonated.[25] "For it is obvious that if a man is entered at the starting line in a race 300 years after another man, the first would have to perform some impossible feat in order to catch up with his fellow runner."[26]

For the black students and parents in Ocean Hill–Brownsville, this was more than an educational experiment: it was an affirmation of racial solidarity, community and, in the idiom of the time, black power.

For whites this was anathema at first because it violated a competing set of values involving individualism, color blindness, and most of all meritocracy. Meritocracy was associated in turn with due process generally and civil service rules in particular.

Of course merit and due process were compromised by the de facto job stratification of Ocean Hill–Brownsville schools.

Black activists had long chafed at the relatively low percentage of black educators in the school system; in the mid-1960s, only 8 percent of its teachers, and 3 percent of its administrators, were black,[27] despite a black student enrollment of over 50 percent.

In theory, blacks had, in 1968, an equal opportunity to take civil service exams but it was equal in the sense of the stork and the fox. In the fable, the fox invites the stork to dinner and gave the stork a flat plate. Both the stork and the fox had the same meal, offered in the same container, but differences between them, here in their anatomical makeup, made a mockery of the opportunity. Speaking of tests that were neutral on their face but produced racially disparate results, Burger stated famously in the case *Griggs v. Duke Power*, "Congress has now provided that tests or criteria for employment or promotion may not provide equality of opportunity merely in the sense of the fabled offer of milk to the stork and the fox."[28]

Let me say this another way. There are two conceptions of equality: there is equality as sameness and equality as difference. Equality as sameness and color-blind notions of equality are interchangeable here. Equality as difference takes the unique historical experience of blacks into account. This historical difference here—the different experiences of blacks— was quite relevant, blacks had historically—by law—been discriminated against in what schools they could attend. One cannot correct the wrongs of history simply by treating blacks the same. Educational equality in a meaningful sense must take this historical context into account. Otherwise one risks perpetuating racism.

No serious advocate of colorblindness disputes the reality that a history of racial subordination has caused enormous inequalities of wealth, political power, educational opportunity, and inequities in many other measures of well-being. Colorblindness advocates, however, demand neutrality now that formal, overt efforts to subjugate persons of color have dissipated. The decontextualized, undifferentiated demand for colorblindness in a society marked by vast racial inequity accepts current conditions as a legitimate baseline; it compels prospective equal treatment, but prohibits affirmative steps to dismantle historical and present-day maltreatment. *In other words, colorblindness preserves status quo of racial inequity. Only whites benefit from such an approach to equality.*[29] (emphasis added)

The tests may have been fair in form but they were discriminatory in operation. The tests although neutral in an abstract and formal sense were not race neutral in context but rather perpetuated a system of de facto Jim Crow in civil service. Merit was a rhetorical device for silencing black claims of historic wrongs and denying the legitimacy of a recently created means of democratic participation.

The local control board clashed with white teachers who they felt were trying to sabotage their efforts. On May 9, 1968, the local board voted to end the employment of Fred Neuman and nine of his colleagues at schools in the Ocean Hill–Brownsville district.[30] Neuman immediately received support from the then 90 percent white United Federation of Teachers. The UFT launched a series of three citywide strikes directed at the reinstatement of Neuman and nine of his union colleagues.

The strike that would affect more than 1 million school children lasted until November 19, 1968.[31]

According to Podair, the public discourse divided between competing sets of lofty ideals: claims of meritocracy versus claims of black autonomy, individual rights (civil service/due process) versus social change for blacks. But there was an element of racism involved as well.

The city's white labor leaders, nearly all Catholics, were at the bar at night at the old Toot Shor's in Manhattan, to them the strike was personal and afar beyond school teachers. The great white unions, the electrical workers and heavy equipment and bricklayers and carpenters

wanted to keep blacks out forever. Gerry Ryan of the fire union put the strike in one sentence: "They want a piece of the pie and they are not going to get it!"[32]
The strike galvanized labor, the white middle class which was solidly anti-busing and anti-integration forces. It also split the Jewish community.

According to Podair, Manhattan Jews supported the strike, whereas "outer borough Jews identified with working class whites."[33] Arrayed against them was a fragile coalition involving the mayor, blacks, and white elites.[34] In part because government support was based on pragmatic considerations, they wanted to avoid violence as the mayor was a weak ally. By holding the functioning of New York public schools hostage with the strike weapon—the might—not right—of the white majority won the day. A brilliant social experiment was cancelled: the white teachers reinstated. The boundary lines of white privilege remained intact. Black empowerment was rejected in the name of color blindness and meritocracy. The crisis of social isolation experienced by black students in New York was now the new normal.

But the significance for us of this tragic but emblematic chapter of urban history is what happened in the interregnum between the time of the strike and the time local control was crushed.

For a brief moment New York experimented with liberatory as opposed to authoritarian education for black students, and a level of democracy for urban blacks, which is quite rare. The experiment brought in—in place of the regular teachers—teachers from Ivy League schools, lawyers trained at New York University,[35] Catholic Nuns who handled behavior problems, and innovation in classroom methods.[36] There was a Montessori style Kindergarten, the Madison Math Project, extensive use of parents in the community as paraprofessionals, and an African American Center.[37] Then famous literary critic I.F. Stone and Alfred Kazin wrote glowing reviews.[38] Said Rhody McCoy, chairman of the local board, "These kids are beginning for the first time to enjoy school. Things are beginning to happen to them. Things are beginning to happen to the teachers."[39]

My proposed solutions are drawn almost entirely from the writings, testimony of the leaders, educators, and social theorists involved in the Ocean Hill–Brownsville moment of decolonization. Although separated by 40 years, the problems are essentially the same. The Ocean Hill–Brownsville experiment arose out of the crushing defeat of black aspirations for integration. The wheel of history has come full circle. Although there was a period of de-segregation, schools have been resegregated across the United States.[40] The same dual school systems that existed in New York City are replicated today all over the country. What we find in Ocean Hill is, if not a detailed blueprint for a strategy, at least the elements of what that strategy must be. Reread-ing that moment, the strategy for change involves three interrelated projects: changing the pedagogy that is dominant in inner city schools, changing the cultural orientation, and re-creating nationally the Ocean Hill–Brownsville experiment, this time with a twist.

Project One—The Pedagogy of Oppression: The Imperial Teacher

The pedagogy of the educational establishment is imperial. It treats social, cultural, and pedagogical norms of the dominant society as the norm and the cultural idiom of blacks as ignorant, pathological, or bad. This ped-agogical imperialism is sometimes referred to as structural whiteness.[41] By structural here we mean that some forms of marginalization that are so deeply embedded in a society that they become invisible both to the dominant group and the group being dominated. Here, concomitantly, the superiority of the perspectives and norms of the dominant society is deeply assumed.

One aspect of this imperial attitude is that the white teachers, much like missionaries to African countries, look down on and stereotype the natives whom they view as urban primitives.

This imperial attitude is rationalized through the rhetoric of a culture of poverty. Originated by Oscar Lewis, the culture of poverty was a de-scription of lifestyles of "the poor," which was characterized by rejection of or indifference to the dominant values of society.[42] This "includes . . . non-traditional family structures, strong present-time orientation, propen-sity to violence and lack of sexual inhibition."[43] Lewis, ironically, saw the "culture of poverty" as "superficial," an effect of social conditions. Ripping this idea from its original framework as a structural critique, Moynihan ap-plied this perspective on the culture of the poor specifically to blacks.[44] By 1966, James Coleman introduced this to government policy makers. In his report he concluded, "Funding levels, quality of facilities, class size had little effect on black achievement."[45]

This perspective, which is quite racist, is a self-fulfilling prophecy. As Kenneth Clark noted culture of poverty is an alibi.

> Black children by and large do not learn because they are not being taught effectively and they are not being taught because those who are charged with the responsibility for teaching them do not believe they can learn, do not expect them to learn, and do not act toward them in ways which help them to learn.[46]

Stimulation and teaching based on positive expectation seem to play a more important role in the child's performance than does environment.

This deterministic notion that blacks are hopelessly trapped in a culture which is itself dysfunctional is played out by a parallel theory that blacks resist learning because in their culture academic achievement is white. This is the oppositional culture thesis, which is misleadingly attributed to Dr. Ogbu. Ogbu argues that " 'involuntary minorities'—black slaves—had no choice but to come to this country. Blacks developed an oppositional culture in response to a glass ceiling that was imposed on them."

> It would appear from the tradition of collective struggle in the field of education that caste-like minorities have looked to formal education as a means of improving their social and occupational status, if not for achieving full status in the dominant group. But their expectations have not been met because their education has not been designed to help them to do so and because of institutional barriers against them in adult life. They have responded to this situation it appears, in a number of ways that have actually tended to reinforce their educational preparation for marginal economic preparation. Some of these responses include conflict with the schools, disillusionment, lowered efforts, and survival strategies.[47]

Ogbu's theory, which presupposes structural conditions as the predicate for cultural adaptation, was hijacked, decontextualized, and pressed in the service of neoconservative ideology.

It is true that black students feel this peer pressure, that students who excel are stigmatized as whites. But there is a missing context.

Students do use this terminology but it means something different in context.

Project Two—The Problem of Eurocentrism: Changing the Cultural Orientation

Our current educational culture is Eurocentric. It is a hegemonic assumption of Eurocentrism that disciplined writing and desiccated logic are the proper means of education. But black children growing up in urban culture find this emotional strangulation. In addition, the Eurocentric quality of the enterprise represents a different mode of thinking than is native to black culture.

Eurocentric culture embraces a reasoning style that is dichotomous. That is, the world is known and described through the comparison of incompatible opposites. Virtually all of reality is split into paired opposites. According to Marimba Ani, "this begins with the separation of self from 'other,' and is followed by the separation of the self into various dichotomies (reason/emotion, mind/body, intellect/nature)." Dichotomous reasoning leads to either/or conclusions and makes it difficult to process information holistically. The dichotomous reasoning found in Eurocentric cultures may be contrasted to the diunital form of reason prevalent in African and other non-European cultures. Diunital reasoning leads to "both/and" conclusions and permits the consideration of information that is not neatly categorized or compartmentalized.[48]

Employment of Hierarchies

Having submitted the material world to a process of fragmentation, the Eurocentric mind organizes the resulting dichotomies into hierarchies of greater and lesser value. Within dichotomies, one pole is valued as superior to its opposite. Thus, reason is considered to be superior to its opposite, emotion, "that is, when 'reason' rules 'passion'." All reality is described in hierarchical terms; consequently, the Eurocentric mind perceives everything as better or worse relative to something else. In this way, grounds are established for relationships based on power, "for the dominance of the 'superior' form or phenomenon over that which is perceived to be inferior. . . .[49]

Ironically hip-hop culture is about destabilizing hierarchies.

Analytic reasoning is the familiar cognitive style within Eurocentric cultural spheres. In analytic reasoning, an item or issue under consideration must first be broken down into its constituent parts before each part is then separately examined. While important information may be gleaned through analytic reasoning, "there are some things that cannot be divided without destroying their integrity." In Eurocentric societies, analytic reasoning is utilized to the exclusion of, and not in addition to, synthetic reasoning processes. Thus, interrelationships are more difficult to perceive, and the fragmentation and seeming disconnection of reality is encouraged.[50]

In hip-hop, analysis takes place at a high level but with a different set of epistemological norms. The goal is to find interrelationships to link and connect rather than fragment.

Nature objectified and rationalized leads to the illusion of a despiritualized universe. In the Eurocentric world-view there is no room for the operation of sacred forces. Nature is reduced to a mere thing, an object that may be manipulated to suit mankind. This is a perspective that is almost uniquely European. Even where God is allowed in Western philosophies, s/he is banished to a separate spiritual realm where s/he can have no effect on quotidian human affairs.[51]

In essence, blacks must abandon their cultural orientation and worldview to achieve in school. This is truly what is meant by acting white.

Ironically, Obama has bought into the same neoconservative ideology. Like the culture of poverty ideologues he externalizes the problem away from the government institutions. He puts the onus on the parents:

Go into any inner city neighborhood, and folks will tell you that government alone can't teach our kids to learn. They know that parents have to parent, that children can't achieve unless we raise their expectations and turn off the television sets and eradicate the slander that says a black youth with a book is acting white. They know those things.[52]

There is no mention or inquiry into structural issues or the extent to which the attitudes, curricula, or practices of the schools themselves might be at the root of the alienation.

At the core of the problem in simplest terms is the fact that the teachers do not respect the students. The students are not only being stereotyped but the stereotypes are deeply defended as commons sense—this is an example of "Reasonable Racism"[53]—(a common sense that is sometimes shared by black teachers as well). This operates as a self-fulfilling prophecy.

The problem is structural in that the reason the teachers stereotype the individual students as unteachable—the meaning of do not "expect the children to learn"—is because they do not respect their "cultural idiom."[54]

Hip-hop represents oppositional culture. Their saggy pants, gold teeth, and twisty braids represent a response to structural conditions.

But teachers and the educational establishment misread this as evidence of ignorance or "unteachability."

Of course being unteachable and being a criminal in waiting is part of a signifying chain: The depth of gulf between the students and teachers is captured by the notion that the teachers view the students in inner city schools as a criminal class who need to be warehoused, watched, and controlled, not taught.[55] Culture plays the role in schools that color played perhaps 30 years ago.

Stereotyping and disrespect have become so pervasive that they come to define the experience of inner city students of the current educational establishment.

These attitudes do far more than create a hostile environment for learning for black students. They legitimate and serve as a foundation for a variety of institutional practices that result in reproducing, within nominally integrated schools, a virtual caste system for black students in the inner city. These practices can be parsed into three categories: school design/maintenance, tracking and testing, and school discipline.

Together these practices blur the distinction between school and prison: they are premised on the notion that the students are hopeless criminals, they are treated as such, and in the manner of all self-fulfilling prophecies they, in vast disproportion, end up behind bars.

Urban School Design

Fortified spaces, which are usually monitored by surveillance, are predicated upon logics of inclusion and exclusion that . . . normalize the exclusion and containment of the most threatening, needy or economically productive.[56]

The criminalization of inner city students begins with the design of the school. Descriptively, many inner city students attend overcrowded and structurally deteriorating facilities that "resemble . . . fortresses, complete with [barbed]-wire . . . fences, bricked up windows, [and] heavy locks on iron doors."[57] Monahan and Torres suggest that this appearance communicates the built pedagogy of the inner city school. (Diana Oblinger defines "built pedagogy" as "the ability of space to define how one teaches."[58]) "The *built pedagogy* of fortification, visibility, and enclosure, communicat[es] to students and others that school discipline will be enforced."[59] (Italics added)

Eric Meiners goes further, "when schools look like prisons the curriculum is geared not toward college but to service labor, and the schools are full of police or other structures that serve only as punitive functions at specific schools to prepare youth to be institutionalized."[60]

The design of urban schools to fit a pedagogy of surveillance and control is exacerbated by the police practices at the schools themselves.

Many of America's poor, urban, and predominately minority schools maintain prison-like atmospheres that make students of color feel like "criminals." Poor, predominately minority schools are regularly placed on "lock-down" by armed police personnel raiding or continuously patrolling school facilities. School districts have even gone as far as completely transferring control over school safety to local police departments.[61]

Tracking

Tracking is the practice of grouping students of similar capability into academic tracks, for example, a college preparatory track and a vocational track. School tracking has resulted in dramatic overrepresentation of blacks and Hispanics as well in vocational and special education programs.[62] Tracking is justified by the idea that the fast learners should not be kept back and the slow learners will learn better among students of similar abilities. (Studies show that tracking inhibits learning for students placed in low-ability groups and does not aid achievement for students placed in higher groups.[63]) Despite this innocent billing, tracking plays a pernicious role for inner city students of color. First black students, who are often placed in lower "tracks" discriminatorily, receive a curriculum which leaves them typically unprepared for college even if they graduate.[64] Also, low-tracked students are subjected to instructional methods that stimulate disruptive behavior.[65] This in turn leads to high push out and incarceration rates.

The sister to the tracking process is the practice of high stakes testing. The No Child Left Behind Act (NCLB) authorizes billions of dollars to state educational systems to address racial achievement gaps. But it comes with a catch.

> NCLB is often identified as America's most problematic federal education policy. Although NCLB distributes approximately $10 billion to school districts each year for the purpose of decreasing racial achievement gaps, NCLB arguably has the opposite effect because it makes federal funds available to states through racially biased standardized testing.[66]

These standardized tests, like the Florida Comprehensive Assessment Test (FCAT) in Florida, have a devastating effect on the students. The FCAT in Florida is a prerequisite to high school graduation: If they fail they are ineligible for a regular high school diploma. The FCAT produces astonishingly high attrition rates for black students in Florida. While the notion is that this tough love approach will make the children study harder, black students tend to simply drop out. In my Constitutional Law class we did a quick mapping of the areas which were highest in poverty in the city. We then located the schools which were failing—because students tended to fail the FCAT. All of the schools, which were failing, were in lowest socioeconomic areas. All of these areas were predominantly black and Hispanic. The entire failing schools in the state of Florida were predominantly black and Hispanic.[67]

Disparate Discipline

Black students between K through 12 are two to five times more likely to be suspended from school than whites.[68] In some state school systems "more than thirty percent of the black student population is suspended each year."[69]

It cannot be reduced to cultural dysfunction. Their acting out is often part of an oppositional identity, in part a strategy of resistance to a pedagogy which annihilates the black child's sense of its own cultural identity. In essence, the school says to the native: you must abandon your primitive modes of thinking and adapt to us. But why is this cultural alienation necessary?

There is a need for a new pedagogy that would involve spontaneity and oral expression—something through hip-hop they are trying to teach themselves.

This new pedagogy would incorporate the language, forms of dress, and cultural idiom into the curriculum. A black arts curriculum that begins with the blues and ends in a study of rap music and an urban studies curriculum that teaches the cultural, social and political history of the community are all examples of changes in the curricula that might help: they would create a sense of respect for the cultural idiom of the students that is currently lacking.

The pejorative perspective that black students are culturally deprived and unteachable is not free standing. It reflects a lack of accountability. According to many of the leaders who participated in creating Ocean Hill–Brownsville, the reason the school can get away with the alibi of culture of poverty as a totalizing explanation for black attrition rates is because "they do not have to answer the community they serve."[70]

This defines the need for new structures of control. Community control of a generalized nature is necessary to accomplish teacher accountability.

We have to change the pedagogy from one that assumes it is the cultural deprivation of the students that is the problem. The premise here is that the students must adapt. We must reverse that: it is the pedagogy that must adapt.

This will not happen through a process of intellectual debate. We cannot achieve pedagogical change without structural changes in who sets the curricula and standards for hiring teachers at the local level. We need to re-create the Ocean Hill–Brownsville experiment in urban areas all over the United States.

How do we get there?

In Herman Wouk's novel *The Winds of War*, he describes how war had transformed a once familiar landscape, "Signposts were gone, place names were painted out, and some towns seemed deserted."[71]

For most of the 20th century, the great signpost pointing in the direction of change was *Brown*.[72] *Brown v. Board of Education* symbolized the notion that the Supreme Court was there for blacks even if the political apparatus of democracy was not. I have taught constitutional law for over 20 years. If anything is true I know was well, as I know my name that *Brown* has been quietly overruled.[73] Inner city schools have resegregated. The Court's opinions merely reflected popular consensus: Just as in Ocean Hill–Brownsville a white backlash has swept away the hard fought civil rights gains of the second reconstruction.

Racial Realism

We need a new racial realism that accepts that neither litigation nor legislative efforts to achieve integration are likely to go anywhere. There is no one to address these arguments to. The Supreme Court will no longer listen, in any meaningful way, and the Congress including the Democratic Party is increasingly deaf to issues of race. I'm reminded of Bill Maher's comment that "the Democrats are the new Republicans."

In a true sense we can't get there from here. Our current strategy for change seems to be a combination of scholarly debate, litigation, and national electoral politics. That hasn't worked. But local grassroots efforts to recreate Ocean Hill might.

Project Three—Revisiting Ocean Hill: The Need for Collective Action

The Ocean Hill–Brownsville experiment rested on norms of racial solidarity and collective action, then in the form of demonstrations and protests. This collective energy represented what Harold Cruse called racial pluralism.[74]

King appealed to a universal humanism. The civil rights narrative exhorted Americans to believe "what unites us is greater than what divides us." Obama's speeches, in a real sense, are derivative of and a reworking of basic Kingian themes.

But King also argued that blacks should not be second-class citizens, a theme that spoke to the historical experience of blacks as a group. The notion that blacks were second-class citizens spoke also to a notion of blacks as a subordinated group, speaking to a lack of power. Since then we have witnessed the canonization of King. But the portrait of King as a saint in our museum of social history includes only the universal humanism theme. This official story accepted the liberal individualism strand of the civil rights narrative but rejected and left out King's claims based on second-class citizenship. With this metaphor, King constantly denounced the historical injustice done to blacks. The canonized, individualist, universal humanist version of the civil rights narrative is thus dehistoricized. This universal humanism becomes a horizon on our thinking. From this perspective, the system easily accepts the notion of formal equal opportunity: the notion that each individual had a right to be treated fairly, but it denies even the coherence of arguments in terms of group rights. Individuals have no history.

So in the civil rights era we have bought into the dehistoricized official story. We simply forget that group identity is constituted by history. Without memory of our history as racial groups no collective activity is possible. This logic helps to explain why in the face of astonishing structural inequality there are no demonstrations about the conditions of joblessness, massive incarceration, or the warehousing of inner city school children. These children are seen as colorless individuals who simply make bad choices.

Wacquant talked about the signifying chain of slavery, segregation, ghetto, and prison. He left out a link: There is a historical continuum between slavery–segregation–ghetto—schools that don't teach—prison. Unless we recognize the historical connectivity between these, there is no possibility of collective action on the issue of education of inner city kids.

The black power narrative rejected this humanism as myth. As Harold Cruse noted, America is not a culturally empty vessel but a bastion of "European cultural and spiritual values," which rewarded groups not unaffiliated human beings. Said another way, in the words of Stokely Carmichael, "blacks have been oppressed as a group, not as individuals. We will not find our way out of that oppression until both we and America accept the need for Negro Americans as well as Jews, Poles, and white Anglo Saxon Protestants, among others to wield group power."

We need a new black consciousness movement and a new racial pluralism. But blackness would have to be updated. Any contemporary black movement for social justice could not be defined by color. I do not see Clarence Thomas—or former Tea Party Candidate Herman Cain—as black, for example. Neither would I see a modern day Che Guevara as white. It would be based on local rather than universal notions of identity. Rather it would be defined, as the hip-hop generation defines themselves by attitude, culture, and values, and where one lives.

As I write many lament the fact that Obama presides over historic levels of unemployment—25 million people are unemployed or underemployed; he has not challenged corporate power and governs from a center-right coalition. Cornel West has gone so far as to say "Obama is the black mascot of wall street."[75] There is some truth to this. But it is a superficial historically disconnected truth.

I would not say it is Obama who has failed. The left has failed Obama. Kennedy, as Harry Belafonte pointed out, had demonstrators in the streets to push him toward progress on issues of race. We need a new civil rights coalition to push Obama. Obama's weakness is our historical moment: it reflects of the fact that the civil rights coalition has fragmented, that the black middle class—the assimilados—have stepped out of history, and the collective action necessary for change is not there.

We need a notion of change that defines the people, those at the bottom as the animating force—from the bottom-up rather than from the top-down notion of change. This is all worked out in hip-hop. The top becomes the bottom and the bottom becomes the top.

Notes

1. James Baldwin, Fred L. Standley, and Louis H. Pratt, *Conversations with James Baldwin* (Jackson: University Press of Mississippi, 1989), 100.

2. Gayatri Chakravorty Spivak, "Teaching for the Times," in *Dangerous Liaisons: Gender, Nation and Post-Colonial Perspectives*, ed. Anne McClintock, Aamir Mufti, and Ella Shohat (Minneapolis: University of Minnesota Press, 1997), 490.

3. Wolfgang Mieder, *Making a Way Out of No Way: Martin Luther King's Sermonic Proverbial Rhetoric* (Leipzig: Die Deutche Nationalbibliothek, 2010), 264.

4. The United Auto Workers strongly supported the civil rights movement in the early years under Walter Reuther. Kevin Boyle, *Organized Labor and American Politics, 1894–1994: The Labor-Liberal Alliance* (Albany: State University of New York Press, 1998). Boyle

describes the civil rights movement as "the coalition the UAW tried for two decades to build." (See Boyle, *Organized Labor and American Politics, 1894–1994*, 222).

5. See Mary L. Dudziak, "Desegregation as a Cold War Imperative," *Stanford Law Review* 41 (1988): 61.

6. See The Voting Rights Act of 1965, 42 U.S.C. 1973 et. seq.

7. George Thomas Kurian and Jeffrey D. Schultz, *The Encyclopedia of the Democratic Party: vol. 3* (Armonk, NY: M.E. Sharpe Reference, 1997), 214.

8. Peniel E. Joseph, *The Black Power Movement: Rethinking the Civil Rights-Black Power Era* (New York: Routledge, 2006).

9. Jerald E. Podair, *The Strike That Changed New York* (New Haven, CT: Yale University Press, 2004), 126.

10. Podair, *The Strike That Changed New York*, 16.

11. Eric C. Schneider, *Smack: Heroin and the American City* (Philadelphia: University of Pennsylvania Press, 2008), 117.

12. Podair, *The Strike That Changed New York*, 12.

13. Podair, *The Strike That Changed New York*, 13.

14. Podair, *The Strike That Changed New York*, 16.

15. Podair, *The Strike That Changed New York*, 17.

16. Podair, *The Strike That Changed New York*.

17. Podair, *The Strike That Changed New York*.

18. Podair, *The Strike That Changed New York*.

19. William Jeynes, *American Educational History: School, Society, and the Common Good* (Thousand Oaks, CA: Sage Publications, 2007).

20. Paul D. Moreno, *Black Americans and Organized Labor: A New History* (Baton Rouge: Louisiana University Press, 2006), 281.

21. Richard D. Kahlenberg, "Ocean Hill-Brownsville 40 Years Later: The Lessons of the New York School Strike," April 28 2008, http://lettrist.blogspot.com/2008/04/ocean-hill-brownsville-40-years-later.html (accessed February 8, 2012).

22. Podair, *The Strike That Changed New York*, 42.

23. Kristen L. Buras, *Rightist Multiculturalism: Core Lessons on Neoconservative School Reform* (New York: Routledge, 2008), 142.

24. Jerald E. Podair, "The Ocean Hill-Brownsville Crisis: New York's An- tigone," *New York Magazine*, November 18, 1968, http://www.gotham center.org/festival/2001/confpapers/podair.pdf (accessed February 8, 2012).

25. R. Martin Luther King, *Why We Can't Wait* (Boston, MA: Beacon Press, 2011; Originally published in 1964); Johnson later paraphrased King in his speech to Howard University in 1968. Randall Bennett Woods, *Lyndon Baines Johnson* (New York: Free Press, 2006), 588. "You do not take a person who, for years, has been hobbled by chains and liberate him, bring him up to the starting line of a race and then say you are free to compete with all the others. Negroes are trapped, as many Whites are trapped . . ."

26. Podair, *The Strike That Changed New York*, 155.

27. *Griggs v. Duke Power Co.*, 401 U.S. 424, 431 (1971).

28. Darren Lenard Hutchinson, "The Majoritarian Difficulty: Affirmative Action, Sodomy, and Supreme Court Politics," *Law and Inequality* 23 (2005): 1, 26 27; Cedric Merlin Powell, Rhetorical Neutrality: Col- orblindness, Frederick Douglass, and Inverted Critical Race Theory," *Cleveland State Law Review* 56 (2008): 823, 848.

29. Neuman was not terminated from employment as a teacher. Under the terms of the letter, he was merely transferred. But Podair's writ- ing about this consistently using the term fired which, counter-histor- ically, adopts the UFT framing the issue.

30. Richard D. Kahlenberg, "Ocean Hill-Brownsville at 40," *The Cen- tury Foundation*, September 2008, http//tcf.org:8080/Plone/commen tary/2008/nc2033.

31. Jimmy Breslin, *The Church That Forgot Christ* (New York: Free Press, 2004).

32. Breslin, *The Church That Forgot Christ*, 6.

33. Breslin, *The Church That Forgot Christ*.

34. New York University was then as now one of the premier law schools in the country.

35. Donna E. Shalala, Mary Frase Williams, and Andrew Fishel, *Readings in American Politics and Education* (Chicago, IL: Scott-Foresman, 1963), 148.

36. Shalala et al., *Readings in American Politics and Education.*

37. Shalala et al., *Readings in American Politics and Education.*

38. Alex Pointsett, *Battle to Control Black Schools Mounts for Ghetto Self-Determination in Education*, quoting Rhody McCoy, *Ebony Magazine*, May 1969.

39. Gary Orfield and Susan E. Eaton, *Dismantling Desegregation: The Quiet Reversal of Brown v. Board of Education* (New York: New Press, 1996).

40. James Kyung-Jin Lee, *Urban Triage: Race and the Fictions of Multiculturalism* (Minneapolis: University of Minnesota Press, 2004), 148.

41. Oscar Lewis and Ruth M. Lewis, *Five Families: Mexican Case Studies in the Culture of Poverty* (New York: Basic Books, 1975). According to Podair this thesis was originally put forward in an article in 1966 in Scientific American, but I have not been able to locate the article. See Podair, *The Strike That Changed New York*, 54.

42. James T. Patterson, *America's Struggle against Poverty in the Twentieth Century* (Cambridge, MA: Harvard University Press, 2000), 3–115.

43. Daniel Patrick Moynihan, *On Understanding Poverty: Perspectives from the Social Sciences* (New York: Basic Books, 1969), 198–296.

44. Podair, *The Strike That Changed New York*, 54.

45. Podair, *The Strike That Changed New York.*

46. John U. Ogbu, *Minority Status, Oppositional Culture, and Schooling* (New York: Routledge, 2008), 247.

47. Kenneth B. Nunn, "Law as a Eurocentric Enterprise," *Law and Inequality* 15 (1997): 323, 334–35.

48. Nunn, "Law as a Eurocentric Enterprise," 335.

49. Nunn, "Law as a Eurocentric Enterprise."

50. Nunn, "Law as a Eurocentric Enterprise," 337.

51. Barack Obama, *Celebrating Change: Key Speeches of President Elect Barrack Obama, From October 2002 to November 2008*, (Rockville, MD: Arc Manor, 2008).

52. On reasonable racism see D. Marvin Jones, *Race, Sex, and Suspicion: The Myth of the Black Male* (Westport, CT: Greenwood, 2005).

53. Podair, *The Strike That Changed New York*, 59.

54. Ronnie Casella, *"Being Down": Challenging Violence in Urban Schools* (New York: Teacher's College Press, 2001), 150.

55. Torin Monahan and Rodolfo D. Torres, *School under Surveillance: Cultures of Control in Public Education* (Piscataway, NJ: Rutgers University Press, 2010), 8.

56. Monahan and Torres, *School under Surveillance.*

57. Chauncee D. Smith, 36 Fordham Urb. L.J. 1009, 1029.

58. Diana Oblinger, *The Future Compatible Campus: Planning, Designing and Implementing Educational Technology in the Academy* (Bolton, MA: Anker Publishing Co., 1998).

59. Oblinger, *The Future Compatible Campus.*

60. Erica R. Meiners, *Right to be Hostile: Schools, Prisons, and the Making of Public Enemies* (Routledge: Taylor and Francis, 2007), 169.

61. Chauncee D. Smith, 36 Fordham Urb. L.J. 1009.

62. Pedro A. Noguera, *The Trouble with Black Boys: And Other Reflections on Race, Equity, and the Future of Public Education* (San Francisco, CA: Jossey Bass, 2008).

63. Jeannie Oakes, *Keeping Track: How Schools Structure Inequality* (New Haven, CT: Yale University Press, 1985), 3; Chauncee D. Smith, 36 Fordham Urb. L.J. 1009, 1037.

64. In 2003, I was asked by then Florida Senator Fredricka Wilson, leading black pastors and other members of a local civil rights coalition, to take point on the issue of the FCAT. See Annabelle Gale, "Coalition Vows Legal Fight over FCAT, Bush Says He Won't Rescind Results," *Miami Herald*, May 18, 2003. (In investigating the facts, I was told by a member of the Miami-Dade school board that blacks in lower tracks lack sufficient advanced placement courses to get into college regardless of their grades.) At Miami-Edison High, a Miami inner city school which is 90 percent black, only 20 percent of the students take even one AP course.

65. Richard Arum, Irene R. Beattie, *The Structure of Schooling: Readings in the Sociology of Education*, (Newbury Park, California Pine Forge Press) 190, See also Gale, "Coalition Vows Legal Fight. . ." (Documenting claims by parents and community leaders about the detrimental effects of tracking and other similar practices.)

66. Chauncee D. Smith, *Deconstructing the Pipeline: Evaluating School to Prison Pipeline Equal Protection Cases Through A Structural Racism Framework*, 36 Fordham Urban Law Journal 1009 (2009), 1038.

67. Of course as William Julius Wilson points out, it's not just race. Blacks in suburban areas did well. Blacks in inner city areas did poorly. But neither is it just "the concentration of poverty." Clearly, bias against culture plays a major role.

68. See Daniel J. Losen, "Challenging Racial Disparities: The Promise and Pitfalls of the No Child Left Behind Act's Race-Conscious Accountability," *Howard Law Journal* 47 (2004): 243, 255–56; (reporting that "between 1972 and 2000, the percentage of white students suspended for more than one day rose from 3.1% to 6.14%. During the same period, the percentage for black students had risen from 6% to 13.2%.") see also, Pedro A. Noguera, *The Trouble with Black Boys*, 126.

69. Chauncee D. Smith, *Deconstructing the Pipeline: Evaluating School to Prison Pipeline Equal Protection Cases Through A Structural Racism Framework*, 36 Fordham Urban Law Journal 1009 (2009) at 1009.

70. Podair, *The Strike That Changed New York*, 208.

71. Herman Wouk, *The Winds of War* (New York: Hatchett Digital 1971).

72. See *Brown v. Board of Education*, 347 U.S. 483; 74 S. Ct. 686; 98 L. Ed. 873 (1954).

73. See D. Marvin Jones, "The Original Meaning of Brown: Seattle, Segregation, and the Rewriting of History: For Michael Lee and Dukwon," *University of Miami Law Review* 63 (2009): 629.

74. Harold Cruse, *The Crisis of the Negro Intellectual: An Historical Analysis of the Failure of Black Leadership* (New York: The New York Review of Books, 1967).

75. Cornel West, "Obama 'a black mascot' and 'black puppet,'" *The Boston Globe*, posted May 17, 2011, http://www.boston.com/news/politics/politicalintelligence/2011/05/west_obama_a_bl.html

7

The Trial of Howard Colvin[1]

Special to *The Herald,* by D. Marvin Jones

BALTIMORE—Captain Howard Colvin calmly confronted his accusers today in a hearing that was open to the public. Colvin created controversy when he permitted an open-air drug market in West Baltimore. The police free zone was dubbed, "Hamsterdam," a cynical fusion of Amsterdam where drugs are notoriously legal and a hamster, an animal often used in scientific experiments. Colvin was charged with Obstruction of Justice and Dereliction of Duty. His testimony, before a Police Board of Inquiry, follows below:

Police Commissioner Burrell:	How do you plead to these charges?
Captain Colvin:	Guilty as charged. I take full responsibility.
Captain Colvin:	Before we proceed to sentencing, I have a statement I'd like to read to the Board of Inquiry.
Commissioner Burrell:	You may proceed.
Captain Colvin:	Many people ask why I would take the risk that I did. Why would I risk my pension, my future? Your honors I was tired of being lied to and tired of lying to my men.

Captain Colvin, continued:

We lock up over 100,000 people a year in Baltimore, most of them black men. Nationally we have spent over a trillion dollars in the last 40 years in the drug war. We currently lock up 800,000 people a year in the United States, for marijuana alone. Yet a global commission made up of presidents and other international figures has said that in the last 10 years drug use is up. It notes that the global consumption of opiates has increased 34.5 percent, cocaine 27 percent and cannabis 8.5 percent from 1998 to 2008. Use of marijuana has risen dramatically to 50 percent of America's youth. The "War" has reduced the inflow of marijuana from outside America but has increased the amount grown inside our borders. After 40 years we've spent a trillion dollars. One writer called it a trillion dollar disaster, I'd call it "a trillion dollar lie."

One way to see how little effect we are having is to look at the level of demand after 40 years. There are over 26 million drug users in the United States. We arrest perhaps 3 percent of them a year. If we are only arresting one out of 30 can we say we are even making dent?

All we have done is create a black market for drugs. On the black market prices are high. Cocaine sells for 300 percent of what it cost to produce in Columbia. Cocaine sells for 10 times the price of gold.

But the higher the price the more the addicts will steal.

Captain Colvin, continued:

In a study of 356 heroin users in Miami, James Inciardi found that they admitted to committing nearly 120,000 crimes (an average of 332 per person) during a single year. In another study of 573 heroin users, Inciardi found them responsible for about 215,000 offenses during the previous year. Included were 25,000 shopliftings, 45,000 thefts and frauds, 6,000 robberies and assaults, and 6,700 burglaries.

Call it the law of unintended consequences. But the end result is we have two epidemics not one. There is still an epidemic of drug use and there is an epidemic of robbery and theft. The drug war is not a cure, it contributes to both infections.

We were led to believe that by fighting drugs we would reduce violence, make it easier for families and the kids.

As we patrol the western district guns are everywhere, everyone has gun. This is what the drug war has wrought.

Guns are essential to carrying on the drug trade, since drug dealers must enforce their own contracts and provide their own protection from predators. Even "mules" who deliver drugs or money need weapons. Packing a gun, like fancy clothing or costly jewelry, has become a status symbol among the kids in the ghetto. In such an atmosphere, other youngsters carry guns in the hope they will provide them with some protection. As a result, disputes

Captain Colvin, continued: that used to be settled with fists are now settled with guns.

But it's not drugs that are causing the deaths. I've met doctors who have told me that drugs lack pharmacological properties to cause violence. Al Capone didn't shoot people because he was drunk, and Marlow Stansfield does not shoot people because he's high. Drug dealers cannot go to the courthouse on street to resolve their disputes so they are forced to settle them in the street sometimes with automatic weapons. I would estimate 50 percent of the murders, which take place, are drug related. We've created a black market, by making drugs illegal. Murder is as much a by-product of that black market—that we created—as the drugs themselves.

Look, the drug war is devastating the black community in the city.

A generation of kids is growing up behind bars. One out of three black kids in Baltimore is under some form of criminal justice system supervision on a given day, much of it because of drugs. All for what? We can't fund schools, we can't fund jobs program, we can't fight violent crime, we can't do anything because we expend all our resources on search, destroy. All we have done is made West Baltimore into concrete Vietnam.

Commissioner Burrell: Since you are lecturing us, what is the answer Captain Colvin?

Captain Colvin, continued: I don't know if Hamsterdam is the answer, "I don't know what the answer is. But I know this— whatever the answer is—it can't be a lie."[2]

New Hamsterdam: "Let a New Earth Rise"

Now when this begins to move, the pig power structure is gonna say, "OK, you have civilian review boards." But all that does is allow the same old fascist power structure to keep control of the police. . . . What we're talking about is righteous community control, where the people who control the police are elected by the people of the community.[3]

I propose at a local level a way to enact Bunny Colvin's transgressive innovation. I develop the idea that each local community in an urban area has the power to decide how police will be deployed. Armed with full information both about the resources available and the level of different kinds of crime, each community will determine their own policing priorities. They could decide to put 100 percent of existing resources in fighting violent crime and no resources toward arresting crack addicts. They could in effect choose harm reduction over a strategy of punishing addicts for what is in effect a public health problem.

This proposal is not new. The Black Panther Party famously proposed this in the 1960s.[4]

PETITION STATEMENT FOR COMMUNITY CONTROL OF POLICE—SUMMARY OF POLICE CONTROL AMENDMENT THAT MUST BE ESTABLISHED IN THE CITIES AND COMMUNITIES OF AMERICA TO END FASCISM

This amendment to a City charter would give control of the police to community elected neighborhood councils so that those whom the police should serve will be able to set police policy and standards of conduct.

The amendment provides for community control of the police by establishing police departments for the major communities of any city; the Black community, the predominately White area, the Mexican American Communities, etc. The departments would be separate and autonomous. They can by mutual agreement use common facilities. Each Department will be administered by full time police Commissioners. (Not single police chiefs.) The Commissioners are selected by a Neighborhood Police Control Council composed of fifteen members from that community elected by those who live there. Each department shall have five Community Council divisions within it. (Or number of departments [sic] ratioed to population.)

The Councils shall have the power to discipline officers for breaches of Department policy or violations of law. (Against the people.) They may direct their police Commissioner to make changes in department wide police policy by majority vote of the said Department Commissioners. The Council can recall the Commissioner appointed by it at any time it finds that he is no longer responsive to the community. The community can recall the council members when they are not responsive to it.

All police officers must live in the department they work in, and will be hired accordingly.[5]

The model of the Black Panther's proposal seems sound. Though groups like the Panthers are marginalized as being outside of the realm of intellectual discourse, their ideas were ahead of the curve, a paradigm shift forward.

A Question of Power versus A Question of Rights

The Black Panthers deftly reframed the issue of police brutality. The legal system individualizes each instance of injustice. It then addresses the problem as a question of whether individual rights were violated. This model puts the problem in perspective: not a question of individual violations but systemic injustice. The problem of the black community can only be understood as something systemic rather than episodic, not the problem of individuals treated badly but the problem of a group without power. Shifting power is the key.

A Post-Colonial Regime

As noted earlier, the Panthers argued that the black community was to the dominant society what the colony is to the mother country. Colonial rule was defined by police who answered to a central command composed of members of the colonizer group. There was no accountability. This replaces the imperial model with one that allows the community to participate democratically—that is, at the neighborhood level.

An End Run around the Ideology of the Drug War

The Black Panthers developed this model to deal with the issue of police brutality. This shift of decision-making authority is quintessentially what is needed in the drug war. The drug war debate has stalled. The frontal assault will not work.

The problem is one cannot talk reason to moral panic. The drug war is driven by politicians who appeal to fear: fear of crime; fear of social decay; fear of stereotypical black men—we see them on our screens—on the evening news; spread-eagled over a police car; in such television series as *The Wire* wearing saggy pants, selling drugs to their kids. The fear has congealed into an ideology of us versus them. This ideology of us versus them anchors the massive incarceration: The drug war tacitly represents the notion that the best way to deal with the dangerous groups who sell and use drugs is to incarcerate and incapacitate them. A corollary is anyone who does not agree with this strategy is, if an academic, a radical, and if a political leader—an enemy. Thus, Kurt Schmoke, the former mayor of Baltimore, who went to high school with me,[6] famously said, after he floated the idea of decriminalizing drugs in Baltimore, "they will call you the most dangerous man in America."[7] So no sitting politician can even suggest they are going to end the war on drugs and survive. But providing each neighborhood with the democratic power to decide how to use the police, as a resource, seems quite plausible, if only in cities with large black electorates. This move to local democracy would pay immediate rewards. I call it a peace dividend. Cash-strapped cities like Baltimore, Newark, and Detroit could use one. Funds saved from drug war—arrest, court processing, incarcerations—could be put to better use in the schools: education instead of jail.

Corrective Justice versus Restorative Justice

Prohibition—which in the drug war context becomes search and destroy—is a creature of the corrective justice approach. Neighborhood councils represent a different model—a model of restorative justice. While the norm of corrective justice is punishment, the norm of restorative justice is healing, the transformation of social arrangements.

This model takes the restorative justice approach.

The deadly combination of the war on drugs and zero tolerance polices (i.e., policies of massive arrest, incapacitation, and quarantine of dangerous groups) has done incalculable damage to the relationship between the police and the community in urban areas.

Law and order, in a democracy, requires that the community served to believe that the laws that govern them are just. The Civil War that took place during the 1960s came about because blacks universally felt that segregationist laws were unjust. Drug laws, as enforced in the black community, together with the cruel hand of zero tolerance, which is an extension of the drug war are, as Michelle has stated, the new segregation.

It is not only racist, it is undemocratic—totalitarian—to impose these drug laws with their enormous destructive impact on communities that don't want the laws. It oppresses the community and it breeds disrespect for law. That disrespect guarantees that any project of law enforcement in those communities is likely to fail. This simple mechanism of community control is transformative in that it will allow the community to embrace law enforcement as just because it will be the community that decides where the enforcement resources go. They have the power to end the segregation—the quarantine, incapacitation, and labeling of the black youth in their communities.

The drug war has defined the world of the inner city. It created a sense of us versus them. The drug war is structurally the reason why there is so much urban violence, the justification for lockdown, the reason why we do not have money to spend on better schools or jobs.

"Hamsterdam" might not be the answer but it would be a new world of possibilities. Quarantine of the drug selling could replace quarantine of huge segments of the black community in lockdown. Harm reduction might replace massive incarceration. But such a shift in policy will not come from a real life Bunny Colvin. There are none. Nor will it come as a result of an academic debate. Political leaders are not listening. Even if they were to listen, they could not openly oppose the war. Walking in lock-step with the ideology of the drug war is an implicit precondition for getting elected to any major office—and if a closet abolitionist were elected, he or she would be removed almost as soon as he or she is outed.

But a new world is trying to be born. We see the beginnings when a former judge, like Timothy K. Lewis, comes out against the drug war in an Amnesty International report[8]; when conservative organizations like the NAACP vote to end the drug war.[9] It is not merely the wasted money, nor even the devastating impact of the drug war on communities of color, it is the fact that after thousands have died in gun battles between rival drug war lords in Mexico and in Latin America international pressure is building to find an alternative to the growing human losses. Obama and other leaders are, in some ways like Bunny Colvin, looking for a way to declare a truce, without being blamed for backing down.

So while a political leader could not propose to end the drug war he or she could propose a shift of power, from a central administration to an Ocean Hill–Brownsville–style neighborhood council (which decides how the police are deployed). There is a poet who says, "let a new earth rise." She says, "Let a new earth rise . . . Let a bloody peace be written in the sky."[10] Let the new world rise.

Notes

1. Howard "Bunny" Colvin was a character in the acclaimed television series, *The Wire*. I think his actions were justified but I don't think Colvin's character would allow him to deny liability. Here I provide a hypothetical speech—which he never gave, the words cannot be attributed to the actual television character—that he might have given had he chose to explain his actions.

2. These were Captain Colvin's actual words in response to a question at a community meeting about poor police protection. See "Amsterdam," *The Wire,* Ernest R. Dickerson (2004; HBO), DVD.

3. Bobby Seale, *Seize the Time: The Story of the Black Panther Party and Huey P. Newton* (Baltimore, MD: Black Classic Press, 1991), 421.

4. Seale, *Seize the Time.*

5. Philip Sheldon Foner and Clayborne Carson, *The Black Panther's Speak* (Cambridge, MA: DA Capo Press), 179.

6. My high school was Baltimore City College. I graduated in 1969. Kurt graduated ahead of me by two years. We attended the same high school for one year. He went on to become Mayor of Baltimore and I became a law professor.

7. Doug Donovan, *"The Wire*, A different Kind of Reality T.V. Local Facts, fictions merge in a show some love, others condemn Baltimore . . . Or less," *Baltimore Sun*, December 19, 2004.

8. See Amnesty International, *Threat and Humiliation: Racial Profiling, Domestic Security, and Human Rights in the Unites States* (Ridgefield Park, NJ: Globe Litho, 2004), http://www.amnestyusa.org/pdfs/rp_report.pdf.

9. See Leonard Pitts, "NAACP's Paradigm Shift on Ending the Drug War," *Miami Herald*, July 30, 2011 (documenting that the NAACP passed a resolution "calling for an end to the war on drugs"). As editorialist Leonard Pitts wrote, "Here's why this matters. Or, more to the point, why it matters more than if such a statement came from Jesse Jackson or Al Sharpton. The NAACP is not just the nation's oldest and largest civil rights organization. It is also its most conservative. Read more here: http://www.miamiherald.com/2011/07/30/2338455/naacps-paradigm-shift-on-ending.html#storylink=cpy

10. Margaret Walker, "For My People," in *The Poetry of Black America: An Anthology of the 20th Century*, ed. Arnold Adoff (New York: Harper Collins, 1973), 145.

8

"We Are Oscar Grant!"

Comin straight from the underground
Young nigga got it bad cuz I'm brown.[1]

It's the wee hours of New Year's Day in 2009. The champagne has popped, the ball has come down, but the fireworks in the Bay Area are far from over. Two groups of revelers are preparing to return to their homes across the bay. They gather at the Fruitvale station in Oakland. Fruitvale owes its name to Cherry orchards, which populated the area years ago. Now it is Oakland's bustling commercial hub.

Police receive a report that a fight has broken out between the two groups of revelers. When the Bay Area Rapid Transit (BART) train comes screeching in, the revelers pile into the train. But before the train could leave, five officers of the BART roll in. Officers haul off several of the passengers. One of them is a young black man named Oscar Grant. Since the officers had not witnessed the fight, it is unlikely the officers knew who among the passengers were involved and what specifically any of those participants did. On what basis did they arrest Oscar Grant? Apparently, Oscar Grant's ordeal began as an instance of racial profiling.

With no specific details of the disturbance, which coincidentally turned out to be nothing more than raucous celebration; no description of the alleged culprits; and no information that the train stopped was the one containing the disturbance; BART officers, acting without an inkling of police corroboration, singled out Grant and three of

245

his friends, all young men of color, among a train that was as racially mixed as it was economically diverse.[2]

First, Grant is handcuffed sitting next to a wall.[3] Perhaps he said something because a moment later a policeman, a BART officer, pushes him face down on the train station platform.[4] The same policeman puts his knee on Grant's neck.[5] Then, a moment later, an officer—who we now know as Johannes Mehserle—inexplicably stands up, draws his gun, and fires point blank into the back of the unarmed man. The unarmed man is Oscar Grant. He is handcuffed and lying face down.[6] "You shot me!" Grant exclaims, shocked as much by outrage as by the force of the projectile.[7] The next morning at Oakland's Highland Hospital, the 22-year-old is pronounced dead.[8]

Why would a policeman shoot an unarmed black man point black in the back? According to Officer Tony Pirone, Johannes said to him, "I thought he was going for a gun."[9] But that explanation would not have made sense. Grant was handcuffed.

Pirone would quickly change his story. He later said that Johannes told him, "I'm going to tase him."[10]

The drama here was that, for once, there was not even a colorable claim of self-defense. Officer Johannes Mehserle killed an unarmed black man who had no means of threatening him or other officers in any significant way.

It was in some ways a repeat of history. Some compared it to the case of Rodney King.

At 12:47 a.m., California Highway Patrol officers are in pursuit of a white Hyundai for failing to yield. The driver is Rodney Glenn King—a black, unemployed construction worker—who will later say he fled from police because he felt the traffic infraction would interfere with his parole. After several units of the Los Angeles Police Department (LAPD) take up chase, Rodney King's vehicle is finally stopped in full view of the Mountain back apartment complex. There, he finds himself surrounded by over twenty armed LAPD officers, several of whom proceed to "beat him half to death" while he is laying defenseless on the ground. King is hit between fifty-three and fifty-six times by officers wielding their batons. The bones holding his eye in its right socket are broken, and he suffers broken bones at the base of his skull. In addition to clubbing him wildly, one officer stomps on his head.[11]

Like the Oscar Grant case, in the case of Rodney King, officers were caught on a video beating King with nightsticks and kicking him repeatedly while he was down. In that case (Rodney King), the officers were acquitted by a Simi Valley jury. (Police claimed Rodney King, while on his back being beaten unmercifully, was not the victim but the aggressor. Rodney King was the prototypical big black man: "He was portrayed as larger than life with superhuman strength."[12]) Outrageously, this deployment of stereotypes swayed the jury.

Others compared the events which took place on a train platform in Oakland to events that took place in Brooklyn in 1999.

12:44 a.m. Images of burned out buildings, empty lots planted thick with broken bottles and the carcasses of old cars. In front of and beside the building trash cans are set alight like torches by homeless denizens of this nameless street in the Bronx. Everything is very still, a horn honking in the distant background. Nearby the weary black immigrant trudges across the threshold of his apartment building at 1157 Wheeler Avenue.

Suddenly a battered Ford Taurus turns the corner . . . [it] careens ominously to a stop. Four men wearing jeans and sweatshirts jump out with their automatic weapons already drawn. The Four men, Kenneth Boss, Sean Carroll, Edward McMellon and Richard Murphy are members of the infamous Street Crimes Unit, a kind of roving patrol. . . . The motto of the Street Crimes Unit is "We own the night!"

A command of "Halt!" shatters the stillness. The officers, still with their guns drawn, approach within 5 feet of Diallo. Diallo in the half-light of the vestibule goes for his wallet, presumably to establish his identity—his innocence. Officer Sean Carroll yells, "Gun, he's got a gun!" Forty-one explosions follow in the deadly space of eight seconds. Some of the bullets find the wooden door which splinters from the force of the fusillade. Intermittently sparks fly as other bullets find the stonewall and ceiling of the apartment house. Nineteen of the bullets explode into the skinny body of the unarmed man. One of the explosions shatters Diallo's spinal cord. Even after Diallo falls to the ground the four police officers continue to fire shells into Diallo's now paralyzed body.[13]

Oscar Grant's case was not the Rodney King case of 21st century. It was not because this was even worse. Oscar Grant was not a big black man, and unlike King, he was handcuffed lying on his face on the ground. Nor was his case a pair to the Diallo case. This was even worse because there was no possibility here that Grant could have been going for a gun. The idea that Mesherle merely made a mistake and was merely trying to use a taser doesn't make any sense either. Why tase a suspect that has already subdued laying face down on the ground? As Grant's attorney Ronald Burris stated, "No. 1, the Taser shouldn't have been used, either. There wasn't any basis for that. And No. 2, the facts on the videotape don't support that."[14]

Nonetheless, Officer Johannes Mehserle was acquitted, by an all-white jury, of murder.[15] He was convicted of involuntary manslaughter and was sentenced to two years in prison. With good behavior his actual time behind bars, for killing Oscar Grant, is about 11 months.

Notes

1. Big K.R.I.T., American Rapstar, Return of 4Eva, Self-Produced Mixtape, March 28, 2011. Interestingly, these hip-hop denunciations of police brutality play an important role in raising consciousness of and creating a foundation for activism against the problem. It drives discussion at least as powerfully as the best books by legal scholars. See Imani Perry, *Prophets of the Hood: Politics and Poetics in Hip-Hop* (Durham, NC: Duke University Press, 2004), 111.

2. Donald F. Tibbs, "Who Killed Oscar Grant?: A Legal-Eulogy of the Cultural Logic of Black Hyper-Policing in the Post-Civil Rights Era," *Southern University Journal Race, Gender, and Poverty* (2010), http://works.bepress.com/donald_tibbs/6

3. www.youtube.com/watch?v=IKy-WSZMklc.

4. www.youtube.com/watch?v=IKy-WSZMklc.

5. www.youtube.com/watch?v=IKy-WSZMklc.

6. "Another BART Shooting: The Public Deserves Answers," *Vallejo California: Times Herald*, July 6, 2011, http://www.topix.com/forum/city/vallejo-ca/T5URKELINUQ1AGNH7

7. Demian Bulwa," BART's Shooting Probe Missteps," *San Francisco Chronicle*, January 30, 2009, http://www.sfgate.com/bayarea/article/BART-s-shooting-probe-missteps-3174551.php

8. Jill Tucker, Kelly Zito, and Heather Knight, "Deadly BART Brawl—Officer Shoots Rider, 22," *San Francisco Chronicle*, January 2, 2009, http://www.sfgate.com/bayarea/article/Deadly-BART-brawl-officer-shoots-rider-22-3178373.php

9. Demian Bulwa, Cop Says Mehserle Yelled I'm going to Tase Him, June 19, 2010, A1

10. Demian Bulwa, "Skeptical Judge Grants Bail to Former BART Cop," *The San Francisco Chronicle*, January 31, 2009.

11. D. Marvin Jones, "Darkness Made Visible: Law, Metaphor and the Racial Self," *Georgetown Law Review* 82 (1993) 437, 490

12. Richard Delgado and Jean Stefancic, *Critical Race Theory, The Cutting Edge* (Philadelphia, PA: Temple Press, 2000), 182. Quoting from Lawrence Vogelman, "The Big Black Man Syndrome: The Rodney King Trial and the Use of Racial Stereotypes in the Courtroom," *Fordham Urban Law Journal* 20 (1993), 317, 571.

13. D. Marvin Jones, *Race, Sex, and Suspicion: The Myth of the Black Male* (Westport, CT: Greenwood Press, 2005), 117–18.

14. Bulwa, "Skeptical Judge Grants Bail."

15. Whiteness itself matters here—both the whiteness of the jury and the whiteness of the police officer. [W]hiteness represents itself as moral and good, while non-white groups are frequently characterized as immoral or inferior. Harry M. Benshoff and Sean Griffin, *America on Film: Representing Race, Class, Gender, and Sexuality at the Movies* (Oxford: Blackwell Publishers, 2004), 56; see also bell hooks, "Representing Whiteness in the Black Imagination," in *Cultural Studies*, ed. Lawrence Grossberg, Cary Nelson, and Paula Treichler (New York: Routledge, 1992) [W]hiteness represents goodness and all that is benign and nonthreatening.

9

Race and Reconciliation

"Good gracious! Anybody hurt?"
"No'm. Killed a nigger."
"Well, it's lucky; because sometimes people do get hurt."[1]

—Mark Twain

It's as though we've seen this movie before. Over and over again black men who are unarmed and defenseless are shot and killed by police. While police are arrested for selling drugs, suspended for sexual liaisons in office, there are no instances in which a policeman has been convicted of murder for killing a black man.[2]

When a certain model of automobile crashes and burns over and over we ask why? We need to ask a similar question in the context of black males and deadly force. In answering the question of why, the mainstream media uses two stories or frames. The effect of the stories makes black men, as a group, invisible as victims.

The first frame is the notion that police brutality is deviant rather than the norm. In one version of this narrative, the notion is that white racism on the part of the individual cop who kills is the root of the problem. In this narrative the goal is to remove the bad apples. This individualizes the problem. The goal is to police 'violations' of the law: To identify law-breakers who simply happen to have a badge." In the Oscar Grant case, the notion seems to be that this was not racism at all but merely an accident. This fits the color-blind version of the story.

The second is the story of the black man as a beast. This story of the big black man, the black man as superpredator, or urban Gangsta, is the same story. It is this story that implicitly underwrites the immunity of the police in the Rodney King case, the Amadou Diallo case, and the virtual immunity in the Oscar Grant case as well.

Both of these stories are false. The individualizing narrative hides the problem through tunnel vision—one cannot see the forest for the trees. The stereotypical narrative of black men hides it in a different way, it short circuits empathy—a superpredator can never be a victim.

The problem of police brutality is systemic and structural. It is not merely a matter of individual racism, though it is that in part. It is a problem of a drug war, which has created a police culture in which the police see themselves as a thin blue line between civilization and the urban primitives. These urban primitives are, of course, black men.

The Historical Context

The culture of impunity with which police use deadly force on black men in urban areas has deep historical roots.

The problem begins with slavery. The plantation was for the slaves themselves no more than a prison. Escape was a constant problem. So was the possibility of rebellion, although a relatively rare occurrence, a constant source of worry for the master. By day the master wielded absolute power, but by night he worried that these same slaves would rise up and slit his throat. Said one Southern gentlewoman, "If they want to kill us, they can do it when they please, they are noiseless as panthers. . . . We ought to be grateful that anyone of us is alive."[3]

This racial paranoia was personified by a stereotype of certain dangerous slaves.

Nat was the incorrigible runaway, the poisoner of white men, the ravager of white women who defied all the rules of plantation society. Subdued and punished only when overcome by superior numbers or firepower, Nat retaliated when attacked by whites, led guerrilla activities of maroons against isolated plantations, killed overseers and planters, or burned plantation buildings when he was abused. Like Jack, Nat's customary obedience often hid his true feelings, self-concept, unquenchable thirst for freedom, hatred of whites, discontent, and manhood, until he violently demonstrated these traits.[4]

For both economic (objective) and psychological reasons, slave patrols were vital to the plantation as an institution. They were vital not only to return escaped slaves but to enforce a sense of terror on the part of slaves: to send a message that any challenge to authority would be met with brutality. To facilitate this, the law allowed the slave master and the slave catcher virtually unlimited power in disciplining runaway or rebellious slaves.[5]

The fear of black men, Nat, is still with us. Richard Wright personifies Nat as Bigger Thomas.[6] The Gangsta rappers as the Nigga or thug. But he represents the focal point of a widely spread and almost radioactive fear. Nat was explicitly a beast in the imagery of the ante-bellum South. In the 21st century this has been updated. While Nat was universal—all black men were potential Nats—the contemporary narrative of black males as dangerous types is more local. Nat is associated with the hood. From Nino Brown in *New Jack City,* to Dough Boy in *Boyz N the Hood; from* Old Dog in *Menace to Society,* to Marcus (50 Cent) in *Get Rich or Die Tryin',* a generation of hood films has fused the images of the hood and black male thugs. Hollywood has taken this so literally that in the movie *Predator* the monster has Dred Locks reminiscent of those that might be worn by members of a Jamaican drug gang.[7] Certain spaces within the ghetto take on an even more sinister connotation. It is no coincidence that the Oscar Grant atrocity takes place at the Fruitvale subway. In popular culture the subway is an iconic site for crime and mayhem. In *Escape from New York,* the president's plane crashes somewhere in Manhattan.

War hero Snake Pliskin is offered a reprieve from a life sentence . . . if he'll rescue the President from the pit of New York but the policeman who briefs Snake on his mission indicates a commute to New York will not be as easy as invading Siberia: "The crazies, they live in the subways. . . . As in Pelham or Planet of the Apes, the New York subway is the Site of Deviancy."[8]

Urban space has been racialized; the strip club, where often drugs and other depravity take place (Sean Bell), and a tenement building where

African immigrants reside (Diallo's apartment building) are notably also scenes of infamous police shootings.

Confrontations between blacks and whites in these spaces of racial anxiety are particularly explosive. The level of firepower expended compares more to what one would expect in war—perhaps Afghanistan or Iraq—than on an American street: 50 shots fired in the Sean Bell case,[9] 41 shots in the Diallo case, etc.

In the United States, police brutality meets lack of accountability. African Americans are nine times as likely as whites to die at the hands of a police officer. American juries have effectively immunized deadly violence by police against black men who have been suspected of crimes.

Unarmed black men have been shot in the back of the head from motorcycles speeding away (Clement Lloyd),[10] shot unarmed after running away from a policeman pursuing them for misdemeanor traffic warrants (Timothy Thomas),[11] shot standing unarmed in their own doorway by police who went to the wrong house (Diallo),[12] beaten to death after being apprehended for speeding on a motorcycle (Arthur McDuffie), and more recently, shot in the back and killed while handcuffed and unarmed (Oscar Grant).[13] But I am aware of no case in which a police officer was convicted of murder for shooting an unarmed black man.

There is an uncanny parallel between the de facto immunity of police in major metropolitan areas like Oakland, Miami, and New York and the customary immunity that the sheriff and his posse of slave catchers had in the era of slavery. The same radioactive fear of black men felt by police is shared by many American juries. The fear creates a race-tinted lens through which the facts of any case are viewed. In the Rodney King case, the racial rhetoric of the big black man served to invoke this narrative. In the Grant trial race was smuggled in when Judge Perry allowed the defense to introduce evidence of Grant's criminal record. This was irrelevant but helped to portray Grant in stereotypical terms. Race and crime are already knotted together. Given this linkage painting Grant as a habitual criminal invoked the notion that Grant was typical of the ghetto—he became Bigger Thomas, he became Nat.

Invoking racial imagery, explicitly or implicitly, encourages the jury to think in essentialist terms. In both the Grant case and the Rodney King case, there were videos which captured the injustice that took place. But in neither case could the jury see the injustice.

How could the film help us to know what happens in the ghetto any-way? Like Africa, the ghetto is a place beyond the experience of whites and, hence, a place of darkness. Who knows what happened? Who knows what happens? King's blackness blended with both the blackness of the setting and the black and white of the video to be-come a screen upon which the image of race and racial fears could be projected.[14]

In both cases—both in the King case and the Grant case—what the jurors saw depended on the extent to which they looked through a race-tinted lens, through the lens of an us-versus-them narrative. Cases like that of Oscar Grant are in a real sense cases in which black people want to see if the promissory note of equal citizenship can be cashed at the bank of the criminal justice system.

If there was going to be a case in which the bank would make good on the check the Oscar Grant case was it. The fact that justice did not show up suggests the promissory note is not going to be honored. Not because of hate, but because there is simply no way to remove the race-tinted lens—the veil.

We need the racial realism to realize that reliance upon the govern-ment to prosecute policemen who have killed black men under suspicious circumstances is not likely to work. It hasn't in the 34 years since I gradu-ated from NYU.

The genius of hip-hop is that as a product of post–civil rights culture it expresses the radical realism that I am talking about. When hip-hop rappers refer to themselves as Niggas they are saying they do not buy into the notion that formal equal opportunity laws have changed their status. The laws did change. It was illegal under police regulations for the police to shoot Sean Bell—police are not allowed to stop an unarmed person fleeing in a car by using deadly force. Similarly the BART officer legally could not have shot Oscar Grant in the back. The problem is that creating rights—formal equality—doesn't necessarily change society.

Rights are not enough. The problem is one of power. Change only hap-pens for blacks when there is a strong demand—in the Civil War Northern troops, in the 1960s urban rebellion.

In many ways blacks in the post–civil rights era are like the Native Americans in *Worcester v. Georgia*.[15] In *Worcester v. Georgia,*[16] the state of Georgia required any white person living on Indian land, to swear an oath to uphold the laws of the United States. Worcester, a missionary, refused to obey the law and was convicted by the state of Georgia. If allowed to stand the principle on which the Georgia law was based would nullify Indian sovereignty. Justice Marshall's opinion said state laws had "no force" in Indian country.[17] The Native Americans had won! The Supreme Court said so. But the Cherokee's right to sovereignty could only have meaning if the federal government was willing to protect it. President Andrew Jackson, who favored Indian removal, was unwilling to do so. He subordinated their rights to his own political ends. President Jackson said, "John Marshall has made his law, now let him enforce it!"[18] Blacks have a right to equal justice. It is just that those rights are sometimes nullified by American juries. They cannot see the injustice due to the distorting effect of the race tinted lens.

"Truth and Reconciliation"

In South Africa, after years of apartheid, Nelson Mandela instituted a process of reconciliation. Police who had murdered blacks and committed unspeakable atrocities were granted amnesty in exchange for confessing their crimes. The parents, family, and loved ones of the victims would be present at the hearing.[19]

Instead of seeking vengeance, I would make the radical suggestion we seek to institute a similar process of reconciliation in urban areas, which have experienced injustices like those in Oakland. In part, the culture of impunity that surrounds the police shootings of black men is a culture of disbelief. The juries believe the police, that the unarmed man in the vestibule of his own home, or on subway platform, prone and in handcuffs, was threatening; they can't accept that the policeman would wantonly take an innocent life.

An urban "Truth and Reconciliation Commission" could bring out facts that would be corrosive of this culture of disbelief. It would compel the media to see that Oscar Grant, Amadou Diallo, and many others no longer as 21st-century versions of Nat, as 21st-century Bigger Thomases. The police who confess could be given not only amnesty but forgiveness. A catharsis could take place. Perhaps there could even be redemption.

Notes

1. Harold Bloom, *Mark Twain's the Adventures of Huckleberry Finn* (New York: City Infobase Publishing, 2007), 7.

2. Officer David Warren was sentenced to 25 years for violating the civil rights of Henry Glover. The case arose when Warren shot Glover, a black man, in the back in the aftermath of Katrina. See Laura Maggi, "Former Police Officer David Warren Sentenced to 25 Years in Henry Glover Shooting," *Times-Picayune*, March 31, 2011.

3. Mary Boykin Chesnut, *A Diary from Dixie* (New York: D. Appleton and Company, 1949), 147–48.

4. D. Marvin Jones, *Race, Sex, and Suspicion: The Myth of the Black Male* (Westport, CT: Greenwood Publishing Group, 2005), 19.

5. Andrew Fede, *People without Rights: An Interpretation of the Fundamentals of the Law of Slavery in the U.S. South* (London: Routledge, 2011), 106.

6. Richard Wright, *Native Son* (New York: Harper Perennial Modern Classics, 2005).

7. Mark Shiel and Tony Fitzmaurice, *Screening the City* (Brooklyn: Verso Books, 2003), 189.

8. Robert Zecker, *Metropolis: The American City in Popular Culture* (Westport, CT: Praeger, 2008), 146.

9. *The New York Times* summarizes the facts in the Sean Bell case:

   > In the early morning hours of Nov. 25, 2006, Sean Bell, a 23-year-old New York City man due to be married later that day, walked out of a Queens strip club, climbed into a gray Nissan Altima with two friends who had been celebrating with him—and died in a hail of 50 bullets fired by a group of five police officers.

   Sean Bell, "Times Topics," *The New York Times*, Friday July 29, 2011. Unbeknownst to Sean Bell, the police had staked out the bar in drug interdiction operation. One of the officers heard one of Sean's friends say, "Yo, get my gun" See Ed Pilkington, "$7 m Settlement Concludes New York Police Shooting Case, *Guardian International*, July 29, 2010, 16. As Sean and his friends tried to exit the building, the police tried to stop them blocking them in with police vehicles front and back. Sean, in his Nissan Altima, continues to try to elude police but is stopped by police gunfire. He was unarmed. Bell, "Times Topics." Prior to the police effort to stop them they had committed no crime. Officers did not have probable cause to arrest them at the time they initially moved to confront them.

10. For a discussion of the Clement Lloyd case, see Jones, *Race, Sex, and Suspicion*, 120.

11. For a discussion of the Timothy Thomas case, see "Cincinnati Officer Is Acquitted in Killing That Ignited Unrest," *New York Times*, September 27, 2001.

12. See Jones, *Race, Sex, and Suspicion*, 120.

13. George Lipsitz, *The Possessive Investment in Whiteness: How White People Profit from It* (Philadelphia, PA: Temple University Press, 1998), 148.

14. D. Marvin Jones, "Darkness Made Visible: Law, Metaphor and the Racial Self," *Georgetown Law Review* 82 (1993): 490, 495.

15. *Worcester v. Georgia*, 31 U.S. (6 Pet.) 515 (1832).

16. *Worcester v. Georgia*, 31 U.S. (6 Pet.) 515 (1832).

17. *Worcester v. Georgia*, 31 U.S. (6 Pet.) 515 (1832).

18. Felix S. Cohen, *Handbook of Federal Indian Law*, 476 (Rennard Strickland et al. eds., 1982), 83.

19. I am quite aware that over the years a consensus has developed that any restoration process after a prolonged period of armed conflict must include both a criminal justice component and truth and reconciliation component. In a setting in which blacks are the majority it is possible to talk in those terms. In the United States our historical experience suggests that true criminal sanctions for policemen who kill unarmed black men is still a way off in the future. But see generally, Naomi Roht-Arriaza and Javier Mariez Currena, eds., *Transitional Justice in the Twenty-First Century: Beyond Truth versus Justice* (Cambridge: Cambridge University Press, 2006) [hereinafter Transitional Justice].

Epilogue

The Last Word: "A Paradise Close at Hand"

In *The Matrix,* machines become the enemy. They create a virtual world that humans are programmed to perceive as reality. This false reality is their means of pacifying humans, keeping them asleep. Joining the rebellion against the machines, Neo (Keanu Reeves) battles agents, the enforcers for the machines. Dressed like CIA operatives with Brooks Brothers' suits, skinny ties, and earpieces, these are computer-generated thugs. When Neo shoots down one of the agents, the agent dies but the program that created it is still running. It simply picks one of the humans in the matrix world, a truck driver or a woman carrying the groceries and they become the new agent.

The virtual world of *The Matrix* is a metaphor for the problem of race. Like the hapless humans in *The Matrix,* we are programmed by society to believe stories about race. For example, segregation was a false reality constructed out of stories—myths—of black inferiority.

The narrative of black inferiority was shot down. But the meta-program—the master narrative is still running. It has simply been rewritten as a narrative of racial fear that sometimes reaches levels of paranoia.

In a weak form the paranoia manifests itself as suspicion that Obama is not really an American citizen. "[T]here was probable cause to believe that Obama's . . . birth certificate was a forgery!" says Arizona Sheriff Joe Arapaio.[1] Bethany Storro claimed that a black woman had thrown acid on her face.

Bethany Storro, Victim of Acid Attack, Said She Could Hear Her Skin Burning

By Sean Alfano
   DAILY NEWS STAFF WRITER
   Friday, September 03, 2010

She could hear her skin burning.

   Bethany Storro was celebrating her new job when a stranger approached her and asked, "Hey pretty girl, do you want to drink this?"

   Storro described her attacker as a black woman in her late 20s wearing khaki pants and her hair in a ponytail.[2]

Media outlets from across the country believed her and treated her case as a celebrated cause.[3]

Random black women who met the very vague description were stopped and questioned. Money for the victim poured in, and fundraising fliers posted around the 83 percent white Vancouver called on the community to "help one of our own." When a few bloggers and online commenters and, later, some mainstream media questioned the credibility of Storro's story, they were attacked for even raising a doubt.[4]

   Storro was a white Tawana Brawley, the perpetrator of a racial hoax. But the hoax was exposed, and skeptical police did not go so far as to arrest a real black woman based on Storro's incredible racial hoax.

   But the most powerful single instance of how real the problem of racial paranoia is takes place in Twin Lakes, a gated community in Sanford, Florida. A 17-year-old black kid from Miami Lakes is visiting his father who is staying in the predominantly white complex of gated estates.

   The National Basketball Association (NBA) All-Star Game is about to come on. "Why not walk down to the 7-Eleven and get some refreshments, some skittles maybe?" He must have thought. Gated communities like Twin Lakes in Sanford, Florida, are architectural efforts to create utopia. They are monuments to a notion that we can create utopia by walling out crime and drugs. "Not in my backyard!," they say. This has led to a "fortress mentality" in which spatial separation from those perceived as different is ideal.[5] Crime and drugs will seep through regardless. What these communities succeed in walling out is racial and cultural diversity: they are overwhelmingly white. They have become not utopia but what one writer calls "Whitopia."[6]

When Trayvon walked from his father's girlfriend's house to the 7-Eleven, it was raining. So the teenager donned a sweatshirt with a hood.

George Zimmerman, captain of the Neighborhood Watch, was driving in his truck as Trayvon made his fateful trip to the store. Zimmerman was armed, looking for anyone who was suspicious. He saw Trayvon:

Zimmerman: There's something wrong with him. . . . He must be on drugs on sump' in
Dispatcher: Are you following him?
Zimmerman: Yes?
Dispatcher: We don't need you to do that?

Zimmerman refused to do as he was told. He continued his pursuit.

To Trayvon no doubt he felt he was being stalked. "Is it a pervert?" He might have asked.[7]

It must have been terrifying for a young man just out to get some skittles.

Trayvon was on his cell phone with his girlfriend at the time:

He said this man was watching him, so he put his hoodie on. He said he lost the man. I asked Trayvon to run, and he said he was going to walk fast. I told him to run but he said he was not going to run.[8]

According to those speaking for Zimmerman, he (Zimmerman) approached Trayvon because there had been several burglaries in the neighborhood committed by blacks, and Trayvon was black.[9] So Zimmerman wanted to question him. If there had been several burglaries committed by whites and Anderson Cooper was walking down the streets of Sanford, would Zimmerman have questioned him? I don't think so.

A few minutes after he spotted him, Trayvon was dead. Zimmerman famously shot Trayvon in the chest and claimed self-defense. Whatever the outcome of the trial the encounter is the aftermath of an incident of profiling. Zimmerman marked Trayvon not because he had done something wrong but because he was black, he was wearing a hoodie, and he was here in Twin Lakes, out of place.

We have said that if Anderson Cooper had been walking through Sanford he would probably have arrived home alive. It is also true that if Trayvon had been dressed in Dockers, with a polo shirt, and sweater neatly tied around his neck, he might have passed for someone who belonged in that affluent area. When Zimmerman says "something is wrong with him" it was not merely that Trayvon was black. The conjunction of Trayvon's race and dress was perceived as evidence of dangerousness. In a famous case called *City of Chicago v. Morales,* the police there refer to this as visible lawlessness. Black skin plus hoodie connotes sociocultural identity linked, in the popular culture, to the ghetto and crime.

From *The Wire* to the evening news, from bright, feel good films like *Precious* to dark movies like *Training Day,* the ghetto is another planet. It is a nightmare world where, as in *Precious,* fathers rape their daughters, where, as in *The Wire,* mothers sell groceries for drugs. It is a place where crack babies are born and grow up to become superpredators, —like Michael Lee in *The Wire*. This tropological or fictional ghetto is as false a vision of social reality as the virtual reality depicted in *The Matrix*.

These images in the social imaginary of blacks as crack addicts, superpredators, and thugs crystallize into racial projects like the drug war. Unanchored and free floating, widely shared images like these have much to do with the fact that of the 600,000 men in New York who were stopped last year, 54 percent were black. This also has much to do with why a black man born today has a "one in three chance of going to prison in his lifetime."[10]

When a person is paranoid it does no good to explain to him that the government is not spying on him or to prove that the television set in the neighbor's living room is not a death ray aimed at him to kill. Paranoia grips the thought process in a vice like grip of fear. Paranoid people do not ask why.

If we asked why, we would see that it is not a culture of poverty at the root of failing schools it is resegregation. If we asked why so much joblessness persists in the ghetto, we would see that the problem is less that blacks do not want to work but that work in the ghetto has simply disappeared.

From Paranoia to Denial

One aspect of paranoia is that the paranoid person must lie to himself. He must come up with a rational explanation for his irrational acts. In *The Cask of the Amontillado* the Italian nobleman Montresor famously says, "the thousand injuries of Fortunato I had borne as best I could, but when he ventured upon insult I vowed revenge." His "revenge" was to brick Fortunato up in wine cellar.[11] We never learned what the insults were. There were none. Montresor made them up. In his delusional state he blamed the victim, Fortunato, for forcing him to kill.

We blame the victims too. The violence in the ghetto is systemic. It is not happening simply because someone wants to take someone else's chain. First people have to lose that aspect of humanity that tells them a human life is worth more than a gold chain. The dehumanizing conditions of the ghetto set the stage for the systemic violence. But we don't see those conditions because those conditions are not what we are afraid of.

As the Trayvon Martin case suggests, the same fear that was once universally associated with black skin is now associated with a hip-hop dress styles, which has been painted as a source of crime. When Derrion Albert was killed in senseless violence, many said, "It's that music that they listen to." So we have demonized the music as well. As we demonize the music, we demonize the people. Real people disappear and become invisible. We don't see them. We see superpredators with twisty braids and gold teeth.

It is Fanon who says the explosion will not happen today, it is too soon. Hip-hop is the explosion that Fanon foretold. It is an explosion of rage against not only the conditions but also the stereotyping, of being invisible. Zimmerman never saw Trayvon. He saw a stereotype of a thug that existed in his mind.

In a real sense, hip-hop music is the purple pill to wake us up from the false reality that substitutes for our image of the ghetto and its people. As the blues chronicled the experiences of blacks during the great migration, hip-hop chronicles the aftermath of the migration of the late 20th century: when seven million blacks moved from the inner city to the suburbs.

Hip-hop is the sound of what it feels like to be left behind. They see the skyscrapers but they live in the projects. They see the limos, but their normal mode of transportation is a bicycle or the city bus. " . . . residents of the ghetto are not themselves blind to life as it is outside of the ghetto.

They observe that others enjoy a better life, and this knowledge brings a conglomerate of hostility, despair, and hope."[12]

Hip-hop in the end is a yearning, a dream of moving "across 110th street,"

> The native never ceases to dream of putting himself in the place of the settler—not of becoming the settler but of substituting himself for the settler. This hostile world, ponderous and aggressive because it fends off the colonized masses with all the harshness it is capable of, represents not merely a hell from which the swiftest flight possible is desired, but also a paradise close at hand, which is guarded by terrible watchdogs.[13]

It is time to declare a state of emergency.

But not against hip-hop—against the conditions that produced it. The emergency is not the N word, it is the fact that one in four black men in New York doesn't have a job. The emergency is the rat-infested houses that are boarded up, the garbage that is not picked up, the almost one million black men—fathers and uncles, husbands and sons—languishing behind barbed wire in prisons across the United States. It is the automatic rifle fire that punctuates the prayers of mothers when they put their babies to sleep, the schools that don't teach, and the dreams of children in Harlem, in South Central, in East Baltimore that rot like raisins in the sun.

Gangstas come as witnesses to the conditions in the ghetto. We can forgive the N word—it means something different to them than it means to us. We can forgive, if we are a mind to, the fact that children have absorbed degrading images of black women like they have absorbed lead from the paint in inner city homes. We can even forgive the Gangstas of their saggy pants and gold teeth. But history will not forgive us if we do not listen to their testimony in rhyme.

Notes

1. Jacques Billeaud, "Arizona Sheriff Joe Arpaio Unveils Obama Birth Certificate Probe," *Chicago Sun Times*, March 2, 2012, http://www.suntimes.com/news/nation/11004216–418/arizona-sheriff-joe-arpaio-unveils-obama-birth-certificate-probe.html

2. Sean Alfano and Bethany Storro, "Victim of Acid Attack, Said She Could Hear Her Skin Burning," *Daily News*, September 3, 2010.

3. Nikole Hannah-Jones, "The Sordid History of Racial Hoaxes," *The Root*, September 21, 2010, http://www.theroot.com/views/sordid-history-racial-hoaxes

4. Hannah-Jones, "The Sordid History of Racial Hoaxes."

5. Caroline O. Moser, *Urban Violence and Insecurity* (Nottingham, UK: Russell Press, 2004).

6. Richard M. Benjamin, *Looking for Whitopia: An Improbable Journey to the Heart of White America* (New York: Hyperion Books, 2009).

7. Donald Jones, "Skittles, Ice Tea and the Right to Stand Your Ground," *The Miami Herald*, April 11, 2012.

8. Jones, "Skittles, Ice Tea and the Right to Stand Your Ground."

9. Frances Robles, "What Is Known, What Isn't about Trayvon Martin's Death," *Miami Herald* (Miami, FL), March 31, 2012. Robles states "there had been a rash of burglaries in the neighborhood attributed to black men." David Morgenstern, a spokesman for the Sanford police, stated he did not know if the burglaries were actually committed by black men. "Were black males actually responsible for any of the crimes reported in the Retreat? 'Impossible to say.' Morgenstern, the police spokesman, said last week" Lane Gregory, "Trayvon Martin's Killing Shatters Safety within Retreat at Twin Lakes in Sanford," *Tampa Bay Times*, March 25, 2012.

10. Rob Cocoran, *Trustbuilding: An Honest Conversation on Race, Reconciliation, and Responsibility* (Charlottesville: University of Virginia Press 2010), 10.

11. Edgar Allen Poe, ed., "The Cask of the Amontillado," in *The Portable Edgar Allen Poe* (London: Penguin Books, 2006).

12. Kenneth Bancroft Clark, *Dark Ghetto: Dilemmas of Social Power* (Hanover, NH: Weslyan University Press, 1965), 12.

13. Frantz Fanon, *The Wretched of the Earth* (New York: Grove Press, 1965), 52.

Bibliography

Books

Acampora, Christa D. *Unmaking Race, Remaking Soul: Transformative Aesthetics and the Practice of Freedom.* New York: State University of New York Press, 2007.

Alexander, Michelle. *The New Jim Crow.* New York: The New Press, 2010.

Andrews, David L., and Steven J. Jackson. *Sport Stars: The Cultural Politics of Sporting Celebrity.* New York: Psychology Press, 2001.

Baker, Houston A. *Betrayal: How Black Intellectuals Have Abandoned the Ideals of the Civil Rights Movement.* New York: Columbia University Press, 2008.

Baldwin, Davarian. "Black Empires, White Desires: The Spatial Politics of Identity." In *That's the Joint!: The Hip-Hop Studies Reader*, edited by Murray Forman and Mark Anthony Neal, 182–203. London: Routledge, 2004.

Baldwin, James. *The Price of the Ticket: Collected Fiction.* New York: St. Martin's Press, 1985.

Baldwin, James, Fred L. Standley, and Louis H. Pratt. *Conversations with James Baldwin.* Jackson: University Press of Mississippi, 1989.

Baraka, Imamu A. *Blues People: Negro Music in White America*, 2. New York: William Morrow and Company, 1980.

Baum, Dan. *Smoke and Mirrors: The War on Drugs and the Politics of Failure.* New York: Little Brown, 1996.

Bertram, Eva. *Drug War Politics: The Price of Denial.* Berkeley: University of California Press, 1996.

Bhabha, Homi K. *The Location of Culture.* New York: Psychology Press, 1994.

Bhabha, Homi. *The Location of Culture*. London: Routledge, 2004.

Bloom, Ken, Frank Vlastnik, and John Lithgow. *Sitcoms: The 101 Greatest TV Comedies of All Time*, 184–185. New York: Black Dog and Leventhal, 2007.

Boothe, Demico. *Why Are So Many Black Men in Prison*. Memphis, TN: Full Service Publishing, 2007.

Bowen, Barbara. "Untroubled Voice: Call and Response in Cane." In *Black Literature and Black Literary Theory*, edited by Henry Louis Gates and Sunday Ogbonna Anozie, 187–205. New York: Routledge, 1990.

Boyd, Herb. *Race and Resistance: African-Americans in the Twenty-First Century*. Brooklyn, NY South End Press, 2002.

Boyd, Todd. *The New HNIC: The Death of Civil Rights and the Reign of Hip-Hop*. New York: New York University Press, 2004.

Boyle, Kevin. *Organized Labor and American Politics, 1894–1994: The Labor-Liberal Alliance*. Albany: State University of New York Press, 1998.

Bracey, John, August Meier, and Elliott M. Rudwick. *Black Matriarchy: Myth or Reality?* Stanford, CT: Wadsworth Publishing Company, 1971.

Breitman, George. *Malcolm X Speaks: Selected Speeches and Statements*. New York: Grove Press, 1965.

Brown, Cecil. *Stagolee Shot Billy*. Cambridge, MA: Harvard University Press, 2004.

Brown, Fahamisha P. *Performing the Word: African American Poetry as Vernacular Culture*. Rutgers: Rutgers University Press, 1999.

Brown, Michael K. *Race, Money and the American Welfare State*. Ithaca, NY: Cornell University Press, 1999.

Brown, Sterling A. "Strong Men." In *Making It on Broken Promises: Leading African-American Male Scholars*, edited by Lee Jones and Cornel West. Sterling, VA: Stylus Publishing, 2002.

Bryant, William C., and Parke Godwin. *The Life and Works of William Cullen Bryant*. Vol. 1, 37. New York: General Books LLC, 2010 (Original publication 1883).

Bynoe, Yvonne. *Stand and Deliver: Political Activism, Leadership, and Hip-Hop Culture*. Berkeley, CA: Soft Skull Press, 2004.

Carr, James, and Nandinee K. Kutty. *Segregation: The Rising Costs for America*. London: Routledge Press, 2008.

Cashin, Sheryll. *The Failures of Integration: How Race and Class Are Undermining the American Dream*. Jackson, TN: Public Affairs Books, 2005.

Chambliss, William. "Drug War Politics: Racism, Corruption, and Alienation." In *Crime Control and Social Justice: The Delicate Balance*, edited by Darnell F. Hawkins, Samuel L. Myers, and Randolph N. Stone. Westport, CT: Greenwood Press, 2003.

Chatterton, Paul, and Robert Hollands. *Urban Nightscapes: Youth Cultures, Pleasure Spaces and Corporate Power*. New York: Psychology Press, 2003.

Clark, Kenneth B. *Dark Ghetto: Dilemmas of Social Power*. Middletown, CT: Wesleyan University Press, 1965.

Coats, Karen. *Looking Glasses and Neverlands: Lacan, Desire, and Subjectivity in Children's Literature*. Iowa City: Iowa University Press, 2004.

Cobb, William J. *To the Break of Dawn: A Freestyle on the Hip-Hop Aesthetic*. New York: New York University Press, 2007.

Cohen, Felix S. *Handbook of Federal Indian Law*, edited by R. Strickland et al., 83. Washington, DC: Office of the Solicitor, U.S. Department of the Interior, 1982.)

Coleman, Beth. *Pimp Notes on Autonomy in Greg Tate, Everything but the Burden: What White People Are Taking from Black Culture*, 68–73. New York: Broadway Books, 2003.

Collins, Patricia H. *From Black Power to Hip-Hop: Racism, Nationalism, and Feminism*. Philadelphia: Temple University Press, 2006.

Conyers, James L., and Andrew P. Smallwood. *Malcolm X: A Historical Reader*. Chapel Hill: University of North Carolina Press, 2008.

Cruse, Harold. *The Crisis of the Negro Intellectual: An Historical Analysis of the Failure of Black Leadership*. New York: The New York Review of Books, 1967.

Currie, Elliott. *Crime and Punishment in America*. New York: MacMillan, 1998.

Currie, Elliott. *Reckoning: Drugs, the Cities, and the American Future*. Boston: South End Press, 1994.

Curtis, Lynn. "Locked in the Poor House: Cities, Race, and Poverty in the United States." *The Review of Black Political Economy*, June 22, 2000.

Dance, Darryl C. *Shucking and Jivin: Folklore from Contemporary Black Americans*. Bloomington: Indiana University Press, 1981.

Davis, Timothy, Kevin R. Johnson, and George A. Martínez. *A Reader on Race, Civil Rights, and American Law: A Multiracial Approach.* Durham, NC: Carolina Academic Press, 2001.

Delgado, Richard, and Jean Stefancic. *Critical Race Theory: The Cutting Edge*, 182. Philadelphia: Temple University Press, 2000.

Drake, St. Clair, and Horace R. Cayton. *Black Metropolis: A Study of Negro Life in a Northern City.* Chicago: University of Chicago Press, 1993.

Du Bois, W.E.B. *Black Reconstruction in America: 1860–1880*, edited by David Levering Lewis, 700. New York: Free Press, 1999.

Du Bois, W.E.B. *The Philadelphia Negro.* Philadelphia: University of Pennsylvania Press, Isabel Eaton, 1899.

Du Bois, W.E.B. *The Souls of Black Folk*, edited by Brent Haynes Edwards. Oxford: Oxford University Press, 2007.

Du Bois, W.E.B. *The Souls of Black Folk.* Rockville, MD: Arc Manor Reprints, 2008.

Dudziak, Mary L. *Cold War Civil Rights: Race and the Image of American Democracy*, 248. Princeton, NJ: Princeton University Press, 2002.

Dundes, Alan. *Mother Wit from the Laughing Barrel: Readings in the Interpretation of African-American Folklore.* Jackson: University of Mississippi Press, 1990.

Dunn, Stephane. *"Baad Bitches" and Sassy Supermamas: Black Power Action Films.* Urbana-Champaign: University of Illinois Press, 2008.

Durrant, Sam. *Post-Colonial Narrative and the Work of Mourning: J.M. Coetzee, William Harris, and Toni Morrisson.* New York: State University of New York Press, 2004.

Effiong, Philip U. *In Search of a Model for African-American Drama: A Study of Selected Plays.* Lanham, MD: University Press of America, 2000.

Ellison, Ralph. *Invisible Man*, 8. New York: Random House, 1995.

Ellison, Ralph. *Shadow and Act.* New York: Random House, 1995.

Fanon, Frantz. *Black Skin, White Masks.* New York: Grove Press, 1952.

Favor, J. Martin. *Authentic Blackness: The Folk in the New Negro Renaissance.* Durham, NC: Duke University Press, 1999.

Fellner, Jamie. *Punishment and Prejudice: The Racial Disparities in the War on Drugs.* New York City: Human Rights Watch, 2000.

Finkelman, Paul, and Peter Wallenstein. *The Encyclopedia of American Political History.* Washington, DC: Congressional Quarterly Press, 2001.

Foner, Eric. *Reconstruction: America's Unfinished Revolution*. New York: Harper Collins, 1988.

Fong, Mary, and Rueyling Chang. *Communicating Ethnic and Cultural Identity*. Lanham, MD: Rowman and Littlefield, 2004.

Ford, Marjorie, and Jon Ford. *Mass Culture and the Electronic Media*. Boston: Houghton, Mifflin, 1999.

Forman, Murray, and Mark Anthony Neal. *That's the Joint!: The Hip-Hop Studies Reader*. London: Routledge, 2004.

Franklin, Donna L. *Ensuring Inequality: The Structural Transformation of the African-American Family*. New York: Oxford University Press, 1997.

Freeman, Jo. "The Bitch Manifesto." In *Notes from the Second Year, Women's Liberation: Major Writings of the Radical Feminists*, edited by Shulamith Firestone and Anne Koedt. Santa Barbara, CA: ABC-CLIO, 2011.

Garland, David. *Mass Imprisonment: Social Causes and Consequences*. Thousand Oaks, CA: Sage Press, 2001.

Gates, Henry L. *Figures in Black: Words, Signs and the Racial Self*, xxvi. New York: Oxford University Press, 1989.

Gates, Henry L. *The Signifying Monkey: A Theory of African American Literary Criticism*. Oxford: Oxford University Press, 1989.

George, Nelson. *Hip-Hop America*. London: Penguin Books, 2005.

Gibbs, Jewelle T. *Young, Black and Male in America*. Boston: Auburn House, 1988.

Gilroy, Paul. *The Black Atlantic*. Cambridge, MA: Harvard University Press, 1994.

Giroux, Henry A. *Breaking in to the Movies: Film and the Culture of Politics*. Hoboken, NJ: Wiley Blackwell, 2002.

Goldberg, David T. *Multiculturalism: A Critical Reader*. Hoboken, NJ: Blackwell, 1994.

Gordon, Robert. "New Developments in Legal Theory." In *The Politics of Law: A Progressive Critique*, edited by David Kairys. New York: Basic Books, 1998.

Gore, Tipper. "Hate, Rape and Rap." In *Rap and Hip Hop: Examining Pop Culture*, edited by Jared Green, 1st ed. Farmington Hills, MI: Greenhaven Press, 2003.

Gramsci, Antonio. *Prison Notebooks*. Translated by Joseph A. Buttigieg. Vol. 3, 169. New York: Columbia University Press, 2010.

Gray, Herman S. *Watching Race: Television and the Struggle for Blackness.* Minneapolis: University of Minnesota Press, 2004.

Grier, William H., and Price M. Cobbs. *Black Rage: Two Black Psychiatrists Reveal the Inner Conflicts and the Desperation of Black Life.* New York: Basic Books, 1992.

Griffin, Farah J. *Who Set You Flowin: The African Migration Narrative.* New York: Oxford University Press, 1995.

Hansberry, Lorraine. *A Raisin in the Sun.* New York: Samuel French, Inc., 1984.

Hansberry, Lorraine. *A Raisin in the Sun.* New York: Vintage Books; First Vintage Book Edition, 1994.

Harper, Phillip B. *Are We Not Men: Masculine Anxiety and the Problem of African American Identity.* Oxford: Oxford University Press, 1998.

Harrison, Alferdteen. *Black Exodus: The Great Migration from the American South.* Jackson: University Press of Mississippi, 1992.

Hemingway, Ernest. *A Farewell to Arms.* New York: Simon and Schuster, 1929.

Hofstede, David. *Planet of the Apes: An Unofficial Companion*, 137. Toronto: ECW Press, 2001.

hooks, bell. *Ain't I a woman: Black Women and Feminism.* Brooklyn, NY: South End Press, 2007.

Jemie, Onwuchekwa. *Yo Mama! New Raps, Toasts, Dozens, Jokes, and Children's Rhymes.* Philadelphia: Temple University Press, 2003.

Jimmy Breslin. *The Church That Forgot Christ.* New York: Free Press, 2004.

Johnson, Cedric. *Revolutionaries to Race Leaders: Black Power and the Making of African-American Politics.* Minneapolis: University of Minnesota Press, 2007.

Jones, D. Marvin. *Race, Sex, and Suspicion: The Myth of the Black Male.* Westport, CT: Greenwood, 2005.

Jordan, Barbara, and Elspeth D. Rostow. *The Great Society: A Twenty Year Critique.* Austin: University of Texas at Austin, 1986.

Joseph, Janice. *Black youths, Delinquency, Juvenile Justice.* Westport, CT: Greenwood Publishing, 1995.

Joseph, Peniel. *Waiting Till the Midnight Hour: A Narrative History of Black Power.* New York: Henry Holt and Company, 2007.

Joseph, Rudolph. *Legalizing Marijuana: Drug Policy Reform and Prohibition Politics.* Westport, CT: Praeger, 2008.

Judy, R.A.T. "On the Question of Nigga Authenticity." In *That's the Joint!: The Hip-Hop Studies Reader*, edited by Murray Forman and Mark Anthony Neal. London: Routledge, 2004.

Justice Policy Inst. *Cellblocks or Classrooms? The Funding of Higher Education and Corrections and Its Impact on African American Men*, http://www.justicepolicy.org/images/upload/02-09_REP_Cellblocks Classrooms_BB-AC.pdf

Keith, Michael, and Steve Pile. *Place and the Politics of Identity*. New York: Psychology Press, August 6, 2010.

Kelley, Robin D.G. *Race Rebels: Culture, Politics and the Black Working Class*. New York: Simon and Schuster, 1994.

Kelly, Robin D.G. *Race, Rebels: Culture, Politics, and the Black Working Class*. New York: Free Press, 1996.

Keyes, Cheryl L. *Rap Music and Street Consciousness*. Urbana-Champaign: University of Illinois Press, 2002.

King, Martin Luther. *Testament of Hope: The Essential Writings of Martin Luther King*, edited by James Melvin Washington. New York: Harper Collins, 1991.

King, Martin Luther. *Why We Can't Wait*. Boston: Beacon Press, 2011.

Klinkner, Philip A., and Rogers M. Smith. *The Unsteady March: The Rise and Decline of Racial Inequality in America*, 89. Chicago: University of Chicago Press, 2002.

Komozi Woodard. *A Nation within a Nation: Amiri Baraka (LeRoi Jones) and Black Power Politics*. Chapel Hill: University of North Carolina Press, 1999.

Kurian, George T., and Jeffrey D. Schultz. *The Encyclopedia of the Democratic Party: Volume 3*, 214. Armonk, NY: M.E. Sharpe Reference, 1997.

Kusmer, Kenneth L., and Joe William Trotter. *African American Urban History since World War II*. Chicago: University of Chicago Press, 2009.

Lehman, Nicolas. *The Promised Land: The Great Black Migration and How It Changed America*. New York: Alfred A. Knopf, 1991.

Leonard, David J. *Screens Fade to Black: Contemporary African American Cinema*. Westport, CT: Praeger, 2006.

Lipsitz, George. *Footsteps in the Dark Hidden Histories of Popular Music*. Minneapolis: University of Minnesota Press, 2007.

Lipsitz, George. *Time Passages: Collective Memory and American Popular Culture*. Minnesota: University of Minnesota Press, 2001.

Locke, Alain. *Harlem, Mecca of the New Negro* (1925) quoted in Lewis Porter. *Jazz, A Century of Change*. New York: Schirimer Books, 1997.

Locke, Alain. *The New Negro*. New York: Touchstone Press, an imprint of Simon and Schuster, 1925.

Lott, Tommy Lee. *The Invention of Race and the Politics of Representation*, 111. Maiden, MA: Blackwell, 1999.

Lott, Tommy Lee. *The Invention of Race: Black Culture and the Politics of Representation*. Maiden, MA: Blackwell, 1999.

Loukides, Paul, and Linda K. Fuller. *Beyond the Stars: Stock Characters in American Popular Film*. Wisconsin: University of Wisconsin Press, 1993.

Löwy, Michael, and Chris Turner. *Fire Alarm: Reading Walter Benjamin's On the Concept of History*. Brooklyn, NY: Verso Books, 2005.

Lubiano, Wahneema. *The House That Race Built: Black Americans, U.S. Terrain*. New York: Pantheon Books, 1988.

Macek, Steve. *Urban Nightmares: The Media, the Right, and the Moral Panic over the City*, 213. Minneapolis: University of Minnesota Press, 2006.

Marable, Manning, and Leith Mullins. *Let Nobody Turn Us Around: Voices of Resistance, Reform, and Renewal*. Plymouth, UK: Rowman and Littlefield, 2009.

Marqusee, Mike. *Redemption Song: Muhammad Ali and the Spirit of the Sixties*. London: Verso Books, 2005.

Massey, Douglas, and Nancy Denton, *American Apartheid: Segregation and the Making of the Black Underclass*. Cambridge, MA: Harvard University Press, 1993.

Mauer, Marc, and Tracy Huling. *The Sentencing Project, Young Black Americans and the Criminal Justice System: Five Years Later*, 12. Washington, DC: The Sentencing Project, 1995.

McCoy, Alfred W., and Alan A. Block, eds. "U.S. Narcotics Policy: An Anatomy of Failure." In *War on Drugs: Studies in the Failure of U.S. Narcotics Policy*, 1. Boulder, CO: Westview Press, 1992.

McNair, Brian. *Strip-Tease Culture: Sex, Media and the Democratization of Desire*. New York: Routledge, 2006.

Meranto, Philip J. *Kerner Commission Report: Final Report and Background Papers*. Urbana: University of Institute of Government Affairs, University of Illinois, 1970.

Meyer, Dirk De, et al. *The Urban Condition: Space, Community, and Self in the Contemporary Metropolis.* Rotterdam, The Netherlands: 010 Publishers, 1999.

Mieder, Wolfgang. *Making a Way Out of No Way: Martin Luther King's Sermonic Proverbial Rhetoric.* Leipzig: Die Deutche Nationalbibliothek, 2010.

Miller, Jerome G. *Search and Destroy: African-American Males in the Criminal Justice System.* Cambridge: Cambridge University Press, 2011.

Millner, Denene, and Bill Condon. *Dreamgirls.* New York: Harper Collins, 2006.

Milovanovic, Dragan, and Katheryn K. Russell. *Petit Apartheid in the U.S. Criminal Justice System.* Durham, NC: Carolina Academic Press, 2001.

Moen, Phyllis, Donna Dempster-McClain, and Henry A. Walker. *A Nation Divided: Diversity, Inequality and Community in American Society.* Ithaca, NY: Cornell University Press, 1999.

Mollenkopf, John. *The Contested City.* Princeton, NJ: Princeton University Press, 1983.

Morgan, Joan. *When Chicken-Heads Come Home to Roost: A Hip-Hop Feminist Breaks It Down.* New York: Simon and Schuster, 1999.

Morrison, Toni, *Race-ing Justice. Engendering Power.* New York: Random House, 1992.

Moses, Robert P., and Charles E. Cobb, Jr. *Radical Equations: Civil Rights from Mississippi to the Algebra Project*, 3. Boston: Beacon Street, 2001.

Myrdal, Gunnar, and Sissela Bok. *An American Dilemma: The Negro Problem and Modern Democracy.* Vol. 2, 525. Piscatawy, NJ: Transaction Publishers, 1995.

Nelson, Emmanuel S. *African-American Dramatists: An A-Z Guide.* Westport, CT: Greenwood Press, 2004.

Norrell, Robert J. *The House I Live In: Race in the American Century.* New York: Oxford University Press, 2005.

Ogbar, Jeffrey. *Black Power: Radical Politics and African-American Identity.* Baltimore, MD: Johns Hopkins University Press, 2005.

Oliver, Richard W. *Hip-Hop Inc: Success Strategies of the Rap Moguls.* New York: Thunder's Mouth Press, 2006.

Palahniuk, Chuck. *Fight Club*. New York: W.W. Norton, 1996.

Parker, Derrick, and Diehl, Matt. *Notorious C.O.P.: The Inside Story of the Tupac, Biggie, and Jam Master Jay*. San Clemente, CA: Tantor Media, 2007.

Pauley, Garth E. *The Modern Presidency & Civil Rights: Rhetoric on Race from Roosevelt to Nixon*. College Station, TX: TAMU Press, 2001.

Pavlic, Edward M. *Crossroads Modernism: Descent and Emergence in African-American Literary Culture*. Minneapolis, MN: University of Minnesota Press, 2002.

Perkins, William E., ed. *Droppin' Science: Critical Essays on Rap Music and Hip-Hop Culture*. Philadelphia: Temple University Press, 1996.

Perkinson, Robert. *Texas Tough: The Rise of America's Prison Empire*. London: MacMillan, 2009.

Perry, Imani. *Prophets of the Hood: Politics and Poetics in Hip-Hop*. Durham, NC: Duke University Press, 2004.

Podair, Jerald E. *The Strike That Changed New York: Blacks, Whites and the Ocean Hill-Brownsville Crisis*, 126. New Haven, CT: Yale University Press, 2004.

Poe, Edgar A., ed. "The Cask of the Amontillado." In *The Portable Edgar Allen Poe*. London: Penguin Books, 2006.

Pough, Gwendolyn D. *Check It While I Wreck It*. Lebanon, NH: University Press of New England, 2004.

Powell, John A., and Eileen B. Hershenov. "Hostage to the Drug War: The National Purse, the Constitution and the Black Community." *U.C. Davis Law Review* 24 (1991): 557.

Quinn, Eithne. *Nuthin' but a "G" Thang: The Culture and Commerce of Gangsta Rap*. New York: Columbia University Press, 2005.

Reeves, Marcus. *Somebody Scream!: Rap Music's Rise to Prominence in the Aftershock of Black Power*. London: Faber and Faber, Inc., 2009.

Reeves, Richard. *President Nixon: Alone in the White House*. New York: Simon and Schuster, 2002.

Reinarman, Craig, and Harry G. Levine. *Crack in America: Demon Drugs and Social Justice*. Berkeley: University of California Press, 1997.

Roberts, John W. *From Trickster to Badman: The Black Folk Hero in Slavery and Freedom*. Philadelphia: University of Pennsylvania Press, 1989.

Roberts, John W. " 'Railroad Bill' and the American Outlaw Tradition in Western Folklore." *Western Folklore*. Vol. 40, 315–28, no. 4 October 1981.

Rodriguez, Nelson M., and Leila E. Villaverde. *Dismantling White Privilege: Pedagogy, Politics, and Whiteness*. Switzerland: Peter Lang Publisher, 2000.

Roediger, David. *The Wages of Whiteness: Race in the Making of the American Working Class,* Brooklyn, New York: Verso Books, 1999.

Rood, Karen L. *American Culture after WWII*. Farmington Hills, MI: Gale Research, 1993.

Rose, Tricia. *Black Noise.* Middletown, CT: Wesleyan University Press, 1994.

Rose, Tricia. *Hip-Hop Wars: What We Talk about When We Talk about Hip-Hop- and Why It Matters*. New York: Basic Books, 2008.

Rose, Tricia. "Never Trust a Big Butt and a Smile." In *That's the Joint!: The Hip-Hop Studies Reader*, edited by Murray Forman and Mark A. Neal, 291. London: Routledge, 2004.

Rutherford, Paul. *Endless Propaganda: The Advertising of Public Goods*. Toronto: University of Toronto Press, 2000.

Saltzman, Jack, David L. Smith, and Cornel West. *Encyclopedia of African-American Culture and History*, 1310. New York: Macmillan Library Reference, 1996.

Sawyer, Diane, and Chris Cuomo. "Reverend Jeremiah Wright: Obama's Pastor Now a Campaign Liability?" *Good Morning America*, 7:07 AM EST, March 13, 2008.

Schaefer, Richard T. *Encyclopedia of Race, Ethnicity and Society*. Vol. 1. Thousand Oakes, CA: Sage Publications, 2008.

Shakespeare, William, Burton Rafael, and Harold Bloom. *The Tempest*. New York: Infobase Publishing, 2006.

Shalala, Donna E., Mary F. Williams, and Andrew Fishel. *Readings in American Politics and Education*. Chicago: Scott-Foresman, 1963.

Sharpley-Whiting, T. Denean. *Pimp's-Up, Ho's Down: Hip-Hop's Hold on Young Black Women*. New York: New York University Press, 2007.

Spivak, Gayatri C. "Teaching for the Times." In *Dangerous Liaisons: Gender, Nation and Post-Colonial Perspectives*, edited by Anne McClintock, Aamir Mufti, and Ella Shohat. Minneapolis: University of Minnesota Press, 1997.

Steele, Shelby. *A Dream Deferred: The Second Betrayal of Black Freedom in America*. New York: Harper Collins, 1998.

Tate, Greg. *Everything but the Burden: What White People Are Taking from Black Culture*. New York: Broadway Books, 2003.

Taylor Gibbs, Jewell. *Young, Black and Male in America: An Endangered Species*. Boston, MA: Auburn House Publishing Co., 1988.

Tolnay, Stewart, and Beck, E. M. *A Festival of Violence: An Analysis of Southern Lynchings, 1882–1930*. Champaign, IL: University of Illinois Press, 1995.

Tonry, Michael. *Malign Neglect: Race, Crime and Punishment in America*. New York: Oxford University Press, 1996.

Wachtel, Paul L. *Race in the Mind of America: Breaking the Vicious Circle between Blacks and Whites*. New York: Routledge, 1999.

Wacquant, Loic. *Deadly Symbiosis: When Ghetto and Prison Meet and Mesh*. Hoboken, NJ: John Wiley and Sons, 2010.

Watkins, S. Craig, *Hip-Hop Matters: Politics, Pop Culture and the Struggle for the Soul of a Movement*. Boston: Beacon Press, 2005.

Watkins, S. Craig. *Hip-Hop Matters: Politics, Pop-Culture and the Struggle for the Soul of a Movement*. Boston: Beacon Press, 2006.

Watkins, S. Craig, ed. "Fear of a White Planet." In *Hip-Hop Matters, Politics, Pop-Culture and the Struggle for the Soul of a Movement*. Boston: Beacon Press, 2006.

White, Walter. *Rope and Faggot: A Biography of Judge Lynch*. Notre Dame: University of Notre Dame Press, 2002.

Williams, Juan. *Enough: The Phony Leaders, Dead-end Movements, and Culture of Failure That Are Undermining Black America - and What We Can Do about It*. New York: Crown Publishing, 2006.

Wilson, August. *Joe Turner's Come and Gone*. New York: Samuel French, Inc., 1990.

Wilson, William Julius. *When Work Disappears: The World of the New Urban Poor*. New York: Alfred A. Knopf, 1996.

Wilson, William J. *Bridge over the Racial Divide: Rising Inequality and Coalition Politics*. Berkeley: University of California Press, 2009.

Winant, Howard. *The New Politics of Race: Globalism, Difference, Justice*. Minnesota: University of Minnesota Press, 2004.

Wright, Richard. *12 Million Black Voices*. New York: Thunder's Mouth Press, 1941.

Yancy, George. *Black Bodies, White Gazes: The Continuing Significance of Race*, 86. Lanham, MD: Rowman & Littlefield, 2008.

Yuill, Kevin L. *Richard Nixon and the Rise of Affirmative Action: The Pursuit of Racial Equality in an Era of Limits*. Lanham, MD: Rowman & Littlefield, 2006.

Articles: From Journals, Magazines, and Other Print Media

Bailey, Ronald. "Is Crime Contagious: Experiments Vindicate the Broken Windows Theory." *Reason Magazine*, November 25, 2008.

Berry, Mary F. *Police Practices and Civil Rights in New York City*. Washington, DC: The United States Civil Rights Commission, 2000.

Cook, Brian. "Joys of the Wire." *In These Times*, Chicago, February 22, 2008.

Cosby, Bill. "Speech at NAACP Gala Celebration of the Brown Decision." *Constitution Hall*, Washington DC, May 17, 2004 quoted in Juan Williams. *Enough: The Phony Leaders, Dead-end Movements, and Culture of Failure That Are Undermining Black America - and What We Can Do about It*. New York: Crown Publishing, 2006.

Dilulio, John J. "The Coming of the Super-Predators." *The Weekly Standard*, Washington, DC, November 27, 1995.

Markus Dubber, *Victims in the War on Crime: the Use and Abuse of Victim's Rights*, New York: NYU Press, (2006), 15.

Dudziak, Mary L. "Desegregation as a Cold War Imperative." 41 *Stanford Law Review* 61 (1988): 66.

Eckholm, Erick. "Plight Deepens for Black Men." *New York Times*, New York, March 20, 2006.

Entman, Robert. "Representation and Reality in the Portrayal of Blacks on Network and Television News." *Journalism Quarterly* 71, no. 3 (1994): 509–520.

Entman, Robert, and Gross, Kimberly A. "Race, to Judgment: Stereotyping Media and Criminal Defendants." *Law and Contemporary Problems* 71, no. 93 (Autumn 2008): 5–6.

Frosch, Dan. "Colorado Police Link Rise in Violence to Music." *New York Times*, New York, September 3, 2007.

Gagan, Bryony J. "Ferguson v. City of Charleston, South Carolina: 'Fetal Abuse,' Drug Testing, and the Fourth Amendment." *Stanford Law Review* 53 (2000): 491, 496.

Harris, Aisha N. "Black Film Genre Fosters Stereotypes." *Hartford Courant*, Hartford, CT, A13, February 17, 2010.

Holland, Robert, and Dan Soifer. "How School Choice Benefits the Urban Poor." *Howard Law Journal* 45 (2002): 337.

hooks, bell. "Sexism and Misogyny, Gangsta Rap, and the Piano." *Z Magazine*, Woods Hole, MA, 1994.

Hutchinson, Darren L. "The Majoritarian Difficulty: Affirmative Action, Sodomy, and Supreme Court Politics." *Law and Inequality* 23 (2005): 1, 26, 27; Cedric Merlin Powell. "Rhetorical Neutrality: Colorblindness, Frederick Douglass, and Inverted Critical Race Theory." *Cleveland State Law Review* 56 (2008): 823.

Jernigan, David, and Lori Dorfman. "Visualizing America's Drug Problems: An Ethnographic Content Analysis of Illegal Drug Stories on the Nightly News." *Contemporary Drug Problems* 23 (1996): 169, 174.

Jones, D. Marvin. "Darkness Made Visible: Law, Metaphor and the Racial Self." 82 Geo. L. J. 427 (1993): 490 .

Jones, D. Marvin. " 'Been in the Storm So Long': Katrina, Reparations, and the Original Understanding of Equal Protection." In *Hurricane Katrina: America's Unnatural Disaster*, edited by Jeremy I. Levitt and Matthew C. Whittaker. Lincoln: University of Nebraska Press, 2005.

Jones, D. Marvin. "No Time for Trumpets: Title VII. Equality and the Fin de Seicle." *Michigan Law Review* 92 (1994): 2311.

Jones, D. Marvin. "The Original Meaning of Brown: Seattle, Segregation and the Rewriting of History: For Michael Lee and Dukwon." *University of Miami Law Review* 63 (2009): 629.

Kempton, Murray. "Bush Tactics Turn Ugly." *Newsday*, October 30, 1988, 7.

Ludden, Jennifer. "Bucking Trend, Homicides among Black Youths Rise." *NPR*, December 29, 2008.

Malcolm, Andrew H. "Prison at a Crossroads: To Punish or to Counsel?" *National Desk, The New York Times*, New York, 1988, 12.

Malloy, Courtland. "Precious: A Film as Lost as the Girl It Glorifies." *Washington Post*, Washington, DC, November 18, 2009.

Nunn, Kenneth B. "Race, Crime and the Pool of Surplus Criminality: Or Why 'War on Drugs?' Was a 'War on Blacks'." *The Journal of Gender, Race and Justice* 6 (2002): 381.

Nunn, Kenneth B. " 'Still Up on the Roof': Race, Victimology, and the Response to Hurricane Katrina." In *Hurricane Katrina: America's*

Unnatural Disaster, edited by Jeremy Levitt and Matthew Whittaker,_ Lincoln: University of Nebraska Press, 2005, 183–206.

Orfield, Gary. *Dismantling Desegregation: The Quiet Reversal of Brown v. Board of Education*, 53. New York: The New Press, 1997.

Ostrow, Ronald. "Sentencing Study Sees Race Disparity." *Los Angeles Times*, October 5, 1995.

Reilly, Bill O'. "Factor Follow-Up Interview with Jackson Bain." *The O' Reilly Factor*, August 28, 2002.

Report of the Nat'l Advisory Comm'n on Civil Disorders. Washington, DC: National Advisory Commission on Civil Disorders, 1968.

Richey, Warren. "Affirmative Action's Evolution." *Christian Science Monitor*, March 28, 2003.

Rothkerch, Ian. "What Drugs Have Not Destroyed, the War on Them Has." *Salon Magazine*, San Francisco, CA, Saturday, June 29, 2002.

Schott Foundation. "Yes We Can: The Schott 50 State Report," www. blackboysreport.org (accessed December 25, 2011).

Senna, Danzy. "Violence Is Golden: The Tupac Shakur Story." *Spin Magazine*, 1994.

Smith, Barbara. " 'Civilization': The Decline of Middle-Class Manlienss, and Ida B. Wells Anti-Lynching Campaign (1892-94)." *Radical History Review* 52 (1992): 9.

Sowell, Thomas. "Tools for Rising above Are Withheld Today." *Ft. Lauderdale, Fl. Sun Sentinel*, November 6, 2001.

Stone, Sasha. "The State of Race: It's the Movies." *Awards Daily*, Valley Village, CA, August 30, 2009.

"Reagan in Radio Talk, Vows Drive against Drugs." *New York Times*, October 3, 1982, at 1:38.

Taylor, Daphne. "Task Force Tackles Grim Graduation Rate for Blacks." *South Florida Times*, Ft. Lauderdale, FL, December 26, 2011.

"Teen's Beating May Be Gang Related." *United Press International*, September 25, 2009.

Vogelman, Lawrence. "The Big Black Man Syndrome: The Rodney King Trial and the Use of Racial Stereotypes in the Courtroom." *Fordham Urban Law Journal* 20 (1993): 571–8.

Willens, Kathy. "Black College Women Take Aim at Rappers." *USA Today*, McClean, VA, April 23, 2004.

"Winning the War on Drugs: A Second Chance for Non-violent 'Offend-
    ers'." *Harvard Law Review* 113 (2000): 1485.
Zunz, Olivier. *The Changing Face of Inequality: Urbanization, Industrial
    Development and Immigrants in Detroit.* Chicago: University of Chi-
    cago Press, 1982.

Films, DVDs, Television Episodes

Across 100th Street, DVD, Barry Shear, Original Release 1972, Los An-
    geles: United Artists, DVD, Los Angeles. Metro-Goldwyn Meyer, Oc-
    tober 16, 2001.
Birth of a Nation. Directed by D.W. Griffith. Original Release 1915. New
    York: Kino on Video, VHS Video Epoch Film Company, 1993.
Dreamgirls. Directed by Bill Condon. Universal City, CA: Dreamworks,
    2006.
Drum Line. Film. Directed by Charles Stone. Los Angeles: 20th Century
    Fox, December 13, 2002.
Foxy Brown. DVD. Directed by Jack Hill. Original Release 1974 by Ameri-
    can International Pictures, Los Angeles. Los Angeles: Metro-Goldwyn
    Mayer, January 9, 2001.
Guess Who's Coming to Dinner. Directed by Stanley Kramer. Culver City,
    CA: Columbia Pictures, 1967.
"Hard Times at Douglass High: A No Child Left Behind Report Card."
    HBO 2008 Documentary Film Series. HBO, July 8, 2008.
Hustle and Flow. DVD. Directed by Craig Brewer. Los Angeles: Para-
    mount Pictures, 2005, B000I52LVS.
Johnson, Lamar C. "Through Viewers' Eyes: Watching Race, Space, Place
    and the Hood Motif in Urban High School Genre Film." Paper posted
    on the web at http://juyc.info/pdf/Lamar_Johnson.pdf (last visited
    March 9, 2012).
Judgment Night. Film. Directed by Stephen Hopkins. Universal City, CA:
    Universal Pictures, 1993.
Malcolm X. Film. Directed by Spike Lee. Burbank, CA: Warner Bros., 1992.
New Jack City. Film. Directed by Mario Van Peebles. Burbank, CA: War-
    ner Bros., 1991.
Shaft. Film. Directed by Gordon Parks. Original Release 1971, Los Ange-
    les: Metro-Goldwyn-Mayer, DVD Warner Bros., June 6, 2000.

Sohn, Sonja (Playing detective Kima Griggs). *The WIRE, "Took,"* HBO Films, Episode 7, directed by Dominic West, aired February 17, 2008.

Superfly. DVD. Directed by Gordon Parks. Original Release 1972. Burbank, CA: Warner Bros., January 13, 2004.

Training Day. Directed by Antoine Fuqua. Burbank, CA: Warner Bros., 2001.

Tresspass. Film. Directed by Walter Hill. Universal City, CA: Universal Pictures, 1992.

Wright, Thomas L., and Barry M. Cooper. *New Jack City.* Film. Directed by Mario Van Peebles. Burbank, CA: Warner Bros., 1991.

Cases

Brown v. Board of Education, 347 U.S. 483 (1954).

Plessy v. Ferguson, 163 U.S. 537 (1896), overruled by, Brown v. Board of Educ., 347 U.S. 483 (1954).

Worcester v. Georgia, 31 U.S. (6 Pet.) 515 (1832).

Discography

Big Punisher. "Fast Money." *Capital Punishment.* Terror Squad/Loud Records B00000K3HL, Compact Disk, April 28, 1998.

Boy, Soulja. "Pow." *Soulja Boy Tell Em.* Collipark Records, B000V9KF0A CD, 2007.

Browz, Ron. "I'll Whip Yo Head Boy" on album called *Get Rich or Die Tryin'* performed by 50 Cent. Santa Monica: G-Unit/Interscope Records, February 4, 2003.

Crosby, Stills, Nash, and Young. "Ohio." *Four Way Street*, 1971. Atlantic Records, audio CD released 1992.

Cry Babies (Oh No) on an album called *Word of Mouf.* Performed by Ludacris. New York City: Def Jam South, 2001.

50 Cent, "I Run New York." *Bulletproof* (Mixtape) (Independent 2005).

50 Cent, "P-I-M-P." *Get Rich or Die Tryin',* 2003.

50 Cent. "The Realest Niggaz." *24 Shots: Brand New Exclusive Material & Freestylers*, F150 Records, B000ANGFCO, *Compact Disk*, Original Release May 2003.

Foxy Brown, "Queen Bitch." *Chyna Doll*, Album, 1999.

Ice Cube. "The World Is Mine." Soundtrack from *Dangerous Ground*. Directed by Daryll Roodt. Los Angeles: New Line Cinema, 1997.

Ice-T. "Rhyme Pays." *6 in the Mornin*, Warner Brothers, MP3 Albums, B001A83H6K, 1987.

Ice-T. "Straight Up Nigga." Original Gangster Album, Sire Records 1991.

James Brown. " 'Say It Loud'—I'm Black and I'm Proud." *Say It Loud-I'm Black and I'm Proud*. Cincinnati: King Records, 1968 on *Say It Loud (Best of James Brown Live)*, audio CD. Cincinnati: Setco Records, 2010.

Ja'net Dubois. "Movin on Up" theme Song from "The Jefferson's," see Bob Lally, Oz Scott, Jack Shea, Tony Singletary, Arlando Smith, *The Jeffersons—The Complete First Season*, DVD, Sony Pictures, August 6, 2002, aired on CBS from January 18, 1975 to June 25, 1985.

Lil' Kim. "Queen Bitch." *Hard Core*, Big Beat, B000000112, Audio CD, 1996.

Mystikel. "Pussy Crook." *Tarantula* (Explicit), Jive December 18, 2001.

N.W.A. Straight Outa Compton, *A Bitch Is a Bitch*. Ruthless /Priority/EMI Records, MP3 Albums, B00138H5YC, 2001.

Robinson, Smokey. "The Tracks of My Tears." Detroit: *Tamla Records*, 1965 on *Motown Legends: Smokey Robinson-The Tracks of My Tears* (CD).

Shakur, Tupac. "Young Black Male." from 2Pacalypse Now, Interscope Record 1991, Audio CD released 1998.

Straight Outta Compton (Vinyl), Ruthless Records, 1988.

The Impressions. "Choice of Colors." *Movin' on Up, The Music and Message of Curtis Mayfield*. DVD. Santa Monica, CA: Hip-O Records (part of Universal Music Group), 2008.

The Temptations. *"My Girl," Single (Vinyl)*. Detroit: Gordy Records (Motown), 1964.

Trick Daddy. "I'm a Thug." *Thugs Are Us*. Atlantic Records, March 20, 2001.

Trina. "Da Baddest Bitch." *Da Baddest Bitch,* Atlantic Records B00004R8Q5, Audio CD, 2000.

Wagner, Richard. " 'The Ride of the Valkyries' from 'Die Valkyrie,' performed by the Vienna Philharmonic Orchestra in Francis Ford Copola, 'Apocalypse Now'." San Francisco, CA: Zoetrope Studios, 1979.

X-Raided, "Bitch Killa," Psycho-Active. Black Market Records, MP3 Albums, B000QQKT2C, 1992.

Fine Art Reproductions

Lawrence, Jacob. *The Migration of The Negro*, panel 15 (1940–1941).

Web sources

AC360°. "Doll Study Revisited, Girl Calls Her Skin Nasty." August 12, 2010, http://ac360.blogs.cnn.com/2010/08/12/ac360°-doll-study-revisited-girl-calls-her-skin-"nasty"/? iref=allsearch.

Black Buffalo. http://ppg-buffalo.wikispaces.com/file/view/Black_Bflo_Profile_Table_2%5B1%5D.pdf.

Divorce Court. *Don Ware v. Tiffany Brown*, September 16, 2009. Ware called himself, "Don Juan the Pimpin Son!" http://divorcecourting.blogspot.com/2009_09_01_archive.html.

Hollander, Michelle. *Unemployment in New York City during the Recession and Early Recovery: Young Black Men Hit the Hardest.* Community Service Society of New York, December 2010, http://www.cssny.org/userimages/downloads/OnlyOneInFourYoungBlackMenInNYCHaveaJobDec2010.pdf.

Levine, Mark V. *The Crisis Deepens: Black Male Joblessness in Milwaukee.* Center for Economic Development University of Wisconsin, October 2010,http://www4.uwm.edu/ced/publications/blackjoblessness_2010.pdf (last accessed February 2, 2010).

Paula Zahn Now. "Hip-Hop: Art or Poison?" *CNN.Com*, February 21, 2007. http://transcripts.cnn.com/TRANSCRIPTS/0702/21/pzn.01.html.

Sunami, Chris. "The Racial Draft." 8/6/07 at http://kitoba.com/entry244.html (last accessed September 28, 2009).

White, Armond. "Pride and Precious." *The New York Press*, November 4, 2009, http://www.nypress.com/article-20554-pride-precious.html.

Index

social disparities, 37; spatial
isolation, 39; stereotypes, 36
*Race, Sex, and Suspicion: The
Myth of the Black Male*, 38–39
Racial coding of violence, 62
Racial identity (Du Bois, W. E. B.),
170
Racial order, 70–71
Racial pluralism, 227
Racial realism, 227
Racism, 8, 159–60; aftermath of
Hurricane Katrina, 159–60;
inside/outside metaphor, 8; top-
bottom hierarchy, 8
Raisin in the Sun, 49
Rap, 198; commercial version,
124; gangsta. *See* Gangsta rap
Rappers, attack on, 5
Reagan, Ronald, 72; Anti-Drug
Abuse Act, 1986, 73; drug
myths and stereotypes, 74;
drug war, 72–76; higher
education budgets, 73; NCIA,
76; self-fulfilling prophecy,
74; Sentencing Project, 75–76;
shrink government, 73; target on
low-income communities, 75
Realism, racial, 227
Reasonable Racism, 223
Reconciliation: confrontations
between blacks and whites,
254; fear of black men, 253;
historical context, 252–56; King
case and Grant case, 254–55;
police brutality, 251–52; power,
255; race and crime, 254;
stereotype of certain dangerous

slaves, 252–53; Truth and
Reconciliation Commission,
256; *Worcester v. Georgia*, 255
Reconstruction, 200
Riot damage in D.C. (Library of
Congress), 2
Run–DMC, 181–82

Savagery *vs.* civilization, 171–86;
barbarism (Smith, Barbara),
171–72; blackness and primitive
culture (Fanon), 172; bleaching
blackness, 180–84; *Briggs v.
Elliot* (Clark, Dr. Kenneth),
172–74; class status (black
people), 175; colonial regime
(feelings of black inferiority),
174; color line, problem of
20th century, 175; Declaration
of Independence, 184–86;
improvisation, essence of
blackness, 176; modern
blackness, 176–78; 1940s doll
test, 174–75; race, cultural
significance of, 176; social
identity, 176; urban blackness,
178–80
Second Civil War, lessons from,
211–29
Second-class citizens, blacks as,
227–28
Second ghetto, 54–60; *Brown
II*, 59; *Brown v. The Board
of Education*, 57; civil rights
era, 54; desegregation, 58;
economic gulf between whites
and blacks, 56–57; fall in Black

About the Author

D. Marvin Jones is Professor of Law at the University of Miami, Florida, where he teaches constitutional law, criminal procedure, and a course called "The Wire." His published works include *Race, Sex, and Suspicion: The Myth of the Black Male* (Greenwood Press, 2005) and numerous articles in the nation's best law journals. He is also a frequent commentator in the press and the electronic media on race in America. He has appeared on PBS' *Frontline*, CNN's *Burden of Proof*, O'Reilly's *The O'Reilly Factor*, and Michael Putney's *The Week in Review*, where he debated Ward Connerly. His commentary has also appeared in *USA Today*, *The Huffington Post*, *The Miami Herald*, and the *South Florida Times*.

Professor Jones has taken a leadership role on many social justice issues. In 2003, Professor Jones, in conjunction with efforts by Senator Frederica Wilson, led an investigation into the impact of high stakes testing in inner city schools. In the same year Professor Jones was hired as a constitutional expert to draft the affirmative action plan for minority contracting in Dade County. In 2006, he was retained by the City of Miami to review their policy on deadly force. In 2007, the National Bar Association recognized Professor Jones as the Outstanding Member for that year.

Professor Jones has lectured nationally for many years. In 1997, he delivered the distinguished James A. Thomas lecture at Yale. Professor Jones has also been a keynote or featured speaker for the Law and Society Association, the National Bar Association, the Florida Association of State Judges, the National NAACP Convention, the Florida Conference of Black State Legislators, and many others. Professor Jones continues to be a sought-after speaker at many universities.